GEOFFREY MACNAB is a journalist and critic. His previous books include *Ingmar Bergman: The Life and Films of the Last Great European Director* and *Delivering Dreams: A Century of British Film Distribution* (both I.B.Tauris); *The Making of Taxi Driver*, *Searching for Stars: Stardom and Screen Acting in British Cinema* and *J. Arthur Rank and the British Film Industry*.

'I found this a page-turning read. It will be a fascinating insight for anyone who has been producing over the last 30 years, as well as for those who are thinking of producing for the first time. It's simultaneously a cautionary tale and an inspirational document for filmmakers.'

STEPHEN WOOLLEY
Number 9 Films

GEOFFREY MACNAB

STAIRWAYS TO HEAVEN

REBUILDING THE BRITISH FILM INDUSTRY

FOREWORD BY DAVID PUTTNAM

I.B. TAURIS

LONDON · NEW YORK

Published in 2018 by
I.B.Tauris & Co. Ltd
London • New York
www.ibtauris.com

ISBN: 978 1 78831 005 5
eISBN: 978 1 78672 409 0
ePDF: 978 1 78673 409 9

A full CIP record for this book is available from the British Library
A full CIP record is available from the Library of Congress

Library of Congress Catalog Card Number: available

Typeset by Tetragon, London
Printed and bound in Great Britain by T.J. International, Padstow, Cornwall

MIX
Paper from
responsible sources
FSC® C013056
FSC
www.fsc.org

CONTENTS

LIST OF ILLUSTRATIONS

FOREWORD

by Lord Puttnam of Queensgate, CBE, President of Film Distributors' Association

Although this book deals with the British film industry since the mid-1980s, its title instantly evokes a life-enhancing British film made much earlier, in the mid-1940s.

Written, produced and directed by Michael Powell and Emeric Pressburger at studios in Denham, Buckinghamshire, under their 'Archers' label, and distributed in the UK by Rank, *A Matter of Life and Death* was set in 1945.

It is the tale of Peter Carter (David Niven), an RAF pilot in a stricken Lancaster falling out of the night sky in flames. He shares what he believes to be his final words with June (Kim Hunter), a USAAF radio controller. With his parachute shredded, Peter jumps – and is lost in the fog. Later in hospital, lying on an operating table, he senses that a miraculous mis-count in heaven has allowed him

1. Lord Puttnam, president of Film Distributors' Association

Tim Whitby for FDA

to survive. Peter meets June and they fall in love. Then, before a vast heavenly tribunal attended by people of many nations, he pleads his case for life over death.

Perhaps the most enduring, iconic image from *A Matter of Life and Death* is the climactic 'stairway to heaven', magnificently envisaged by production designer Alfred Junge. On screen, it stretches seemingly endlessly from this world to the next. Built for the film by London Passenger Transport engineers, it was cleverly enhanced by the use of miniatures. The film was released in the US under the title *Stairway to Heaven*.

The traits and themes of *A Matter of Life and Death*, widely regarded as one of the finest films ever made in the UK, recur and resound throughout this new book on the industry itself.

It embraces questions of national identity and the ties that bind Britain and America (the Ministry of Information suggested that such

2. 'After all, what is time? A mere tyranny.' So observed the celestial Conductor 71 (Marius Goring) in Powell and Pressburger's imaginative romance, *A Matter of Life and Death*. In 2017 the film was reborn for big-screen audiences with a 4K digital cinema release, supported with a subtly refreshed poster.

a film be made, at a time of enormous social turmoil, to foster Anglo-American relations). It is creatively daring and ambitious; original, stylish and moving. It blends fantasy and reality, steely determination, love and sacrifice.

On a personal note, *A Matter of Life and Death* features an early screen appearance, as a fellow airman, by a young Richard Attenborough, who would later become a very close friend. He appears, as a tireless champion of the film industry, in several chapters of this book. It was also the first film to be selected for a 'royal command performance', held in London's Leicester Square in November 1946, an accolade previously bestowed only on stage productions. Today, of course, the UK hosts any number of spectacular world-class premieres every year.

The year 1946 was a landmark for another reason: it marked the all-time peak for British cinemagoing. Over 1.6 billion cinema admissions were recorded, equivalent to an almost unimaginable 32 visits per person. Across the following four decades, as television and then video technologies disrupted and remodelled viewing patterns, cinemagoing declined remorselessly, reaching the nadir of a mere 54 million (equivalent to just one visit per person per year) in 1984.

The resurgence that began in the mid-1980s – I actually cut the ribbon when opening the UK's first multiplex cinema, The Point in Milton Keynes, in 1985 – along with the paradigm shifts caused by digitisation are the subjects of this book.

In its totality, it's a remarkable story of seismic transformation. Cinema visits had tripled by the early 2000s, while the digital platforms on which increasing numbers of films can be experienced have multiplied out of all recognition. As I write today (in early 2018), I feel certain that the true impacts of digital upheaval have only just begun to be felt across the film and media sectors.

Following *Delivering Dreams*, his well-received 2016 book about the first century of British film distribution (also published by I.B.Tauris), Geoffrey Macnab has delved more deeply into a tighter time frame for this, his latest work. His meticulous research has included hundreds of contemporaneous reports, along with fresh interviews with dozens of senior executives and politicians who recount their opinions, dilemmas and decisions during what's been a period of constant change.

Today, as revenues from on-demand streaming services outweigh those from physical discs, the buoyant gross receipts from UK cinema ticket sales exceed £1.3 billion a year. This is 5 per cent of the world's cinema box office – from a country of barely 1 per cent of its population.

Film has become the dynamic heart of our creative industries, a sector which each year is contributing some £90 billion net to the UK economy, accounting for one in 11 of British jobs. Indeed, it's a level of reach that recalls the narrator's opening line in *A Matter of Life and Death*: 'This is the universe. Big, isn't it?'

While it has always had, and will forever confront, many challenges, facing troughs and droughts as well as sunlit uplands along its complex, unpredictable path, you can only feel immensely proud that the UK film industry continues successfully to punch well above its weight in the world.

Keeping its audience at the forefront of its thinking, the business continues to evolve rapidly in these turbulent times. It's a ride this book warmly invites you to join.

DAVID PUTTNAM
www.davidputtnam.com
www.launchingfilms.com

PREFACE

Stairways to Heaven tells the story of how the British film industry has been transformed over the period from the mid-1980s, when it was in a prolonged slump, to 2018, when business appears to be booming as never before. As the book recounts, politicians' attitudes toward the industry have changed from exasperation to pride. They believe that the industry had finally reached the tipping point.

'The force is with us,' the former Chancellor George Osborne boasted of the British film industry in late 2015 as a whole bundle of big Hollywood movies, *Stars Wars* among them, were shot at British studios, using British actors and British crews – and creating 'British jobs'.[1]

'The UK film industry is a great success story,' chimed in Karen Bradley MP, Secretary of State for Digital, Culture, Media and Sport, in the House of Commons in December 2016, as if there was no longer any room for debate on the matter.[2]

By then, British cinema was contributing more than £4 billion a year to the economy and supporting 70,000 full-time jobs. Cinema admissions were steady at the 170 million mark. There were generous tax breaks in place for foreign and domestic film-makers shooting films and TV dramas in the UK. Lottery money underpinned local production. It appeared that the problems that had bedevilled the industry since the silent era had finally been solved. This book looks at how and why the industry began to benefit from such levels of public support.

For generations, the British had fretted about how best to compete with Hollywood. The answer, some believed, had now been revealed. Rather than trying to usurp the US majors' powers, the policy should be to court the American studios and to persuade them to make their movies in the UK. The examples of the British-made James Bond and Harry Potter films were reassuring for the studio bosses. If those franchises had been successfully based in Britain, there was no reason not to bring Disney live-action dramas and Marvel superhero movies to British studios too. The talent liked being in Britain. A weak pound made the dollar stretch further. The UK had a thriving post-production and visual effects sector.

Bradley boasted about the new co-production treaty the British had signed with China, 'making us only the second country in the world to have both film and TV treaties with the Chinese'.[3] She also expressed pride that a 'global franchise' like HBO's *Game of Thrones* had been shooting in Britain, and that films had even been made in the Staffordshire Peak District, the area that she represented.

In the 1980s and 1990s, the picture had been very different. 'The sad history of the British film industry is that it has erratic and inconsistent bursts of real excellence,' Tory politician Kenneth Baker said in a familiar observation in a 1996 House of Commons debate.[4] These 'bursts' of excellence soon 'sputtered out'. The tax incentives and infrastructure that might have guaranteed sustained success weren't in place. There was no 'critical mass'. A few British films won Oscars and some US movies were shot in British locations or at British studios but there was no continuity of production and no sign that the industry would soon be worth billions.

Baker is an ambivalent figure in the story of British cinema in the 1980s and 1990s. He blamed others for removing the tax incentives and yet, in his time as a minister in the Department for Trade and Industry, in the Thatcher government, he oversaw the dismantling of much of the public support that had been available for British producers. He was perceptive, though, in his diagnosis of what was wrong with the British industry.

There is an important paradox that this book also seeks to address. UK cinema may have turned into the great success story that the politicians claim, but this does not mean that all sectors of the industry are thriving in the same way. At the same time that the British film industry has never had it so good, independent producers and distributors are lamenting a system that seems tilted against them. Their businesses are often creaking as the former struggle to hold on to rights and the latter try to secure better rental terms for the films they are releasing.

Baker's remark about the British film industry lacking 'critical mass' is revealing. Since the 1920s, the thinking has been that the British need their own equivalent to the huge American studios, which not only produced big-budget movies but had the means to market and distribute them. In the period that the book covers, several attempts were made to create vertically integrated companies capable of competing with their American rivals. Goldcrest, Palace, PolyGram Filmed Entertainment, FilmFour in its time as a stand-alone company, and even the public body the UK Film Council were all striving to achieve the 'critical mass' that Baker mentioned. They all achieved some success, the executives behind them had long-term strategic visions and yet none of these companies or organisations survived in their original guises. This book asks why not.

There is also the vexed question of the UK film industry's relationship with mainland Europe. This has been brought into sharp focus by the result of the 2016 Brexit referendum, when a majority of British people voted to leave the European Union. The film industry's ties with Europe aren't especially close. Few British producers work regularly with continental partners. Public film policy in the UK is far more focused on the US than it was on Europe. The British aren't members of Eurimages, the Council of Europe's co-production and cultural support Fund. Nonetheless, they are part of Creative Europe, the European Union's funding programme for the audiovisual industries, which had a budget of €1.46 billion for 2014 to 2020.

The tax breaks that so help the film and TV industries in Britain are dependent on EU state aid approval. Laws passed in Brussels concerning such matters as a planned 'digital single market' or 'portability' would have a major impact on British independent film-making and distribution. Leading British production companies receive generous support from Creative Europe to develop new projects. British exhibitors and distributors also receive EU backing and money from Brussels goes to training initiatives and to festivals.

A glance back over the shoulder at British film history of the previous century is enough to arm anyone against complacency. As *Stairways to Heaven* chronicles, there has been a very big upswing in the industry's fortunes. Nonetheless, anxiety persists. There is no predicting how the industry will cope with evolving competition from giant new players like Amazon, Netflix, Google and Apple.

Seasoned observers warn that, as producer Sandy Lieberson puts it, 'any industry that depends on tax subsidies and government subsidies is in dangerous waters.'[5] This is a famously cyclical business. Just as one or two big successes, a *Full Monty* or a *King's Speech*, can transform the mood in the industry, a flop, a *Revolution* or a *Golden Compass*, can depress the entire sector.

Who is to say that the US studios won't go somewhere else to make their movies or that cinema audiences won't dip? At the time of

3. Finding a voice: Tom Hooper's biographical drama *The King's Speech* won four Oscars in 2011 and grossed more than $400 million in ticket sales on its cinema release worldwide. Two-thirds of this haul was generated in international markets outside the US/Canada. In the UK, its box office of £45 million makes *The King's Speech* one of the highest-grossing independent (non-studio) releases of all time.

Momentum Pictures

writing, the UK industry is thriving on the back of the most sustained period of inward investment it has ever experienced. British film has benefited from the unprecedented public support that successive governments, Labour, Coalition and Tory, have offered it. So much infrastructure has been put in place that it is inconceivable to many that the activity might stop again. But the disappearance of home video, which (as the book chronicles) rescued the film industry in the 1980s and 1990s, is evidence that formats and tastes can change very quickly. So can government policy.

Stairways to Heaven looks at the personalities who have moulded film policy over the last 30 years. The book acknowledges the importance of Richard Attenborough and David Puttnam as lobbyists and strategists, working closely with ministers in both the Thatcher and Blair governments. It considers the impact of a new generation of entrepreneurs who galvanised British film-making at Palace, PolyGram and then at the UK Film Council. There is a chapter on Working Title, the most successful British production company in the period the book covers. The role of the broadcasters is assessed in detail and it is explained how BBC Films and Film4 became key supporters of independent British cinema. The book tells the story of the creation of the Film Council, its destruction and its replacement as lead film agency by the British Film Institute.

A perennial complaint about British film policy over the period covered is that it has so often been production-led. Due attention wasn't always paid to the audience or to the distributors and exhibitors who serviced that audience. *Stairways to Heaven* seeks to acknowledge their contribution and to look at the importance of marketing in putting British cinema back in the public eye. The book also considers the plight of those who were left behind – the independent film-makers, small exhibitors and distributors for whom there wasn't always a place in the brave new world the Film Council was striving to create. The book touches on film education and on attempts to reach younger generations of cinemagoers as well as those who aspired to work in the industry. It looks at the huge impact of the Harry Potter films, the revival of the James Bond brand and the crucial role they played in British cinema over the period.

This is a complex and sometimes contradictory story. It is also an uplifting one. In the 1980s and 1990s, even some of Britain's most prominent producers had dismissed their national cinema as, at best, a cottage industry. 'It's like comparing the space programme with people in the Hebrides knitting scarves,' Stephen Woolley, a film-maker who features prominently in these pages, commented in the early 1990s of where the British film industry stood in comparison to Hollywood.[6] By 2018, though, there was no more talk of knitting in the Hebrides or of film-making as a hobby for dilettantes. Many of the biggest global box-office hits of the period were being made not in Hollywood but in Britain – a state of affairs that not even the most optimistic industry observers from 30 years before would ever have considered to be either likely or remotely possible.

The Downing Street Summit

'It was, however, the coming of cinema to Grantham which really brightened my life.'

—Margaret Thatcher, *The Path to Power*

There are conflicting reports as to how the Downing Street summit in June 1990 came about. Some say that the idea for a meeting between Prime Minister Margaret Thatcher and a film industry delegation was first floated after a lunch between Peter Palumbo, chairman of the Arts Council, and Richard Attenborough, then about to make his biopic, *Chaplin*. As Alexander Walker recounts in his book *Icons in*

4. Smile: Richard Attenborough's all-star biopic brought Robert Downey Jr, who had been acting in films since the mid-1980s, to greater prominence. His leading performance in *Chaplin* was rewarded with a Best Actor BAFTA and an Oscar nomination. Geraldine Chaplin played the role of her own grandmother, Hannah. The film opened with a royal charity premiere in London in December 1992. Robert Downey Jr's acclaimed performance as *Iron Man* (2008) would later help to propel Marvel's universe of superheroes to sustained big-screen success.

David James/Carolco

the Fire, Palumbo was shocked by Attenborough's revelation that he couldn't even begin to finance *Chaplin* in Britain. 'We've hardly any film industry left,' Attenborough is said to have told Palumbo, who responded: 'Does the boss (Thatcher) know all this?'[2]

Wilf Stevenson, then the Director of the British Film Institute (BFI) and one of the leading figures in the Downing Street delegation, has a different memory.[3] He says that the idea of a film summit was hatched after an encounter between Attenborough and Tory Party chairman Lord (Alistair) McAlpine at a Christie's sale of French impressionist paintings. Attenborough had been bemoaning the fact that British film-making was going through a renaissance but couldn't secure any government support. McAlpine then brought the matter to the attention of the Prime Minister.

Since the Films Act 1985 dispensed with the Eady Levy, there had been a perception in the industry that the government simply didn't care about British film culture. During the Thatcher era, there were constant changes in the ministers overseeing the film industry (a situation that would recur during Tony Blair's premiership). No one stuck around for long. It didn't help either that different government departments dealt with different aspects of the film industry. The commercial side was overseen by the Department of Trade and Industry while the cultural side was overseen by the Office of Arts and Libraries. The ministers were happy to applaud when British film-makers and actors won Oscars but seemed to regard cinema as something essentially frivolous when compared to 'real' industries.

'Intellectually, politically, they [the Tories] felt they shouldn't do it,' Stevenson remembers of the Conservative government's attitude toward intervening in cinema. 'They said that the failed industrial policy of the past of backing state-owned companies didn't work, that nationalisation was terrible, it all should be pushed back to the market.'

What began to swing the politicians in favour of helping the industry was a change in the way British film-makers portrayed themselves. It had been customary for producers in particular to lambast the Thatcher government. The arguments they made for being helped by the public purse tended to be cultural ones. They were being stifled by the Hollywood competition and deserved the chance to tell their own stories. They couldn't compete in the marketplace – distribution and exhibition were dominated by the US studios – and therefore argued that they needed a little tender, loving subsidy.

By the time of the Downing Street summit, the film industry representatives realised that such special pleading wouldn't work with the politicians. 'The dialogue changed from being one of a begging bowl for funding to allow public good to happen to investment to create a sustainable thing that will repay through tax,' Stevenson remembers of the shift in approach. 'You don't just make cars. Cars are made up of components from lots of different supply chains all around the world. If you're going to support the industry of car making, you have to support all the things that lead to it.'

This wasn't just about the warm, fuzzy feeling of pride that audiences and politicians alike felt when films like *Chariots of Fire* and *Gandhi* won Academy Awards. The Downing Street summit convinced the government that there were practical reasons for supporting the British film industry: reasons to do with job creation, tax revenue and inward investment, as well as prestige.

'The cinema has an importance in the popular mind out of all proportion to its economic significance,' a government research paper published the year after the Downing Street summit pointed out.

> Film production stands at the centre of a web of industrial and market operations; if it prospers, it promotes a range of activities which collectively have much greater economic weight than film production proper; if it declines, it inhibits these activities and causes reductions in output considerably greater than it suffers itself.[4]

Employment, tax, inward investment, export – these were the drivers for government support. Rather than being regarded as a sclerotic industry on its last legs, film began to be seen alongside the so-called 'sunrise industries' that were expected to grow as technology improved.

Margaret Thatcher herself was far more of a film lover than the industry might have suspected. The Prime Minister writes in tremulous fashion in her autobiography of how, when she was growing up as a grocer's daughter in Grantham, the arrival of the cinema 'brightened' her life. She had been worried that her parents would disapprove of her going to the movies, but one of the grocery's best customers was the Campbell family, who owned three cinemas in the town.

Her father, who was a councillor, alderman and mayor of the town, let her go to what he considered to be 'good' films – and that meant she was allowed to see Fred Astaire musicals and anything made by Britain's pre-eminent producer of the 1930s and early 1940s, Alexander Korda. The future prime minister and Iron Lady writes of spending her ninepence for 'a comfortable seat in the darkness'.[5] She waxes nostalgic about the film programme with the British Movietone news followed by a public service item and then, finally, the 'big picture', a rousing British imperial yarn like *The Four Feathers* or a melodrama like *Stella Dallas*.

Thatcher even claimed that some pictures, for example *The Scarlet Pimpernel*, starring Leslie Howard as a dashing aristocrat and set against the backcloth of the French Revolution, helped with her political education. Another favourite was Carol Reed's wartime biopic *The Young Mr Pitt* (1942), starring Robert Donat. 'England has saved herself by her exertions and will, I trust, save Europe by her example' was a line she would quote fondly later in her life, saying that it 'encapsulated' her own political vision. When law student (and later to become a film distributor) Frank Mannion met her briefly at a book signing for her autobiography, *The Downing Street Years*, she spoke with enthusiasm about her childhood love of musicals, especially those of Astaire and Ginger Rogers.

Her biographer, Charles Moore, quotes an entry from her diary about going to the cinema as 'a last splash' before she started school again. In a breathless entry, she writes of her excitement at seeing a double bill of *This England* with Constance Cummings, Emlyn Williams and John Clements ('we enjoyed it, although it was a historical film, for the most part') and *Romance of the Rio Grande*, starring Cesar Romero and Patricia Morrison. Afterwards, she and her friends gorged on salmon salad: 'We happened to strike a lucky day for there was also jam and chocolate biscuits,' she confides to the diary. Her biographer suggests that attending both these films was 'an act of minor defiance against the wishes of Mr and Mrs Roberts' (her parents), who thought that their children should go 'only to those films properly chosen on their merits, rather than watching whatever happened to be on'.[6]

The man who had brought cinema to Grantham, and had had such an effect on the young and impressionable Margaret Hilda Roberts, was John Arthur Campbell, OBE (1878–1947), described in the local paper as 'the wild one of the family'.[7] Campbell, who had been born Gamble, came from North Runcton, near King's Lynn. After failing in several apprenticeships, he had run away to join a company of actors. It was through the stage he met his wife, Mary Fulton (real name Mary Worger). She was the one who persuaded him to go 'front of house' and to run his own theatres and touring companies. During World War I, this provincial impresario opened what was to become Grantham's best-loved cinema, the Picture House on St Peter's Hill, and he later turned the Exchange Hall on the High Street into the Central Cinema. He was a playwright, amateur film-maker and a Freemason as well as a cinema owner. The local press has stories about some of his publicity ruses, for example distributing Charlie Chaplin rag dolls to spectators in the silent era.

The young Margaret's friends, the Campbells, were indeed an intriguing family. John Arthur's daughter, born in 1916 and nine years older than Thatcher, was the actress Judy Campbell. She was known as Noël Coward's muse, starred in the original productions of several of his plays, and racked up numerous film credits, including *Green for Danger*. She was the mother of singer and actress Jane Birkin. The Campbell dynasty continues through Birkin's children with her lover, the French crooner Serge Gainsbourg.

John Campbell's biography of Thatcher has a revealing anecdote about Judy Campbell being sent by her mother to buy a cauliflower from the Roberts' grocery shop. The precocious and bossy young Margaret, aged only ten or so, was serving behind the counter. Judy had been told by her mother that Margaret was 'a remarkable little girl'. Contradicting the accounts elsewhere, the biographer claims that the Campbells didn't tend to shop in the Roberts' grocery store and that Judy had been sent there really just so she could get a glimpse of Margaret, who even then was regarded as a prodigy who (Judy's mother told her) would go very far. Campbell suggests that, although Judy was in 'no way a friend of the young Margaret', she provided inspiration to her when

> her adolescent imagination was being fired by visits to the cinema [...] and dreams of London. Judy had got away: her picture was in the *Grantham Journal* every other week. Judy was glamorous: as an actress, she got to wear pretty clothes. Yet as the daughter of Mr and Mrs Campbell, she was also respectable: a local girl of whom Grantham could properly be proud.[8]

This detail about Thatcher's childhood may seem trivial but it underlines her enthusiasm about cinema. In spite of her government's previous reputation for callous treatment of the UK film industry, that childhood passion for the movies meant she was ready to listen to the delegation of producers and grandees and to help them if she could.

'Why didn't you come years ago?' is how Thatcher is said to have greeted Attenborough and the others.

'Because I wasn't asked, darling,' Attenborough replied.[9]

One attendee, Jeremy Thomas, the Oscar-winning producer of *The Last Emperor* and *Merry Christmas, Mr Lawrence*, remembers 'the Thatcher meeting' as an attempt to give 'the failing film industry a shot in the arm'.[10] He felt, though, that everything on the agenda had been decided in advance.

This was indeed the case, although there was nothing necessarily sinister about the way that the summit was stage-managed. Wilf Stevenson talks about the frantic work by the film delegates and the civil servants behind the scenes to ensure that everything went to plan.

David Puttnam remembers, 'If you'd seen myself, Dickie, John Brabourne and Simon Relph walking in, you'd see we are all carrying stuff. What we'd done was prepare a lot of material for the Treasury. We came very well prepared that day.'[11]

One of their key goals was to identify a senior figure in government who would accept their ideas. This turned out to be the unlikely figure

5. A sumptuous cinematic experience: tracing the story of Pu-Yi (John Lone), ruler of China at a time of tumultuous change, *The Last Emperor* (1987) won nine Oscars, four Golden Globes and three BAFTAs, including the Best Film prize for director Bernardo Bertolucci and producer Jeremy Thomas.

bafta.org

of the eccentric Eurosceptic Nicholas Ridley at the Department of Trade and Industry. Stevenson recalls of Ridley:

> Early on, we went to see him to explain what was going on and he said you've probably got a point. I do think this is an industry that could work very well but you've lost control of your distribution. Why are there no British distributors? Is that something we can sort out? Is it a monopoly? These were all the kind of questions we had been raising. He got it very, very quickly. He was very, very impressive.[12]

Producer David Puttnam had been less enthused, remarking around the time of the summit: 'In Nicholas Ridley, we've got a Secretary of State (for Trade and Industry) [...] who gives the impression that he would regard it as his greatest success [...] if he could close the British film industry down.'[13]

Stevenson remembers:

The government didn't want any surprises. You actually write the press release for the end of the meeting before it starts and that is what we did. Two things were astonishing. One was that Thatcher was very good and stuck to the script. The second was [the presence of] Lew Wasserman, with whom she flirted outrageously. That was Downing Street's invitation, not the DTI's. We would have run a mile if we had known. We would have thought he'd spike the whole thing.[14]

Wasserman was the mystery guest at the feast and it is easy to understand why the British producers were so startled to see him there. The American executive, then the chairman and chief executive of MCA Universal, is often dubbed 'the last of Hollywood's moguls'. When he died in 2002, the *New York Times* obituary described him as 'arguably the most powerful and influential Hollywood titan in the four decades after World War II'.[15]

Biographers and contemporaries portray Wasserman, the music business talent agent turned studio boss, as a formidable and, at times, terrifying figure. He was very close to US President Ronald Reagan and was an extraordinarily skilful lobbyist who (as his biographer, Connie Bruck, notes) made Hollywood a force in Washington.[16] Wasserman was also responsible for several groundbreaking deals. In his talent agency days, he negotiated with Universal for actor James Stewart to have 'points' in the profits of his films, starting with western *Winchester '73*, taking a reduced salary in return for a hefty share of the profits.

Wasserman and Jules Stein, his partner at MCA (Music Corporation of America), embraced TV at a time when other studios shunned the medium, acquiring the Paramount library and persuading his client Alfred Hitchcock to direct for TV. In 1962, MCA acquired Universal Studios – and Wasserman became the studio boss. He originated Universal's studio tours and oversaw the production of Steven Spielberg's *Jaws* (1975), the first of the summer blockbusters.

There are conflicting reports about the reasons for Wasserman's presence in Downing Street that day. Hansard reports that Thatcher had met with Wasserman earlier in the summer of 1990 to discuss his proposals for building a studio complex in Rainham in Essex. After Thatcher's death in 2013, former minister Norman Lamont (now Lord Lamont of Lerwick) gave a speech in Parliament which recounted the story of what Lamont claimed was Thatcher's first encounter with Wasserman on a plane returning from the UK to the US.

'Somehow on that journey he [Wasserman] persuaded her that her crowning glory as prime minister would be the state financing of film studios in Rainham Marshes in Essex,' Lamont, who was chief secretary to the Treasury at the time, remembered. He expressed bewilderment at the proposal, and told her,

> 'But I thought we believed in controlling expenditure.' I received a glare. I said, 'I thought we believed in low taxes. I thought we didn't believe in subsidies to inefficient industries.' I got more and more desperate and said, 'Prime Minister, there's no unemployment in Essex. We would have to build the roads in order to get to Rainham Marshes.' I remember her glowering at me very fiercely and in desperation I said, 'You do know, Prime Minister, that we'll have all the environmentalists against us because there's a very rare bird' – I knew about these things – 'called the Brent goose that breeds there.' She looked at me and said, 'You are utterly hopeless. All you ever say is "No, no, no." You do not have a constructive idea in your head.'[17]

A British producer attending the summit suggests that Wasserman had another motive in being there. He wanted to protect the preferential terms on which US studio revenues were taxed in the UK. (The producer believed that the Wilson government had struck a special deal to repatriate funds to the US studios with no withholding of tax, but this is difficult to verify.) Puttnam remembers:

> What actually had happened was that she [Thatcher] had socially met Lew Wasserman. What he said to her was 'Margaret, I don't understand. You won the Oscars in '82 and '83, you clearly make good films, you've got wonderful film-makers here, the opportunity to build a wonderful film industry

and I don't understand why it doesn't happen. She said, 'Neither do I, but would you be prepared to help?'[18]

Any analysis of the British film business from the time of the Downing Street summit to Brexit just over a quarter of a century later can't help but acknowledge that all UK public film policy invariably ended up benefiting the US studios. Perhaps Thatcher had realised that rubbing up to Hollywood was in the long-term interests of British cinema.

'Margaret Thatcher had a great will of wanting the British film industry to succeed as an employer. She thought it was a great business, which it turned out to be,' Jeremy Thomas remembers, adding that very little came out of it to the advantage of independent producers like himself. 'It was already in my mind that it was a cartel against the smaller film-makers – that it was very hard to break in.'[19]

Whatever the case, Wasserman managed to charm not just Thatcher herself but most of the producers in attendance. Producer Simon Perry remembers the Hollywood executive standing up and telling the Downing Street audience that, twice in his lifetime, the Hollywood system had been saved by government intervention:

> One was with the Fin Syn [Finance and Syndication] Laws, which stopped the US studios from becoming TV companies, and once with the tax credit system in the early 1980s, where the studios got tax credits for the money they put into film. He [Wasserman] said, 'Without that, Hollywood would not be anything like it is today.'[20]

This was intriguing both for the government, which could see the logic in supporting the industry, and for the delegates. It scotched the idea that Hollywood ran purely on free market principles.

Wilf Stevenson remembers that Thatcher called on Wasserman to say a few words to sum up at the end of the summit.

> She said, 'Now, Mr Wasserman, what do you think?' We thought he would say this is stupid, why are you throwing money [at the film industry], but what he said was 'I think what we've

heard today is a really, really important contribution to the growth of the film industry in the world and I can tell you that as a studio head trying to get the most money I can out of the films I make, I would rather be 50 per cent of a growing market than 100 per cent of a dead market.' It was fantastic. It wasn't part of the script.[21]

There are very different recollections of what the summit achieved. Jeremy Thomas suggested that nothing much changed from the point of view of the independent producer. Film-maker and screenwriter Bruce Robinson suggested the government could best help the film industry by resigning and there was a certain amount of sarcastic fatalism about what benefit the producers' meeting with Thatcher was likely to bring.[22] Stevenson says:

> It [the Downing Street summit] brought together a community that had previously been split and there was a relatively straightforward agenda with simple ideas. You can't do anything in Whitehall unless you've got a single message and a single voice.[23]

To outsiders who hadn't been invited to the summit, it didn't seem as if a community had been brought together at all. Almost all the attendees were producers. There were one or two directors (Attenborough and John Boorman) but no independent distributors or exhibitors. The fact that the delegates were almost all men reflected the gender bias in the industry at that time. There were very few female executives then in senior roles in production companies.

'I think it became a production group because of the way it started, not because we had a particular thing in mind,' Stevenson states. He suggests that the distributors and exhibitors weren't invited because the leading ones 'were largely not British companies'. They were also seen by some attendees as being 'part of the problem'.

The choreography and the advance planning appeared to pay off. Several short-term goals were achieved quickly. Thatcher committed the money for the UK to rejoin the European Union's Media

Programme. The British Film Commission was set up in 1991 to woo overseas film-makers to come to Britain. Perhaps surprisingly, given the anti-European animus of ministers like Ridley and of Thatcher herself, a European Co-Production Fund was also established in 1991, to be run by British Screen. The idea was to promote collaboration between British film producers and other film producers in the European Union. The new fund received a grant of £5 million, spread over three years.

There was a hiccup. Nicholas Ridley was forced to resign not long after the summit. 'This is all a German racket designed to take over the whole of Europe,' Ridley told journalist Dominic Lawson in the *Spectator* of plans for greater European integration. 'I'm not against giving up sovereignty in principle, but not to this lot. You might just as well give it to Adolf Hitler, frankly.'[24] This left the film lobbyists without a key ally. Thatcher herself resigned in November 1990.

'The big thing we didn't really get going was that we couldn't get into the DTI when Ridley fell,' Wilf Stevenson remembers of the departures.

> When he left, the powers of darkness in the department said, 'Well, we don't need to do film any more. Thatcher's gone, Ridley's gone. That's that.' They just squashed it right down. They set up a series of working groups in the basement of the DTI and we were just being pushed back. We couldn't do anything to stimulate distribution or to deal with the monopoly situation.[25]

Stevenson remembers that Lamont, the Chancellor of the Exchequer during the early 1990s, overcame opposition from his own civil servants to help the film industry.

> We got in to see Norman Lamont quite quickly after he became Chancellor. This was after Thatcher had fallen. He and Dickie had a previous relationship. He was quite keen to help. I am not sure he carried his officials with him. We were summoned to a meeting he had arranged. There was Lamont, myself and

Dickie. There were 14 people around the table, quite senior officials.

Every time Lamont suggested a measure to benefit the film industry, his civil servants shot him down, saying either it wasn't feasible or it was too expensive. The Chancellor grew ever more exasperated.

At the end of it, he just got fed up. He said, 'This is ridiculous. I want to help the film industry. I've got a budget coming up. I want something in the budget,' and stormed off.

In the end, Lamont was able to provide accelerated write-offs of development costs and, under Section 42 of the Finance Act 1992, a three-year write-off of production costs for investors. (The real boost for British producers was to come five years later, in 1997, when Section 48 tax relief was introduced for British films with budgets of £15 million or less. The then Chancellor Gordon Brown hailed this as 'a three-year measure at a cost of £30 million, that will not only boost the number of British films but the British economy by boosting our exports.')

Just as significantly, the lobbying began which would lead in the mid-1990s to lottery funding coming on tap for British film production. Stevenson argues that 'you can't overstate' the importance of the summit and that it laid the foundations for everything that was to follow, from the introduction of lottery money into the industry to the formation of the UK Film Council.

To understand just why the summit needed to be called in the first place, it is necessary to take a step back in time to the 1980s, when the British film industry was in one of its biggest, most prolonged slumps and the Thatcher government was being blamed not just for abandoning it in its hour of need but for exacerbating the problems it already had.

CHAPTER 1

Back to the 1980s

The year 1984 is a fitting date at which to begin a survey of recent British cinema. As is often pointed out, this was the nadir – the point at which British cinemagoing slipped to its lowest ever level, with admissions falling to 54 million (a tiny fraction of the 1,635 million tickets sold in the record year of 1946).

In the early 1980s, the atmosphere in Wardour Street, Soho, the home of the main film companies, was akin to that of the City of London before the 'Big Bang'. It is instructive to speak to those who worked within the industry in this period. There was an air of defeatism. The culture within the business was one of long lunches and very heavy drinking.

Then *Screen International* editor Terry Ilott remembers the gloomy forecasts that some were making:

Puttnam made a speech in which he predicted that soon there would be ten cinemas in the country. That would be where you would have the gala openings in Glasgow, Edinburgh, Manchester, three in London – and after that, there would be nothing else because it would go onto video and TV.

'It [the industry] was awash in alcohol,' Ilott also recalls.

It was extraordinary to be offered drinks, hard drinks, whisky, when you went to see somebody at nine o'clock in the morning. To get in at ten, to go to lunch at 12, to finish lunch at half past three, to wander into a strip club for an hour, to get back to your office for half past four to pick up your coat and go home was completely acceptable. It was tremendously inefficient and the culture was dreadful, truly dreadful.[1]

His observations are borne out by Puttnam himself, who talks with mixed feelings about a restaurant called the Braganza in Soho, at which the industry converged.

All the distributors – among them senior executives from United Artists and Columbia – they would all gather at lunchtime. They would meet around 12.30. The bar was on the ground floor, the restaurant was on the top floor. They would go up to the restaurant at two and they would roll out at four. It was ludicrous. They'd either go off and play golf or they'd put their feet up and have a sleep. All business was done between nine in the morning and [lunch] and then they'd have to get on the phone to LA at 7pm.[2]

There was more business done in the Braganza than in the whole of Wardour Street, says Odeon chief booker Stan Fishman.

I could walk up Wardour Street, going on my way to lunch, seeing various people up there, and do as much business as I could in the office. The entertaining and drinking in those days played an interesting part in the business. I was taken to lunch most days by distributors. I am not a big drinker and I never went to pubs and clubs, and most afternoons I was viewing pictures with my viewing panel.[3]

'It was an industry that lunched,' agrees a former trade journalist. 'A lot of business was done over lunch or on the golf course.'[4] In an era before email and mobile phones, and when so many of the companies were based close to each other in Soho, it made sense to meet face to face.

There were still films that were engaging audiences. *Star Wars* had been released a few years before. *E.T. the Extra-Terrestrial* had been an enormous hit. However, cinemas were in a shocking state of disrepair.

Many independent venues were closing down. Trade journalists from the period talk of attending monthly meetings organised by the Cinema Exhibitors' Association and sister organisation the Association of Independent Cinemas. These would be depressing occasions at which members made it clear they were struggling to stay afloat. Odeon and ABC had dominated the British landscape for as long as anyone remembered and they too were creaking.

Even then, it was clear that the new Tory government wasn't ignoring the industry. In fact, British cinema was about to be given some extreme Thatcherite 'shock treatment' in an ill-conceived bid to revive it. On 19 July 1984, the Minister for Information Technology, Kenneth Baker, presented his White Paper on 'Film Policy' in Parliament. In hindsight, the White Paper's recommendations seem very brutal indeed. Baker made the usual remarks about the British film industry undergoing 'a renaissance' and paid tribute to the outstanding technical skills of its producers, writers, directors and actors. He then proceeded to explain just why he intended to remove almost every system of state support for that industry.

The decline in cinema attendance provided the pretext for getting rid of the Eady Levy, which Baker said was now 'outdated'. Introduced on a voluntary basis in 1950 and made compulsory by the Cinematograph Films Act 1957, this was a tax on a proportion of the price of cinema tickets. Half of the money raised stayed with exhibitors but half went to producers, to fund new production. To be precise, the rules for Eady instructed that a twelfth of the price of a cinema ticket would be paid to the British Film Fund Agency, and that payments would also be made to the National Film Finance Corporation and the Children's Film Foundation. Later on, some of the Eady revenues also went to the British Film Institute Production Board and the National Film School. The Levy was collected every month by Customs and Excise and paid over to the British Film Fund Agency, which oversaw its administration.

Eady money had helped fund James Bond and Superman movies. It had attracted international production to the UK while also helping local film-makers. Nonetheless, by the mid-1980s, neither the exhibitors nor the distributors supported the Levy. Both groups lobbied

hard for it to be scrapped. Odeon's booker Stan Fishman and leading distributor James Higgins, who headed up United International
Pictures (UIP) UK, joined forces to lobby the government.

> I took a stand with James Higgins. He and I approached the
> British government. We explained the situation: the amount
> of money that both the distributors and the exhibitors were
> putting into the industry and the costs. It was producers that
> were benefiting. The irony was that the formula that was set
> basically gave money from the levy to the more commercial
> British pictures. Therefore, films that it should have been for,
> maybe those that were difficult to find finance for, British films
> or independent films, suffered.[5]

It wasn't just commercial films receiving Eady support. 'All kinds of
very odd short films were being made,' Fishman recalls.

One of the unlikely beneficiaries of Eady largesse was the enter-
tainer, gameshow host and radio and TV personality Nicholas Parsons.
He had a production company and was making 16 mm films which
would be blown up to 35 mm and shown in cinemas. Parsons recalled:

> I used to write, direct and produce them. The most successful
> one was called *Mad Dogs and Cricketers*. I approached the charity
> the Lord's Taverners, of which I am a member, and said, 'Would
> you like to have a film about your activities?' We went and made
> a film about their activities. I took a team to Corfu where they
> play cricket. I made another one about their golfing activities.[6]

Mad Dogs and Cricketers was narrated by comedian Eric Morecambe. It
showed celebrities and ex-professional cricketers playing in a match
for charity against Oxford University at Blenheim Palace. The film also
followed them on their trip to Corfu. It all made for a perfectly pleas-
ant travelogue but was hardly a groundbreaking piece of British film-
making that showed off what Eady money could achieve to best effect.

As director Alan Parker later wrote, distributors had used the Eady
Levy in a very opportunistic way.

In 1973 we were approached by EMI to make two short films. Just what their logic was is still a mystery to me. I think it had something to do with the old British Eady Levy still in place in British cinema exhibition. If the distributor could tag on a short British film to the main feature, then they could gather a (disproportionate) percentage of the boxoffice – sometimes as much as 30%.[7]

Among the apparently most notorious (mis)uses of Eady money was from Paramount on a short skateboarding film called *Hot Wheels*. By programming it with *Grease* (1978), the American company was able to work the system and lawfully earn itself a £123,000 public pay-out.[8]

Fishman warned Baker that if the Eady Levy was maintained or (worse) increased, Odeon would respond by printing on cinema tickets the extra amount that customers were being forced to pay in tax. Baker realised this could make for very bad publicity for the government. With the exhibition sector in near crisis, Baker was able to argue that the Levy had become 'an extra tax on seats which cinemas cannot afford [...] an elaborate and unfair burden on the industry's weakest sector'.[9]

This move to scrap Eady had also been encouraged by the Cinematograph Films Council, the industry body set up in 1938 to advise the government on film policy. In its annual report in March 1983, the council had warned that 'many cinemas were not in profit because of having to pay Eady. Others were closing altogether.' The council itself was destined to be abolished as part of Baker's cuts. Its recommendations had given the government the chance to argue that the film industry itself wanted the Eady Levy removed.

David Puttnam recalls fighting 'tooth and nail' to save the Eady Levy. He acknowledged that he owed his career as a producer at least partly to the Levy. One of his first hits, *That'll Be the Day*, had been funded because the comedy *Holiday on the Buses* had raked in so much money for Nat Cohen at EMI that he was prepared to invest in Puttnam's movie. As a trustee and later chair of the National Film School, which was supported by Eady money, he had a second motive for wanting to keep the Levy.

6. Bridge to industry: the National Film and Television School opened in 1971 (as the National Film School), using a grant from the Rank Organisation to acquire the freehold of Beaconsfield Studios in Buckinghamshire from then owners, King's College, Cambridge. Its first director, Colin Young, was succeeded by Henning Camre, Stephen Bayly, Nik Powell and, in 2017, Dr Jon Wardle. Today the NFTS is widely regarded as one of the world's finest film schools, equipped to professional industry standards, and with an impressive network of alumni.

Photograph © NFTS

7. Passion and commitment: in addition to his successful career as a television and film producer, Duncan Kenworthy has played numerous industry roles. He chaired BAFTA from 2004 to 2006 and was a governor of the NFTS for 13 years from 2001. In February 2015, the School's then Director, Nik Powell, presented Duncan (right) with an Honorary NFTS Fellowship, recognising his contribution.

Photograph © NFTS

The two main chains, Odeon and ABC, were determined to get rid of Eady. They didn't appreciate Puttnam's efforts at saving it.

> I had some vicious fights with the duopoly to the extent that at one point I was threatened that my films would not be played on British circuits. It came down to that, except they couldn't do it because that would prove it was a duopoly.[10]

Another casualty of the 1984 White Paper and the Films Act of the following year was the National Film Finance Corporation. The NFFC had invested Eady Levy money in British films for many years, among them such striking recent productions as Bill Forsyth's *Gregory's Girl* and Lindsay Anderson's *Britannia Hospital*. Baker announced that a new private sector company, British Screen, was to be set up.

In truth, the NFFC was beginning to creak. This was one of those government organisations in which decisions were reached by committee. The most it could invest in a single project was £500,000. The fund, which generally liked to take a one-third stake in a film, was struggling to find suitable films at the right budgets in which it could invest. *Sight & Sound* noted:

> Even when the old board did finally agree to support a project, there was no guarantee that other finance was available. As a result, money was often on offer for months or even years while the producer scrambled after the rest of the budget […] The Corporation found itself in the peculiar and invidious position when it was fighting closure, that it was pleading with the government for more money while having £5 million in the bank, all committed to projects that had not yet found the balance and might never do so.[11]

Baker's observations that the NFFC had not established itself 'as a major force in the world of film production' and that it was 'a subordinate source of finance, rather than an important means of initiative and support' weren't wide of the mark.[12]

At one stage, the NFFC entered into negotiations with Channel 4 (which went on air for the first time in November 1982) to see if the two organisations could invest in films jointly. The sticking point, though, was Channel 4's insistence that it be allowed to show any films it backed within 18 months of their cinema releases. The industry standard was still for a three-year holdback and the NFFC certainly wasn't going to break ranks by accepting a shorter 'window'.

According to Puttnam, Kenneth Baker had some regrets about dismantling the Eady Levy support system:

> He said, 'I've failed [with Eady]; what we've really got to do is see what to put in its place.' I negotiated with him a half-million-pound capital grant [for the National Film School]. We came up with a cluster of good ideas including British Film Year. That was all decided that day. These were all ways of him trying to make up for the fact that he had lost Eady to the Treasury.[13]

Baker later wrote in his autobiography that Richard Attenborough had told him that the Eady Levy was so small that all its money was not enough to finance even 'half a Hollywood film'. Furthermore, the money tended to go 'toward low-budget UK films – sometimes even soft porn'.[14]

Just as the exhibitors had predicted, cinemagoing rates did indeed begin to pick up rapidly once the Eady Levy was wound up (as part of the 1985 Films Act). However, whether the end of Eady had anything at all to do with the increase in admissions remains a moot point. The major factor in the revival in the exhibition sector was the investment by American companies, including National Amusements and AMC, in glossy new multiplex cinemas like The Point in Milton Keynes. These multi-screen venues were infinitely more comfortable and luxurious than the decaying old one- and two-screen cinemas in Britain's city centres, which fully lived up to their label of 'fleapits'. They were also able to programme films in a far more flexible fashion. With several screens at their disposal, they could give popular movies much longer runs, thereby maximising their box-office potential.

Steve Knibbs (later to become Chief Operating Officer at Vue International and one of the leading figures in UK exhibition) took his first job in cinema at The Point shortly after it opened. At the time, he had been working for Allied Lyons, running pubs and hotels in Yorkshire. AMC executive Millard Ochs hired him, telling him, 'We are looking for bright young managers like you.'

Although his friends teased him about working in Milton Keynes, a 'new town' scorned by outsiders and then best known for its concrete sculptures of cows, Knibbs knew that he had come to somewhere special. 'Walking into The Point at that time, it was like stepping into a new world,' he told *Screen International* of AMC's glossy new multiplex. 'At the time, it was like putting an alien spaceship down.'[15]

Knibbs oversaw the opening of other multiplexes and remembers the effect they had on their local communities. One was in Warrington, in Cheshire. He took a taxi to the venue, which was in the middle of a housing estate. The taxi driver asked how many screens the new venue had. The reply was ten. 'How do you watch ten screens at the same time?' the driver asked.

In his time at AMC, Knibbs helped convert the British to salted popcorn with butter on. 'The British palate was very sweet,' he remembered. He still speaks in admiration of the level of service that exhibitors like AMC and National Amusements provided in an era when a lot of older cinemas were becoming very run down. 'It was just simple things like cleaning the auditoriums between shows – and when I say clean, I mean clean.'

On any Saturday night at The Point, the venue would be heaving. All of the screens would be sold out and there would be the same sense of anticipation found at a big rock concert or nightclub. Cinemagoers shared the sense they were somewhere special.

The abolition of the Eady Levy had cut the cord between exhibition and production. It meant that British producers saw no benefit whatsoever from the resurgence in cinemagoing. This was an example of making a change to benefit one side of the industry without considering the damaging impact on another side. Baker didn't seem to acknowledge that there was any connection between exhibition and British production. If cinemas in Britain were to prosper by showing

American films, that seemed fine by him. Quotas had also been removed. As cinema attendance rose, there were soon calls for the Eady Levy or an equivalent measure to be reintroduced.

'No sooner had they got rid of Eady than the fortunes of the exhibition sector revived. Six or seven years later, everyone was saying we need a levy to support production,' remembers the then *Screen International* editor Terry Ilott.[16] 'You had one, it's gone and it is not going to come back' was the tacit response to the pleas. A video levy was proposed as the video rental business took wing in the 1980s, but the video industry was utterly opposed to the idea.

When Eady disappeared, British production immediately dipped. At a British Screen Advisory Council (BSAC) conference in London in 2013, James Bond producer Michael G. Wilson explained that Albert 'Cubby' Broccoli (who had launched the Bond films alongside Harry Saltzman) had been drawn to the UK in the first place by the Eady Levy and that after its abolition the UK industry went into a 'terrible decline'.[17] It was no coincidence that Broccoli took *Licence to Kill* to shoot in Mexico in the late 1980s, a decision he would have been unlikely to make if the Eady support had still been in place.

One idea briefly floated was imposing an Eady-style levy on the broadcasters to benefit film. However, this notion was soon dismissed. Baker didn't want the BBC licence fee to go up and was well aware the ITV companies were already paying a subscription to the recently launched Channel 4 for the new company to invest in feature films.

What was bizarre about Baker's recommendations, which eventually found their way into the Films Act of 1985, was the clear sense the government felt that its measures would actually help the industry. It was as if the ministers believed that, by removing its crutches, they would enable the industry to walk on its own feet. Baker himself was later sharply critical of Tory Chancellor Nigel Lawson for abolishing capital allowances for film production in the 1984 Budget – a decision Lawson took without any consultation with his colleagues. In his autobiography, *The Turbulent Years*, Baker wrote that Lawson had dealt a 'near-mortal blow' to any potential investment in British films.[18] However, at the time, he defended the Thatcher government's free-market philosophy to the hilt, declaring:

Our policy is to free the film industry from Government intervention and from an intrusive regulatory regime dating from
the days of the silent films. Our policy will clear the way for
the industry to operate in a more confident framework and to
consolidate upon its success.[19]

'There is a widespread belief that the Government are confusing the
film industry and its needs with their monetarist policies in other sections of British industry,' Labour MP Tom Clarke observed during a
House of Commons debate in May 1984.[20]

In Parliament, Kenneth Baker was unapologetic about the removal
of the allowances. 'I do not accept the argument that the future of the
British film industry depends entirely and exclusively upon the tax
regime under which it will operate,' he told the House of Commons.[21]

One point that Baker and his fellow ministers continued to make,
even as they cut away at public support for the industry, was that
British cinema was thriving. Oscars for *Gandhi* and *Chariots of Fire*
proved as much. The government may have got rid of the Eady Levy
and the NFFC but it was still very keen to be associated with British
Film Year, the grand, tub-thumping event on behalf of the country's
cinema which was to run from April 1985 until March 1986.

'It [British Film Year] will be a real coming together,' promised
Baker. 'It involves not only the producing side but the exhibition,
the television, the video and the creative sides. To pull all of them
together is an imaginative and huge project.'[22] Baker's remarks are
revealing. He didn't mention distribution. Baker appeared to regard
the idea of a 'coming together' between different sides of the industry as a one-off novelty, not as something that should happen as a
matter of course.

Baker's fellow minister Norman Lamont likewise appeared convinced that film could thrive without public support, whether through
tax breaks or levies on tickets. 'Overall, in our view, the industry is in
a healthy enough state to take advantage of the increased opportunities that are becoming available through video, cable and DBS [direct
broadcast by satellite],' Lamont commented during the second reading
of the Films Bill on 19 November 1984.

These are massive changes, and they are not all so far away. DBS is due to start in 1987. These changes, which will open up the market for films, pose the problem as to whether we can create enough films, and cause me to refuse to believe that the future is bleak.

'I believe that there are tremendous new opportunities,' Lamont continued.

I do not think that with these growing sectors it is an appropriate response to say 'levy' everywhere. Take a growing and successful sector and impose a levy on it, to recycle money to an industry which will face growing markets and growing opportunities for its products.[23]

What his remarks overlooked was the huge competitive disadvantage under which British producers were working. New markets may indeed have been opening up, but the satellite and cable providers had little interest in the health of the British production sector. Their movie channels showed almost exclusively American product.

Home video and pay TV had indeed taken off in the UK in the 1980s, and 1984, the *annus horribilis* for British cinemagoing, had seen the passing of a new Video Recordings Act. The legislation was introduced in response to the so-called 'video nasties' of the era. From the autumn of 1985 onwards, video recordings all had to have British Board of Film Classification (BBFC) classifications. In effect, this helped give the burgeoning British video business an air of respectability. No longer was it a case of consumers furtively renting films like *Straw Dogs* or *Driller Killer* from murky side-street video stores. Now, the video shops were just as likely to be bright and airy establishments in the middle of the high streets, catering for families as well as fans of 'World Cinema'.

When Sky launched its four-channel satellite service in February 1989, its film channel Sky Movies was one of the major draws for potential pay-TV subscribers. Its rival British Satellite Broadcasting (soon to become its partner) likewise traded heavily on the lure of its 'Movie Channel'. Both companies recognised the British public's voracious appetite for movies. The downside was that they were far more interested in programming Hollywood movies than British fare. It was to become a perennial complaint among independent British distributors that they simply couldn't sell on their films to the new pay-TV outlets – and that on the rare occasions that they managed to do so, it would be on terms far less attractive than Sky was apparently striking in its package deals with the US studios.

There were surprisingly prosaic reasons for Sky not picking up independent British films in greater numbers. It appeared that the new satellite broadcaster simply couldn't afford to do so. Sky had been formed in November 1990 after the merger of the two rival organisations, Sky Television and British Satellite Broadcasting. By then, though, the damage had already been done. Before the merger, both had gone 'running after the studios' (as producer Simon Perry puts it) to get hold of big US movies. Perry recalls:

> The studios saw them coming and bid them up and up and up. They paid a ludicrous amount of money for output deals with the studios. That's what they existed upon. Sky had spent a huge amount of money on those packages, those output deals. They were very disparaging about anything from the independents not only because they didn't think those films would play but also because they didn't have any money left.[24]

After the 1984 White Paper was presented to Parliament, Labour MP Bryan Gould called it 'a black day for the British film industry' and accused the government of 'misplaced ideological zeal for turning the future of the industry over to market forces despite the fact that, as the Monopolies and Mergers Commission found, nothing remotely resembling a free market exists in this area'. Gould also pointed out the hypocrisy in the minister extolling such films as *Chariots of Fire* and *Gregory's Girl* at exactly the same moment he was introducing policies that would 'bring much closer commercial and cultural surrender to the Americans'.[25]

One paradox was that British Film Year (see Chapter 11) was

launched in 1985, at exactly the same time as the new Films Act was undermining the industry. The government was tub-thumping for the industry at the precise moment that it was passing measures bound to undermine the production sector.

The goal of creating sustainable, vertically integrated British companies which could produce, market and distribute their own films, and compete with Hollywood in the process, was as far away as could be conceived. Nonetheless, the British industry has always been bullish about its own prospects. Against the odds, the late 1980s turned out to be a lively period in British film history. Whatever the underlying structural problems of the industry, film-makers, distributors and exhibitors alike were looking for new ways of doing business.

In the Thatcher government, the film-makers found a common (and surprisingly inspirational) enemy. Opposing Thatcher seemed to energise them. The most vivid and memorable British features of the period (many of them backed by Channel 4, which became the lynchpin of the industry in the Thatcher years) – *My Beautiful Laundrette, Mona Lisa, The Ploughman's Lunch, Letter to Brezhnev, Sammy and Rosie Get Laid, Angel, Hidden Agenda,* and so on – relished attacking Thatcherism on every level. The Thatcher government's policies in Northern Ireland, its views on gender, ethnicity and sexuality and its 'greed is good' style of capitalism were all excoriated with considerable vigour.

At the same time, the sections of the industry that most deplored the Thatcherite ideology behind the 1985 Films Act showed an entrepreneurialism that Thatcher herself might have admired. Producers set up their own distribution companies (for example, Oasis, which was set up by Jeremy Thomas and Chris Blackwell and run by Chris Auty). Distributors moved sideways into production (Palace Pictures, run by Stephen Woolley and Nik Powell, had started as a video distribution company but soon began making its own movies too).

Alongside the low-budget films made by directors like Stephen Frears, Neil Jordan and David Leland, the Brits were still making big international movies. Goldcrest, before its collapse, had backed such epics as *The Mission, The Killing Fields* and, less auspiciously, the American civil war saga *Revolution* starring Al Pacino. Producer

Deep in the jungles of South America
two men bring civilization to a native tribe.
Now, after years of struggle together,
they find themselves on opposite sides in a
dramatic fight for the natives' independence.
One will trust in the power of prayer.
One will believe in the might of the sword

THE
MISSION

8. Friendship and sacrifice: hot off *The Killing Fields* (1984), Roland Joffé directed another sweeping epic, *The Mission*. Shot on beautiful locations including the Iguazu Falls on the Argentina/Brazil border, it was written by Robert Bolt, a master of epic screenplays with *Lawrence of Arabia*, *Doctor Zhivago* and *A Man for All Seasons* under his belt. *The Mission* starred Robert De Niro and Jeremy Irons as Jesuits defending an outpost in the South American jungle of the 1750s. It won the prestigious Palme d'Or at Cannes, a precursor to numerous international awards. David Puttnam produced *The Killing Fields* and *The Mission*; Chris Menges won Oscars for his cinematography on both films.

Warner Bros./Goldcrest

Jeremy Thomas, still in his late thirties, had won a Best Picture Oscar for Bernardo Bertolucci's *The Last Emperor*, for which he had managed to secure permission to shoot in the Forbidden City in Beijing. At the same time, film-makers like Terence Davies and Bill Douglas were making intimate and autobiographical dramas – and Douglas managed to secure a hefty budget to shoot *Comrades* (1986), an epic about the Tolpuddle Martyrs, the rural activists in nineteenth-century Dorset who were deported to Australia as punishment for setting up a trade union. Meanwhile, Peter Greenaway, who had made his debut feature *The Draughtsman's Contract* for Film on Four, emerged as a British director whose offbeat and experimental movies were savoured as much in continental Europe as back home in Britain; Derek Jarman was shooting feature films on 8 mm stock; and Nicolas Roeg was in his pomp.

There was continual fretting about the UK losing its best talents (Alan Parker, Ridley Scott and others) to Hollywood in this period. Nonetheless, look back on the British films produced during the late 1980s and it seems like an extraordinarily fertile period. The debate around British cinema was also very lively. The film-makers railed against Thatcher, and the more conservative commentators in turn railed against the film-makers.

'For pointless sensationalism, sloppy attitudinising, and general disgustingness it deserves some sort of prize,' Professor Norman Stone wrote in a memorably splenetic article on Stephen Frears' *Sammy and Rosie Get Laid*.[26] Stone attacked the film's scriptwriter Hanif Kureishi, bemoaning the 'feeling of disgust and decay' in his work and calling his films (which also included *My Beautiful Laundrette*) 'worthless and insulting' primarily because of the way they ran down Margaret Thatcher.

Kenneth Baker's credibility with the industry was diminishing. By now, the Tory politician was nicknamed 'Half-Baker' because he wasn't able to follow through on his free-market promises. When the government failed to raise the money needed for new quango British Screen to be established from private sources, it simply went back on his principles and gave the new body a grant anyway.

Against the odds, British Screen Finance, which went 'live' in 1985, proved to be relatively successful. It was a strange organisation, a hybrid between a public and a private body. It was supported both by the Department of Trade, which agreed to provide £10 million over five years, and by Rank and Thorn EMI, the two British 'majors'. the British director Alan Parker remembered of the period:

> There were only two places that you could go for money in those days. There was Rank at one end of Wardour Street and EMI at the other. If you didn't get money from one of those two places, you didn't make your film [...] They [Rank] owned all these cinemas. They had a distribution company. They had a wonderful studio at Pinewood and they had a laboratory, and yet they made very few films.[27]

When it came to British Screen, it was in the interest of the two majors to lend at least some token support to this new company. Between them, they controlled 60 per cent of the exhibition market and therefore stood to become the main beneficiaries when the Eady Levy was abolished. As part of the new settlement, they each committed to investing around £250,000 per year for a period of three years. Channel 4, which provided £300,000, was the third of the private partners in British Screen – and the only one with any real commitment to investing in independent film production. The British Videogram Association invested £250,000. Complementing all this private money was a government grant of £1.5 million a year. Perhaps surprisingly, Rank and Thorn EMI did not stop funding British Screen after three years. In fact, both companies remained on board until the closure of the company in 2000 – but Rank had become Carlton by then, while Thorn EMI had been acquired first by Cannon for a while and then by MGM.

The public–private model under which British Screen was run was unusual. The new outfit was tasked with supporting projects that would not otherwise 'proceed to production'. This was the so-called 'additionality' clause – British Screen was helping green-light projects which the market would otherwise have spurned. At the same time, the new organisation was supposed to be run on 'a commercially successful basis'. As trade paper *Moving Pictures* pointed out, 'this was the same topsy-turvy Lewis Carroll-like logic which applied at the NFFC, which was obliged to back films which were commercially viable but couldn't get funded (which, of course, they would if they were commercially viable).'[28]

In other words, British Screen was skewered on the horns of a familiar dilemma, unsure whether it was there to support art or to make a profit – and aware that it would rarely be able to do both.

The government had expected British Screen to make a 'modest' contribution to British production overall. However, in the absence of other funding sources, the new organisation became almost the only place that independent British producers could approach. As Jeremy Thomas remarked, 'In the 1980s, Channel 4 and British Screen were the only games in town.'[29] Thomas might have added that, given that Channel 4 and British Screen were joined at the hip, there was only really one game in town.

British Screen's first chief executive was the well-liked Simon Relph, founder of Skreba Films. As a producer himself and as the son of a producer (Michael Relph), he had a very keen idea of the challenges facing British film-makers in putting together the budgets for even the most modest of movies. He himself had just been through the ordeal of producing Bill Douglas' troubled epic, *Comrades*, which had shot in England and in Australia with backing from the NFFC. He and Douglas had begun working on the project in the early 1980s. 'I think, unfortunately for Bill, he hit a period where it was very hard for original film-makers like him to get anything done,' Relph later remembered.[30] His own experiences made him very sensitive to the plight of fellow film-makers. Relph, who died in late 2016, stands as a pioneering figure in British cinema of this period – someone who was trying his best to bridge the chasm between production and distribution and who pursued a long-term strategy. British Screen was only able to invest in around ten films a year but Relph wanted to provide film-makers with a support system that would both help get their films into the marketplace and open up opportunities to develop new and bigger projects.

Relph used the National Film Trustee Company, formed in 1971, to collect revenues from old NFFC movies and the films that British Screen was itself supporting. This brought in an extra £500,000 a year. He hired business affairs executives and supported a National Film Development Fund under former trade journalist Colin Vaines.

One of Relph's boldest moves was to combine with production outfits Palace Pictures and Zenith to create a new company to sell

9. Widely respected: producer Simon Relph (1940–2016) served as CEO of British Screen Finance from 1985 to 1991 and chair of BAFTA from 2000 to 2002.

bafta.org

British films abroad. Palace had pushed hard for the new sales arm to be set up because of its frustration that distributor HandMade, who had zero expectations for Palace's 1986 film *Mona Lisa* and had disliked director Neil Jordan's cut of the film, which they tried to alter, were the sole beneficiary as a sales company of all the work Palace had done to persuade the Cannes Film Festival to take the movie. The Sales Company, as it was called (not very imaginatively), was breaking new ground. 'At that time, British films had such a bad name one could almost be sectioned for trying to sell them internationally,' British Screen Finance Director Kim Ballard later recalled.[31] There was an obvious logic behind the Sales Company, which was run by Carole Myer (former Head of Sales at FilmFour International). It gave the producers more direct influence over how their films were marketed. It also offered them better commission rates than they would have received from outside sales agents.

Relph saw British Screen not just as a source of production funding but as a support system for British film-makers at every stage of their careers. One initiative he hatched with Channel 4 in 1987 was 'Short and Curlies', a programme of short films made to the highest feature-film standards. The thinking here was to give young directors the experience of working with top professional crews and shooting their movies on 35 mm. Rank and EMI had already made it abundantly clear that they weren't much interested in investing in new British production in the long run, even if they did support British Screen in the short term.

The late 1980s was a colourful period in British production, but the major hitch was that British films still accounted for a tiny percentage of overall British box office (little more than 2 per cent in some years). The British studios were struggling. The industry had a very lopsided look. British Screen was doing sterling work but Relph and his team were receiving 350 or more scripts a year – and were able to back only a handful. They had Channel 4 as partners, which meant their films would eventually find a slot on TV. There were plenty of critical successes in the first years of British Screen (*Prick Up Your Ears*, *The Belly of an Architect*, *The Last of England*) and some features (*Personal Services*, *White Mischief* and *Scandal* among them) were given big mainstream releases – but few were real box-office hits. The producers fretted that so little money came back to them.

When you read the trade papers from the period, they highlight the difference in mood and expectation between the producers, distributors and exhibitors. On the production side, everyone canvassed by *Screen* seemed pessimistic in the extreme. The year 1986 'saw the lowest level of film production in the UK for some years – fewer than forty films going before the cameras', lamented an editorial in *Screen International*.[32] Theatre impresario turned movie producer Michael White (*The Rocky Horror Picture Show*) was making a familiar observation when he told the magazine that it was 'disgraceful that the film industry, which is so crucial, is not better supported'.

'Independent producers are the cornerstone of the new industry, yet many of them, with good projects, cannot raise finance,' lamented another leading independent producer, Simon Perry (whose credits include *1984* and *White Mischief*).[33]

'The truly British feature film is becoming something of an endangered species,' agreed David C. Patterson of production company HandMade Films (owned by the former Beatle George Harrison). 'The problem, and the solution, lie with television,' Patterson continued, pointing out that 'whereas a US film producer would expect to recover about 30 per cent of his cost from domestic television, the UK producer would consider even 10 per cent a triumph'.[34]

Even bleaker was the assessment of the industry from Alan Sapper, the general secretary of the Association of Cinematograph, Television and Allied Technicians (ACTT). 'We are still confronted with a deepening crisis of the British film production industry,' Sapper wrote. 'This is based on the lack of indigenous finance and the inability to attract foreign finance owing to the lack of a tax regime that makes high-risk capital investment attractive.'[35]

'There's an extraordinary paradox occurring,' David Puttnam agreed, talking to Thames TV in 1990. 'Audience figures are zooming and every indication is that, as the multiplexes continue to get built, those audience figures will continue to zoom. This is happening at precisely the moment when production is dropping like a stone.'[36]

An editorial in *Screen International* noted the anxiety caused by the lack of funds available for development and production. The Goldcrest crash has frightened off potential investors from the City, and the withdrawal of capital allowances and the Eady Levy has had a devastating effect on investment from industry sources in the US.[37]

Alongside these downbeat commentaries, *Screen International* also included a range of articles from distributors and exhibitors. Their tone was very, very different. James Higgins, president of the Society of Film Distributors (as it was then named), contributed a notably optimistic article, highlighting how multiplexes had transformed the cinemagoing landscape for the better. While acknowledging that the UK box office was still 'predominantly product driven' and that there was 'no firm bed-rock audience' for whom visiting the cinema was a regular habit, regardless of what was showing, he hailed the box-office growth the industry was already experiencing.[38]

Exhibitors like AMC, Rank, Cannon, CIC and Maybox were all upgrading their venues or investing in multiplexes. A cynical view would be that these exhibitors were relieved they were no longer burdened with the concerns of production. There were no quotas to force them to show a percentage of British films and they didn't have to divert any of their box-office profits toward producers. It had become a familiar grumble among producers that the UK's major companies, most notably the Rank Organisation, were ignoring home-grown production and concentrating on showing Hollywood fare instead.

By the mid-1980s, film and television services were just a small part of the overall Rank portfolio. The country's biggest film company was diversifying into restaurants, theme parks, photocopiers (Rank Xerox) and bingo. Nonetheless, the mid-1980s were banner years. As the media reported, Rank's film and TV division had made a £13 million trading profit in 1986. This constituted a small but important part of overall profits at the Rank Organisation that year, which were at £164.1 million, up 21 per cent on the previous year. Jim Daly, direc-tor of Rank Film and Television Services, pointed to the very robust performance of the cinema business, 'with an 8 per cent increase on audiences (in 1986) on top of the 50 per cent increase last year'.[39] Daly listed the films that were drawing the audiences back: *Santa Claus: The Movie* (which had done better in the UK than anywhere else), *Rocky IV*, *The Karate Kid II*, *Hannah and Her Sisters*, *Aliens* and *The Jewel of the Nile*. At least *Aliens* and *Santa Claus: The Movie* had been shot in Pinewood Studios, but every title that Daly namechecked was distributed by an American company.

Outspoken film-maker Michael Winner claimed that British producers were entirely responsible for the pickle in which they found themselves. 'The problem with the English film industry is its producers,' he told Thames TV.

> The producers have throughout decades that I have watched it made films to please their friends at the dinner table who don't actually pay to get in and without any serious regard for the large international audience you need to attract to a motion picture.[40]

The industry itself recognised that something wasn't working. Close to 85 per cent of the gleaming new multiplexes that were helping drive up admissions were owned by American companies. Distribution was dominated by the Americans. Local production levels were variable but had fallen as low as only 30 films in 1989. Venture capital simply wasn't coming into the industry. The optimism voiced by Conservative ministers like Norman Lamont and Kenneth Baker that British production, if left to its own devices and weaned off public support, would flourish turned out to be completely misplaced.

To visit Pinewood in this period was to get a sense of the trough into which British film-making was then sinking. By the end of the decade, the sound stages at Britain's flagship film studios were all but empty. As noted, the most recent Bond film, *Licence to Kill* (1989), had become the first in the 007 series to shoot entirely outside the UK, decamping to Mexico because Britain was considered too expensive. To the immense relief of the local industry, Tim Burton's *Batman* (1989) was lured to Pinewood. Gotham City had been built in its entirety on the Pinewood backlot and the film had demonstrated yet again the excellence of British technicians and craftsmen – but this already seemed like a last hurrah. In the early 1990s, some of the

Gotham sets had been left standing and a huge statue of the Joker was still on display, but Warner Bros. had long since left. *Batman Returns* (1992) was shot entirely in the US.

Pinewood's glories seemed all very much in the past and the studios, like British film-making itself, were in a prolonged slump. Some Hollywood movies were still coming, occasional British films and TV dramas were made at Pinewood too, but business was, at best, desultory. The studios were steeped in history but there was a dispiriting sense that their glory years were in the past. British production levels had plummeted. In 1991, America made 455 films for the cinema – and Britain made all of 15, excluding TV movies.

Every so often British features were still winning Oscars but their one-off successes only served as a reminder that the production sector as a whole was floundering. By the early 1990s, the best-known production companies of the previous decade, Goldcrest and Palace Pictures, had gone bust. (The former survived in name as a post-production services company but the glory years of *Gandhi* and *The Mission* were long behind it.) The 'Go-Go Boys' at Cannon, brash businessmen Menahem Golan and Yoram Globus, who had caused such exasperation and indignation by taking over large swathes of the British film industry, were also a spent force in the UK.

It was instructive to read the British newspaper response to the Oscar successes of British films. In March 1993, *Howards End* and *The Crying Game* both won Academy Awards. As customarily happened, this prompted a mini orgy of self-congratulation among the politicians and media commentators. In particular, Peter Brooke, the National Heritage minister, was quick to trumpet the Academy Awards as an indication of the wealth of talent that British cinema still possessed. Just as at the time the Eady Levy was dispensed with, there was a dispiriting perception within the movie business that the Tory government simply didn't care about the film industry. Derek Malcolm warned in the *Guardian*:

> Those, however, who think the Oscar success will make a difference to government policy, which is to do as little as possible to help the industry in this country, are probably in for

a disappointment. If we do well, the government suggests that we don't need any assistance. If we don't, it complains that we hardly deserve support.[41]

What made the parlous state of British film production all the more frustrating was the knowledge that cinemagoing in the UK was on an upsurge. Box-office admissions had reached their lowest point of 54 million in 1984 but, by 1992, that figure had almost doubled to 103.64 million – and would continue to rise throughout the 1990s.

In theory, if the British public was buying the tickets, the industry as a whole should have benefited. In practice, the box-office hits were almost all films made by US studios and released by American distributors. Columbia, UIP and Warner Bros. dominated the distribution market. There was no longer any mechanism in place to divert money from the box office to the British producers. Newspapers were quick to spot the imbalance. 'Lots of Oscars, No Film industry' ran the headline in one newspaper story and 'Camera, Lights, Inaction for British Cinema' was the headline on another.[42]

One positive result of what Simon Relph called 'our great summit with Mrs Thatcher' was the setting-up of the European Co-Production Fund, a UK-based initiative overseen by British Screen to 'promote collaboration between British film producers and other film producers in the European Union'.[43] This new fund was to have a grant of £5 million, spread over three years.

As critic and historian Alexander Walker noted in his book *Icons in the Fire: The Decline and Fall of Almost Everybody in the British Film Industry 1984–2000*, the Downing Street summit wasn't just an exercise in public relations. It had yielded practical benefits or, at least, as he put it, 'a financial mouse crept timorously out of this mountain of misplaced faith.'[44] What happened was that two working parties (one run by the Department of Trade and Industry, the other by the Treasury) were put in place to examine structural modifications to the industry and investment incentives.

The public debate over film policy in the early 1990s is fascinating. Even as producers continued to grumble that the government had abandoned them, lines of communication were opening up between the politicians and the industry. Ministers wanted to be associated with British cinema successes. There was a growing acknowledgement, too, that the film industry created jobs and that British movies helped put British goods and services in the shop window. American movies that shot in Britain created jobs and brought inward investment. At the same time, many of the old tensions and suspicions remained, both between politicians and the film industry and between different sectors of that industry.

The politicians' ambivalent attitude toward British film-makers was apparent in notorious remarks made by Labour MP Joe Ashton during the National Heritage Select Committee session in December 1994 when three of the country's most distinguished directors, Mike Leigh, Alan Parker and Ken Loach, met the politicians. Ashton told the film-makers:

> When we have arts versus entertainment it always seems that the arts people are really moaning and groaning, they are wanting to make films that they want to make which the average person does not want to see. You people have an elitist attitude that the public must adjust to what you want to put before them and if they do not then it is the public's fault.

'Ninety-nine per cent of my constituents are Philistines; maybe I represent them,' Ashton also commented during the session. 'It is just your industry run at the top, making stuff for each other, quite frankly. There is no feedback from the consumers at all.'[45]

Ashton's rhetoric was deliberately provocative. However, he was tapping into an 'anti-luvvie' mood that was becoming increasingly apparent in the mainstream media and for which the precocious actor–director Kenneth Branagh had become a lightning rod. Branagh's *Henry V* (1989) had been, in the words of critic Alexander Walker, a 'vividly visceral, populist experience'. Branagh seemed, in his youth, ambition and in the ease with which he switched between stage and screen, to be Britain's answer to Orson Welles. Nonetheless, there was a distrust of the cheery and effusive manner in which he went about tackling his 'art'.

Ashton's words also pointed to a strain of thinking that would become increasingly influential in British film culture in the Film Council years. There was a perception, as critic Raymond Durgnat put it, that '[a]n upper crust of quality product has been doing fine' as prestige productions won Oscars and plaudits, but that downstairs the view was grim.[46]

The three directors were incensed at being baited by the politicians. Mike Leigh protested that they were all driven to make films by 'a commitment to entertainment, not to lofty ideas', and called Ashton's jibes 'the most dreadful and dangerous generalisation and I do resent it deeply'.

Ken Loach, the director of *Cathy Come Home* and *Kes*, was revered within the industry. At the time of the committee hearings in December 1994, his career was picking up again. He had made three successful films in a row: *Hidden Agenda* (1990), *Riff-Raff* (1991) and *Raining Stones* (1993). Nonetheless, Loach had also endured a dismal period in the 1980s when he simply couldn't get any of his films financed. He was appalled by Ashton's 'personally abusive' remarks. 'I have heard some confused Philistines in my day but I think this beats the lot,' he told the committee.

The third of the directors, Alan Parker, had just made *The Commitments* (1991), a hit film about a bunch of music-loving, working-class Irishmen. He bristled at the idea that he was 'elitist', ignoring the public and making films for his friends. *The Commitments* stood both as a corrective to Ashton's hectoring and, on one level, as an endorsement of what the politicians were saying. Parker explained that it was a film 'no one in Britain would finance'. His backing had come entirely from the US; it was released in the UK by 20th Century Fox.

The film-makers were asked what had happened to the good old British film industry that 'used' to give the public what it wanted. Parker responded: 'We never had one. What is this film industry? Name it.' Asked to pinpoint the kind of movies that once made British cinema great, one politician came back with the example of the *Carry On* films.

In many ways, this was an extraordinarily dispiriting occasion. A group of politicians, used to being lobbied far more aggressively by other industries, were blasé and offhand. They didn't seem to realise that the three directors they were browbeating were among the most distinguished film-makers of their era. Nonetheless, it was significant that the directors were there at all. That, at least, was a sign that the Conservative government recognised there was a problem, and one partly of its own making.

There had already been attempts to undo some of the damage done by the 1985 Films Act. It was recognised by the politicians that, as James Clappison MP put it,

> British film making is not living up to its full potential. Investment has declined. In comparison with our European neighbours, we are investing less and producing fewer films [...] we must produce big-budget British films and also, importantly, we must attract to Britain producers from overseas, especially from America, to use our film infrastructure.[47]

In 1991, the government had set up the British Film Commission to promote the UK's attractiveness as a location for filming. After the 1992 election, now under Prime Minister John Major, film was moved under the wing of the Department of National Heritage. The government also arranged for the UK to join Eurimages (the Council of Europe's Cinema Support Fund) and introduced tax relief for the industry through the Finance Act.

The Labour Party, which had been in opposition for so many years, was busy plotting its own cultural policies and set out aggressively to woo the film industry and score points against the Tories while doing so. The opposition was quick to blame the government for the ongoing 'brain drain' in the British film industry that was driving 'skills, both creative and technical, to the West Coast of the USA'. As Labour noted in a policy document in the early 1990s,

> The one cultural industry which is not currently successful is the film industry. Britain is the only country in Europe which gives no substantial support to its film industry. As a result, our industry has declined to the point where only nine British financed films were started in the first six months of 1991.[48]

Labour was already floating the idea (soon to be embraced by the Conservative government) of establishing a National Lottery to support the arts.

As both parties sought support from the 'creative industries', there were again signs of rifts between the different interest groups in British cinema. The distributors, for example, felt that the lobbying was being led by the producers, who were putting their own interests first. After the Downing Street summit of 1990, there had been Working Party discussions between the Department of Trade and Industry (DTI) and representatives from the film sector. Percy Livingstone, who preceded James Higgins as president of the Society of Film Distributors (SFD), could not help but notice that the Working Party was led almost entirely by producers following 'a divide and rule policy'. Livingstone wrote to the DTI:

> It [the Working Party] seems to be making a fundamental mistake in focusing on theatrical distribution in isolation from other sectors of the industry which we believe will result in an unbalanced perspective [...] the only correct perspective is of course that of the audio-visual industry as a whole.[49]

Livingstone pointed out some home truths about distribution that he didn't believe the Working Party understood at all. It was a familiar list: 65 per cent of box-office receipts were retained by exhibition; distributors had 'huge' prints and marketing costs as well as hefty overheads. He questioned many of the points in the 'background paper' which the Working Party had already drawn up.

'Even when there is no common ownership, the largest distributors have substantial power in bargaining with exhibitors,' this paper had claimed.

> The big distributors are the source of the lower risk, mass audience material. They can use the leverage of those films to get their less obviously commercial material on the screens and to secure the best play dates for all their product.

Livingstone responded:

> Mass audience material is almost always expensive, high budget
> and high risk, therefore the term 'lower risks' is not true. The
> losses through disappointing rentals from a major release are
> enormous. The distributor cannot use the leverage suggested
> as linkage between titles is not allowed following the MMC's
> report and the Films (Exclusivity Agreement) Order 1989.

The SFD president was also aghast at the suggestion in the background
paper that 'UK distributors do not invest in production on a major
scale any longer, although there is still integration with the exhibition sector'. The disengagement from production arose from the high
costs and risks involved and the ready supply of cheap and popular
American films. He countered that

> the term 'cheap' is completely untrue. A review of the most
> successful films shows that they are actually very expensive
> […] if the UK distributors find it cheaper to purchase rights
> of American films than to invest in UK production, their deci-
> sion must be related to the higher cost of UK production and
> the commerciality of the actual production in question. This
> emphasises that an appropriate fiscal incentive for a UK investor
> could be significant for UK production.

In September 1991, Labour held a special conference on the film
industry at the National Film Theatre in London, giving its plans for
'Regenerating Britain's Film Industry'. Some of the more conservative
elements in the distribution and exhibition sectors grumbled about
the speakers, who included many leading young film producers.
'Practically all the speakers, as may be imagined at a Labour Party
seminar, were Left Wing with snide comments about the present
government and Mrs Thatcher in particular,' an SFD attendee notes
in a memo.[50]

Shortly after the seminar, Livingstone wrote to one of the
seminar's organisers, Gordon Brown, again trying to warn him

about the dangers of looking at the film industry solely from the perspective of the producers. Livingstone pointed to a continuing paradox:

> In spite of the undeniable fact of the decline in British film production, the cinema industry as a whole in the UK is show-ing steady growth and this is expected to continue for the next 4–5 years at least. It should not, however, be assumed that these conditions create a ready source of funding to be tapped to develop British production. Such a move could well prove to be counter-productive.[51]

The SFD president was also quick to let Brown know that the sharp rise in British box-office revenues didn't mean that the distribution sector was prospering. Out of the estimated UK cinema box office of £250 million in 1990, the distributors had total earnings of £15 mil-lion – and from that, they had to deduct prints as well as marketing and overhead costs. They therefore didn't have much spare to contribute to the industry fund which was being proposed.

One of Livingstone's sharpest observations regarded the failure of the Labour proposals to make any reference to the public. This was a perennial problem in discussions between the film industry and the government. Sometimes, the industry representatives became so enwrapped in their own particular problems that they failed to notice that, in the words of a later government paper, 'it all starts with the audience'. Policy makers needed at least to try to remember to come up with ways not just of revitalising British production, but of ensur-ing British films had the opportunities to be distributed properly and to reach British cinemagoers.

During this period, British cinema's most prominent figures were themselves striking a determinedly despondent note about their own business. 'I just don't think there is a film industry any more,' producer Simon Relph, who (as mentioned) had spent several years as chief executive at the government-backed funding agency British Screen, told one newspaper. 'There's a collective of British filmmakers but… well, an industry implies more than that.'[52]

Even Richard Attenborough, director of *Gandhi* and lobbyist extraordinaire on behalf of British cinema, was fretting to journalists that there was 'no industry' in the UK.[53] The British didn't have tax incentives for production or much in the way of training schemes either. Distributors and exhibitors were often at loggerheads – and neither were going out of their way to support British-made films.

Oscar-winning actress turned Labour politician Glenda Jackson made the same point:

> There is no British film industry. It's always a one-off situation. A question often asked is: is the British film industry dead, dying, or only worrying too much? Or is it alive and well and hiding in our television sets – a parochial wonder, but entirely incomprehensible to anyone but us?[54]

Jackson's words were truer than she might have guessed. British production in the 1980s was surviving – and prospering to a degree – not just because Channel 4 was starting its Film on Four strand but because these were blockbuster years for the video business.

CASE STUDY
HENRY V (1989)

Stockbroker turned film producer Stephen Evans likes to say that he became involved with Kenneth Branagh by 'going to the wrong house on the wrong day'. In the late 1980s, Evans was an admirer of the youthful and still largely unknown Branagh's theatre work. He saw that Branagh had launched the Renaissance Theatre Company and felt that, with his 'background in the City', he might be able to help.

'He (Branagh) hadn't got a clue what he was doing but I admired his chutzpah,' Evans recalls. In order to assist Branagh, though, it was necessary to meet him first. Evans tried calling the Riverside Studios, where Branagh was then performing, but couldn't get through. The actor wasn't returning his calls.

One afternoon, Evans went to visit his friend Michael, who had just moved into 51 Eaton Terrace, Belgravia. When he rang the doorbell, it was answered by a woman he didn't know. Evans assumed that this was Michael's new girlfriend.

'Where's Michael?' he asked. The woman replied that he wasn't back yet but that he would be home in 45 minutes. She invited Evans into the house and offered him champagne. He lit up a cigar and waited for Michael to return. He asked if he could make a quick telephone call and tried to ring Branagh again. This time, he called the box office at the Riverside and, by chance, Branagh himself answered. Evans told him, 'I might be able to help you with your theatre company.' Branagh agreed to meet. At that point, Michael returned.

'His first words to me were "Who the fuck are you?" I was in the wrong house. It just happened be a guy called Michael.'

If Evans hadn't reached Branagh then, he insists he 'wouldn't have bothered the following day'. He would have stayed a 'loaded stockbroker' rather than losing his money in the film business.

His anecdote about how he first spoke to Branagh underlines the part that luck and coincidence play in British film history. The actors in Branagh's theatre had been wary initially about having a stockbroker as patron but were eventually won round.

Under Evans, Renaissance Films became one of the biggest names in the British industry until its eventual collapse in 2005. Credits as a producer included *The Madness of King George* and *Wings of a Dove*.

Evans raised close to $10 million for Branagh's adaptation of *Henry V*, calling in favours from old City friends and investors, most of whom knew they stood little chance of making any profit. This was a period when there were no significant tax breaks for film production beyond a Business Expansion Scheme system, which didn't yield much. Eventually, the BBC invested a small amount too for the broadcast rights but Evans clawed together most of the budget on his own.

Branagh hadn't made a film before. This was a case of an unknown actor who was even less well known as a film director taking on a Shakespeare play that had already been done with huge success by Laurence Olivier 45 years before in 1944.

Nonetheless, Branagh's *Henry V* (1989) was a triumph of sorts. It secured two Oscar nominations and turned Branagh, then in his late twenties, into an international celebrity – Britain's very own answer to Orson Welles when he was making *Citizen Kane* and was considered a wunderkind.

'There was no upside,' Evans recalls. 'The film did very poorly in the UK. It did well in the US and funnily enough, given what the subject matter was, it did very well in France.' It was enough, though, to launch Branagh's career and to pull Evans out of the City and into the film business.

CHAPTER 2

The Video Revolution

'The key to it all was the explosion of VHS,' Stephen Woolley, co-founder of Palace Pictures, says of the phenomenon, still not properly credited, that revived a near-moribund British film industry during the 1980s.[1]

There has always been a certain snobbery about video within the British film industry. Even 30 years after the event, the industry was still loath to acknowledge that it had effectively been rescued at one of its very lowest ebbs by something as tawdry and unseemly as the VHS cassette.

At first, no one seemed to like video. The National Viewers' and Listeners' Association (NVLA), the scolding and censorious pressure group which had been founded by self-appointed moral crusader Mary Whitehouse in the mid-1960s, campaigned vigorously throughout the decade against what became known, largely thanks to its efforts, as 'video nasties'. Conservative MP Graham Bright, from Luton South, introduced a Private Member's Bill to enforce government regulation of the video industry. This would eventually lead to the Video Recordings Act of 1984.

'I was convinced that action was required to deal with the sale of video recordings depicting unrestrained violence, sexual abuse, mutilation and murder. Everything that I have learnt in the intervening months has confirmed that view,' Bright commented during a House of Commons debate. Bright and his fellow politicians had been treated the week before to a compilation of clips from so-called video nasties featuring (as he put it) scene after scene of revolting violence, including sickening sexual abuse, mutilation and even cannibalism. I know that several Hon. Members had to leave the room before the end of the showing and I do not blame them for that. Many others, like me, had to turn away from some of the scenes.[2]

There were moves among right-wing politicians to forbid any film with an 18 or X certificate being allowed to appear on video at all. The idea was scotched only after the politicians were convinced that banning X-rated titles would only play into the hands of the pirates. Liberal film lovers were almost equally suspicious of the burgeoning new business because of what they perceived to be the shabby quality and dubious provenance of the videos themselves. The cinema owners didn't like video either – it was perceived as a threat to their businesses. The broadcasters were equally hostile. The film-makers, meanwhile, chafed at the very idea of their masterworks being watched on small screens from fuzzy magnetic tape.

The impression Woolley gives of the early days of the video industry is of himself as a prospector exploring a modern-day Klondike. Woolley spent a year on his own acquiring the movies that Palace would release on video. In the early 1980s, he went to all the festivals and markets to negotiate rights for Werner Herzog and John Waters movies; for David Lynch's *Eraserhead*, István Szabó's *Mephisto*, some Godard, some Kurosawa and for anything from Rainer Werner Fassbinder that he could get his hands on. Woolley was often able to get at least some of the films for a song. The sales agents at the major independent companies hadn't even begun to legislate for video. 'People had no idea what video was.'[3]

The sales agents would have pieces of paper detailing what they might expect to receive for theatrical or TV rights but there was nothing for video. Woolley would estimate how many copies he might sell, work backwards from that and suggest a number. 'Anything I offered for video seemed like a good price. They had nothing to compare it to. The market was literally a blank piece of paper […] the companies were overjoyed to get anything.'

As it turned out, the foreign-language classics he bought on those initial trips didn't have that sizeable a market on rental video. What he did realise, though, was that there was an immense appetite for cult movies, horror pictures and genre fare on video. Fans liked music films too. When Palace Pictures launched in May 1982, one of its sales ploys was to allow stores who wanted to rent out Gary Numan's *Micromusic*, recorded at the pop star's farewell Wembley Arena concerts, to send in blank tapes. 'For $7.50 plus post and packing the company will copy the program onto the tape and return it,' reported *Billboard*.[4] This was a considerable saving on the $40 they'd have had to pay otherwise. The fact that the quality of a second-generation video copy might be less than pristine wasn't mentioned.

Stars also helped propel VHS rentals – and the video boom created a new generation of them over the next decade: Belgian kick-boxers like Jean-Claude Van Damme, American martial arts experts like Chuck Norris and Swedish musclemen like Dolph Lundgren among them. At the same time, the new format gave an unlikely impetus to the faltering careers of many older names – and not just when they were making films. (For example, Jane Fonda may have been an Oscar winner from a distinguished Hollywood family, but the lead actress from such 1970s classics as *Klute* and *Coming Home* was to become far better known for her *Jane Fonda's Workout* videos in the 1980s than for her movie roles.)

'Home video was driven very much by names, not by reviews. If you had a star, you could pretty much guarantee there would be a home video sale,' recalls Terry Ilott, editor of *Screen International* from 1984 to 1987.

> You couldn't get major [Hollywood] movies because they held out for three or four years. There was lots of B-movie stuff, lots of porn, but also lots of good films being made where 40 per cent of the cost was being set against the home video value. This also revived the independent distribution marketplace. All of a sudden, independent distributors had a way of bypassing the hold the majors had on distribution.[5]

To those in senior positions in the British film industry, just as to those in charge of the Hollywood studios at the time, the video business in the late 1970s and early 1980s seemed like a furtive back-street enterprise populated by pirates and pornographers. In a way, it was. That was its attraction. Ilott remembers:

> The majors wanted nothing to do with it. They tried to block the selling of video cassette recorders in America on the grounds that they were an incitement to piracy and copying. They shunned it and thought it would cannibalise their core business.

With the US studios ignoring video, there was, at first, very little for the early video dealers to license. With no films to show, they turned toward pornography and horror as a matter of necessity, thereby confirming the worst suspicions that the mainstream industry had about them.

'There was a dearth of legitimate material because the studios would not release films on video. They thought they would lose control of it,' video pioneer Iain Muspratt says of the early days of VHS. 'That gave rise to the beginnings of piracy but also what it meant was that what people would license was pretty disreputable stuff.'[6]

The actions of the British Board of Film Classification (BBFC) didn't help. Its then director James Ferman had a showreel of especially grisly scenes the BBFC had cut out from films. 'He used to show it at the Houses of Parliament and all these MPs and peers would stagger out, thinking it was dreadful,' Muspratt remembers. The fact that these scenes had been taken out of context was ignored as their shock value was foregrounded.

Ferman had understandable reasons for taking a wary line. The Video Recordings Act gave the BBFC responsibility for licensing videos as well as feature films – a huge increase in its workload – and confronted Ferman and his examiners with a new set of challenges. With video cassette recorders (VCRs) in people's homes, the fear was that kids would end up watching films intended for their parents. Ferman was very well aware of the furore that had greeted his prede-cessor Stephen Murphy's decision to 'pass' such films as *Straw Dogs*, *A Clockwork Orange* and *Last Tango in Paris* to be shown in cinemas in his time at the Board, from 1971 to 1975. He didn't want to be caught up in a moral backlash against permissiveness.

Muspratt chaired the conference at Central Hall, Westminster, at which Mary Whitehouse came out with the phrase that brought blight on the video industry – 'video nasty'. During the event, she was asked about a film that had a controversial reputation. She immediately declared that the film was 'dreadful' and 'should be banned' forthwith. Someone asked if she had actually seen the film. 'No,' came the inevitable reply. She was then asked if someone else from her organisation had seen the film if she hadn't. Again came the inevitable reply, 'Oh, no.'

Ironically, Whitehouse may ultimately have helped to give the video business the respectability that she had so long been attacking it for lacking. The Director of Public Prosecutions used the Obscene Publications Act to prosecute distributors and impound their titles. The newspapers relished the scandal of it all and were ready to fan the flames at any opportunity. As academic Julian Petley has noted, the press played a leading part in whipping up the 'video panic'.[7] 'How high street horror is invading the home' was the headline of a typically sensationalist story in the *Sunday Times* in the summer of 1982.

> Uncensored horror video cassettes, available to anybody of any age, have arrived in Britain's high streets […] They exploit extremes of violence, and are rapidly replacing sexual pornography as the video trade's biggest money spinner. The nasties are far removed from the suspense of the traditional horror film. They dwell on murder, multiple rape, butchery, sado-masochism, mutilation of women, cannibalism and Nazi atrocities.[8]

The *Daily Mail*, meanwhile, warned about the potential corruption of minors: 'More and more children, well used to video recorders in school, are catching on to the fact that their parents' machine can give them the opportunity to watch the worst excesses of cinema sex and violence.'[9]

All this overheated rhetoric prompted action from the politicians. The end result was the Video Recordings Act 1984, which required that all videos released after the beginning of September 1985 be submitted for classification from the BBFC. There was some heavy-handed censorship. Films that had received BBFC certificates for being shown in cinemas had scenes cut for their video releases. However, the legislation gave the industry a new veneer of respectability and ultimately enabled it to take its place on the high street.

Woolley talks of the way that the video revolution gave power to the independents. 'The independent distributors, the licensors, the shops – everybody who was involved in those early days of video was very maverick […] there were no majors there who were elbowing us out of the way. There were literally no rules.'[10]

Ilott agrees:

No one knew what would happen. It took off like a rocket, home video. There's no precise figure but I think about $3 billion was pumped into independent production driven by video. It was the home video revenue that enabled companies like Hemdale to make *Platoon* or Goldcrest to make *The Mission*. These independent companies were suddenly able to hedge the bets they made with film production with home video revenue.[11]

Given how quickly it grew, it was startling how slow the UK video market had been to take off, even given the 'video nasties' furore.

'Video was never designed to be anything other than a time shift mechanism. Nobody believed there would ever be a domestic market in pre-recorded video,' Iain Muspratt remembers of a period in which the most likely application of video technology appeared to be to allow viewers to record live TV and then to watch it at their leisure.[12]

One of the very first pre-recorded video cassettes ever sold in Britain was an education programme about elephants, bought from the Guild Group by Lancaster Education Authority in 1974. Muspratt, then Guild's managing director, remembers that the retail price of cassettes in this period was anything between £350 and £700. They were sold to institutions, not to individuals.

UK companies Intervision, formed in 1972, and VCL were early entrants into the video market. At first, their focus was on supplying video equipment and pop promos to discos. Their early attempts at licensing feature films, releasing 'rubbish Italian spaghetti westerns and that kind of thing', hadn't been profitable.[13] However, when the VHS and Betamax formats became easily available, they saw their chance. As Julian Upton points out, their business models had always been based on having an eye for the main chance:

> Intervision and VCL had been opportunistic long before they entered the home video market – their very existence was down to an opportunity created by the then UK licensing law that stated a club or disco had to offer 'entertainment acts' in order to be able to sell alcohol.[14]

Video films of pop bands performing counted as entertainment (however hastily or ineptly shot) and enabled club owners to get the licenses they needed to sell beer, wine and spirits.

In the late 1970s, Intervision struck a deal with the US studios to release such movies as *Rocky, Jaws, Carrie* and *Casablanca*. These sat alongside the adult titles in its catalogue. Guild followed suit, releasing Sam Peckinpah's *Straw Dogs* (the subject of a furious censorship row) and *The Stunt Man*, starring Peter O'Toole, on video in 1980.

In its early years, Palace Pictures, founded in 1982 by Woolley and Nik Powell (the former business partner of Virgin mogul Richard Branson), made an instant killing through video. The speed of the success took both of them by surprise.

'Nik Powell came to me with the idea of starting this company [Palace] alongside another dozen companies he was starting as a farewell to Richard Branson,' Woolley recalls.[15] The other companies included a video editing centre, a satellite dish company, a record distribution company in Holland and a post-production company. He also had plans for a vegetarian restaurant.

'I was importing satellite dishes that were bigger than the moon and that people installed in their back gardens – and they could only get Russian ice hockey on them.'[16] Powell acknowledged that not all of his business ventures were immediately successful. Even before the launch of Palace Pictures in 1981, he had launched the Video Palace megastore in Kensington High Street, London, selling dishes, TV sets and laser players as well as videotapes.[17]

There was no expectation that Palace Pictures would take off as quickly as it did. The plan agreed between Powell and his new partner was that Woolley would acquire and release the kind of exploitation and art-house movies that he had already been showing at the Scala, the independent cinema he founded in 1979 on Tottenham Court Road and that was later based in King's Cross.

Woolley had bought the rights to American horror film *The Evil Dead*, directed by the then little-known Sam Raimi. It was a movie which had screened at the American Film Market in Los Angeles. Some saw it as just another splatter-filled exploitation picture but Woolley immediately spotted its cult potential and persuaded his business partner that they needed to acquire it. 'We must have offered about five times more than anyone else [...] at that point, we didn't have a clue about the prices,' Powell is quoted as saying in Angus Finney's 1996 book, *The Egos Have Landed: The Rise and Fall of Palace Pictures*, seemingly contradicting Woolley's remarks about sales agents having no idea of the price of video. However, Woolley was referring specifically to the acquisition of video-only rights, whereas Powell was referring to the acquisition of theatrical, video and TV rights where the prices were pegged much higher, which left Palace 'somewhat at sea' and at the mercy of the sales companies.[18]

Palace blithely broke with convention by releasing *The Evil Dead* simultaneously on VHS and in cinemas. The transition to buying all rights was made in Los Angeles in March 1982 at AFM/Filmex, where Palace bought *The Evil Dead* and *Diva*. It took a lot of persuasion for Woolley to convince Powell to pay more for theatrical rights because he had told him a year before that the theatrical market was a drain on resources, but by the time the company had spent a year unsuccessfully releasing subtitled films, it became apparent that the best way to make video work was through theatrical release and exposure, as Palace proved with *The Evil Dead*. The video retailed to stores at around £50 and Woolley remembers that the company sold 50,000 copies in the first year alone, grossing more than £2.5 million.

'It wasn't a debate. We didn't tell anybody, we didn't ask anybody, we just did it,' Woolley says of the decision to open the movie in cinemas on around 50 copies at exactly the same time that it appeared in video stores.[19] Such a strategy would have been unthinkable just a few years later – the 'windows' system was rigidly enforced and

'THE MOST FEROCIOUSLY ORIGINAL HORROR FILM OF THE YEAR'...
...STEPHEN KING BEST SELLING AUTHOR OF *THE SHINING* AND *CARRIE*
THE ULTIMATE EXPERIENCE
IN GRUELLING TERROR
SAM RAIMI'S
THE
EVIL
DEAD
NOW
ON VIDEO

10. Don't go into the woods: mixing dark humour and grisly violence, *The Evil Dead* was an effective calling card for 21-year-old Sam Raimi, its inventive writer/director, who has worked extensively in film and television. *The Evil Dead* spawned a franchise and continues to exert a huge influence on film-makers across the horror/suspense genre.

Palace Pictures

distributors had to wait months or more after a film's cinema release to issue it on VHS. There used to be a five-year interval between a film's cinema release and when it was allowed to be broadcast on TV. 'There was a dawning after a few weeks that we shouldn't have done that and we had our knuckles rapped. But our response was that nobody had said we shouldn't.'

Their topsy-turvy theory was that releasing the film on video would get people talking about the film. Those who had seen it would tell their friends – who would then go and see it in the cinemas. They hoped that the formula would work the other way around too and that cinemagoers would convince their friends to see the film on VHS.

Nik Powell recalls that chief Odeon booker Stan Fishman 'almost killed me' for ignoring a holdback.[20] Nonetheless, the Palace bosses were able to argue that they were 'new boys' behaving with the raw exuberance of youth and hadn't meant to hurt anyone's feelings. They got away with it. Holdbacks, though, were soon enforced, starting at three months and gradually growing longer.

Woolley acknowledges that he paid a big price for Jean-Jacques Beineix's highly stylised thriller *Diva* (the other notable success from the early days of Palace). There was a logic, though, behind doing so. He wanted to shake up the traditional way of releasing foreign-language fare in the UK market. This was a commercial film in his eyes and that was how Palace was going to treat it.

Palace's freewheeling approach to marketing was to do the precise opposite of most of the UK's theatrical distributors of the period – and of Rank in particular. Powell and Woolley hired from outside the industry. Their publicist Phil Symes was from the music business and was best known for looking after rock band Queen. The publicity material for *The Evil Dead* was designed by Graham Humphreys, an art school student from Salisbury who had only recently moved to London.

'I had a friend who was working at a small design agency. Their secretary knew somebody who was working at Palace Pictures. She said it might be a good place to take your work,' Humphreys recalls.[21] He approached Palace, set up a meeting, left some samples of his work and then, a few days later, was rung by Palace to say they'd like him to have a go at a poster for a new film.

> When it was described to me, it was described as a low-budget B-movie horror film which was very gory. They asked me along to the Scala Cinema one afternoon and it was screened just for me to watch. I sat there on my own and watched the fully uncut version.

As a horror fan, Humphreys immediately spotted the references to British Hammer films and 'trashy B-movies' from the 1950s.

> That was what I was really trying to emulate [in the poster]: the trashy B-movie aesthetic. At the same time, having been to the Scala as a punter in the past, they had a jukebox there which was full of punk rock and 1950s stuff. It was very much a transgressive, teenage rebellion mix of music. In many ways, that was the key for the aesthetic for me.

A particular inspiration was the music of American goth punk band the Cramps, who were famous for having given a free concert a few years before in the California State Mental Hospital. In their image and music, the Cramps were very influenced by 1950s horror, exploitation, gangster and sci-fi movies like *Robot Monster*, *Plan 9 from Outer Space* and *Gun Crazy*.

The poster Humphreys came up with was lurid and ingenious. 'It was what I would describe as a punk rock, fifties B-movie aesthetic. There were no natural colours. I didn't use flesh tones or anything. It was day-glo and loud and quite brash.' In the film, a tape recorder is featured. Humphreys therefore came up with an image of reels of magnetic tape (which look like film cans) with a skull peering over them. Behind, as if peering through a window, are terrified (and terrifying) faces which are green-tinted. Nobody knew the names of the actors and so he wasn't obliged to foreground the stars.

At the time, there was a nightclub called the Bat Cave which attracted the goths and the punks – the people Humphreys was sure would like the movie. He tailored the image to them. 'People who used to go to the Bat Cave loved *The Evil Dead*. That [enthusiasm] expanded out into the music scene.'

As Humphreys' memories attest, the film tapped into the punk spirit. The marketing and poster work did likewise, getting away from 'the fatigue of the big-budget American horror films' with their 'photographic' imagery of knives and eggs. His poster was adapted for the VHS sleeve. 'Video was fairly new and nobody had thought how if you do a quad [rectangular] poster [for the cinema], that wouldn't really translate to a portrait format [for video].'

Humphreys ended up 'repainting' the *Evil Dead* poster for the book-cover-like format of the video sleeve. He wasn't happy with the work, which he had to complete very quickly, but says now that it's rough-and-ready quality gave it 'a nasty, subversive look very far removed from the very slick packaging everybody else had'.

'We almost intentionally hired people who didn't have any connection at all with the business or certainly with Rank,' Woolley recalled of Palace's recruitment practices. 'We were trying very hard to do the reverse of everything Rank had done. We were trying to be flamboyant, less conservative and not to follow a formula.'[22]

'I also thought that the British film industry needed some more rock and roll' is how his then business partner Powell described the irreverent Palace approach. Powell was from the music world and when he came into the film business he was startled to discover that 'the producers still wore jackets and ties, even young producers wore jackets and ties. It was oil and water compared to the record business of that era.'[23]

Predictably, the older players in the British industry looked askance at this upstart in their midst. Woolley recalls:

> They thought we were too big for our boots and that Nik was coming in throwing money around and that it would all end in disaster and work against everyone else. In fact, Palace was a big shot in the arm for the industry. People began to realise that we didn't have to have these staid, boring campaigns that Rank was shoving down people's throats.[24]

Woolley was withering about Rank's approach to marketing and distribution. He bemoans the fact that Palace came into existence too late to have the opportunity to release films like Nic Roeg's *The Man Who Fell to Earth* or *Don't Look Now*, films that were handled in inept fashion.

> The spark that ignited the industry was Palace, but Palace's spark came from the VHS world, the video world. It [video] was really this opportunity for independent companies and independent people to suddenly partake in the business. Someone like me, who was a big film fan, could suddenly jump in. There was this brief moment when the pool was open to everyone.

Palace was a tiny company specialising in cult films – *Diva, The Evil Dead, Nightmare on Elm Street, Blood Simple* – and yet it was outperforming the established players. Woolley and Powell were consummate networkers who befriended the film-makers. For example, the Coen brothers were the editors of *The Evil Dead*. When they went into production with their own films, Palace was a natural partner for them.

'At Palace, it was us against the world. Palace epitomised the new guard,' recalls Robert Jones, who joined Palace in his early twentiess as a sales manager and was later to become a successful producer and financier as well as to head up the UK Film Council's Premiere Fund. 'At Palace, we were all young and single and became very much a family.'[25]

Jones' initial job was going around all the wholesalers and retailers who had heard that video was a 'good wheeze' and might have been butchers the week before but had now decided to open video stores in a spirit of opportunism. Jones recalls the freewheeling way in which Palace did business in the early days:

> I remember going to south London to collect £35,000 in cash in an airline bag from a guy who wanted to buy a consignment of *The Evil Dead*. We wouldn't give him any credit. He asked me when I was leaving if I wanted to buy any guns at the same time. It was a bit Wild Westy [...] and it [video] was certainly the thing that kept Palace going through thick and thin.

Palace couldn't afford to set up its own full sales team with reps to go into every venue to sell the tapes. It therefore set up Palace Virgin Gold in partnership with Virgin and the Golds, enterprising East End wholesalers who had a warehouse in Leyton.

Some of Palace's competitors may have seemed world-weary and apathetic but Woolley, Powell and co. were hard-working, passionate cinephiles who felt an evident pride in being able to represent work by the directors they loved. 'That's why we went to festivals and saw seven or eight films a day. We wanted to find the next *Cinema Paradiso*. We wanted to find the next *Reservoir Dogs*. We wanted to be wowed,' Jones remembers.

Palace may have been under-capitalised but it quickly grew from within. 'Whether through altruism or just lack of money, they built a fantastic team,' Jones says. The company had no compunction about 'pissing people off' by releasing day and date and it transformed the way that foreign-language movies were marketed. 'You can look at it through rose-tinted glasses but it was an incredible company,' Jones says of an era in which video was the cash cow.

Palace's success allowed (and arguably compelled) the company to diversify into production. 'The video industry was absolutely crucial in terms of pumping money into production,' Ilott states. 'Also, it proved to be hugely important in terms of the education of the audience, which no one had expected at all.' He argues that the video boom broadened tastes and brought the customers closer to the film-makers whose work they watched.

> You're talking about an audience that suddenly has a handle on film and film history [...] it enabled people to educate themselves about film. The audience became much more sophisticated. They were building up their own libraries. That had a fantastic impact. There was a moment when video stores were like record stores were with music, staffed by film buffs. They were repositories of real expertise.[26]

'I do think that video introduced a more direct relationship with an audience that has now gone,' agrees Iain Muspratt, who went on to run Choices, Britain's second-biggest video chain after Blockbuster. 'Our shops were centres of the local community.'[27]

What had previously seemed like marginal independent titles from directors like Sam Raimi, the Coen brothers or David Lynch eventually became regarded by viewers as if they were part of the mainstream. Nik Powell suggests:

> The higher proportion of the population that in the eighties and nineties started having a higher education meant that the market for middlebrow product and independent films grew exponentially. That's what underwrote the success of Palace, Miramax and many other companies around the world.[28]

It helped too that, early on, the independent video pioneers had so few direct competitors.

There had been seemingly sound business reasons for Hollywood to ignore the nascent video market. In the pre-video era, the US studios were able to sell films to free TV and to pay TV for vast amounts.

In the mid-1970s, NBC had paid MGM a reported $15 million for a package of films including *Gone with the Wind* and *Doctor Zhivago*. The former title reached an audience of 34 million when it was shown on US television for the first time in 1976.

'In the mid-1970s, before the explosion of video, subscription pay-TV channels accounted for as much as 20% of domestic revenues of US theatrical distributors,' David Waterman wrote in his book *Hollywood's Road to Riches*.[29] Hollywood didn't want to kill what looked like a very fat golden goose by striking illicit new alliances with the video companies.

It was a similar story in the UK, where Rank and EMI, then the major players, were very cautious about the video market. That only changed when Cannon, run by flamboyant businessmen Menahem Golan and Yoram Globus, took over Thorn EMI in highly contentious circumstances in 1986. Ilott remembers the deal:

> EMI was part of a bigger company, Thorn EMI. They decided that screen entertainment had no future and sold the screen entertainment business en bloc to [Australian businessman] Alan Bond, who sold it on within a week to Golan and Globus for about three times [the cost].[30]

At the time, the British film 'establishment' had closed ranks against Cannon. No one on Wardour Street wanted one of Britain's most powerful film companies to fall into the hands of the two producers whose best-known film was smutty teen comedy *Lemon Popsicle*. Sir Colin Southgate, CEO of Thorn EMI, was left looking foolish after selling off EMI's film interests to Bond for £125 million when the Australian sold those interests on only a week later for £175 million.

'You wouldn't book our films in your cinemas,' Menahem Golan told the EMI staff immediately after the takeover was completed and the Cannon logo began to be put up on all of the country's ABC Cinemas. 'So we bought your company!'[31]

Unlike their peers, the 'Go-Go Boys' embraced video. They were schlockmeisters and by far their most successful movies were the action pictures and B-films which performed so well on video.

Golan would talk in later years about how he drew up a contract with Sylvester Stallone on a napkin for Stallone to play an arm-wrestling lorry driver in *Over the Top* – a strong seller on video, even if the critics derided it. It was also Golan who discovered the so-called 'Muscles from Brussels', Benelux bruiser Jean-Claude Van Damme. The Belgian had given a kick-boxing demonstration in an LA restaurant to Golan, who was so impressed that he quickly hired him to star in *Kickboxer* (1989). Golan and Globus also did a roaring trade with their unsavoury vigilante movies in the *Death Wish* series, directed by Englishman Michael Winner. 'They saw the power of video,' says Muspratt, who oversaw the release of many Cannon titles through Guild Home Entertainment.[32]

However, already debt-ridden, the Cannon bosses were forced to sell the 2,000-title EMI Library to US producer Jerry Weintraub in 1987 to raise funds. This library included such recent EMI-backed titles as *The Deer Hunter* and *Rambo: First Blood* but also a host of classic British movies, among them the vintage comedies made at Ealing Studios under Michael Balcon in the 1940s and 1950s. The library was eventually to end up in the hands of French company StudioCanal, who used fledgling British distribution company Optimum to manage it. Throughout the video and then the DVD era, the library was a cash cow. The best-known titles were reissued again and again.

The video industry became so lucrative that it was easy to forget the teething problems it had faced. Videotape had been used by the television industry since the mid-1950s. In the 1960s and early 1970s, film and TV companies had been exploring the possibilities of film-playing video machines for the domestic market but in Britain, at least, this seemed a very distant prospect indeed.[33]

During the mid-1970s Japanese electronics companies were busy developing rival systems for home use. Sony was pushing Betamax, launched in 1975. JVC had VHS, Toshiba and Sanyo had something called V-Cord II and Matsushita Panasonic also had its own format, launched a year later.[34] The VHS system was cheaper and could offer 90-minute tapes (as opposed to the 60-minute ones for Betamax). The war over formats would eventually be won by VHS.

'I put it down to commercial skullduggery, politics […] and

technology,' Alan Pritchard, executive vice president at Sony Pictures Home Entertainment in the 1980s, later said of the way Betamax and other formats, including the Philips 'Video 2000' two-sided system, were bypassed in favour of VHS (perceived by many to be an inferior product).[35] The format wars would have a sequel a generation later when Hi-Def DVDs were pitted against Blu-ray. Sony was pushing Blu-ray while Toshiba championed HD DVD.

Companies like RCA and Philips had experimented with video discs with very mixed results. These were the size of dinner plates or 78 rpm records and predictably weren't successful commercially. '100 reasons to buy an RCA Video Disc Player' reads the advertisement in a 1981 issue of entertainment trade magazine *Billboard*.[36] The 100 reasons were the 100 films that RCA had rights to, everything from *The Godfather* to *The Graduate* and *Rocky*. The video disc players cost $499.95 and the cheapest Video Disc sold at $14.95. These were prohibitive prices for most consumers, given that a single disc only stored a maximum of sixty minutes of video.

Another question was whether the video market would operate on a rental or a retail basis. The studios were far more comfortable with the former idea. At first, they didn't want anybody to own their films. 'They had a natural customer base with a rental mentality,' Alan Pritchard remembers of the early Hollywood tendency to see rental as an extension of the theatrical market. 'It was built on the studio mentality that the product was never sold.' Gradually, the studios realised this model was unmanageable. 'That changed because of the difficulty of the administration. It was going nowhere and I think the business would have been strangled by that complexity,' Pritchard notes.[37] Instead, the US majors agreed to allow dealers to buy videos but on the strict understanding that they would rent the films on to their customers. The dealers would pay around £30 for library titles and £50 or more for newer films.

When the studios belatedly entered the video market in earnest in the early 1980s, a transition was already under way. The porno years were coming to an end. In *Inherent Vice*, his history of video in the US, Lucas Hilderbrand points out that the adult industry sold 950,000 tapes in 1979 and 1.3 million the following year, but that its market share began to dip in the 1980s.[38] Anti-obscenity laws were enacted. Family-friendly chains stopped renting porn. Hollywood's increasing prominence in the market meant that there was far more choice available.

The studios were convinced that their vast catalogues would be a gold mine. This turned out not to be the case. Pritchard was an executive at RCA who came into the video business after Columbia sold its home video division to RCA in 1981. He remembers that the studios were all releasing between eight and ten library titles every month. In the case of Columbia, these were acknowledged classics such as *The Bridge on the River Kwai* and *Lawrence of Arabia*.

However, it was the newer films that sold the best. One quirk the studios quickly noticed was that certain films which had flopped in the cinemas sometimes turned out to be big successes on VHS. Audiences would discover new stars (for example, comedian Steve Martin) on video and then go and see their next films in the cinemas. Video was seen as a 'safety net' or a 'cushion'. It gave films a second chance to find an audience and extended their commercial life in the process. Frank Darabont's Stephen King adaptation *The Shawshank Redemption* (1994) is a famous example of a film that did only modest business in the cinema but went on to become a huge success on rental video.

Video changed the nature of production as well as that of distribution. 'The back end of the business needs 20 titles a month. The problem was that the studios could only make 20 or 25 movies a year,' Pritchard recalls.[39] With such a voracious pipeline to feed, budgets came down, production levels rose, and there were opportunities for new players, especially those producing action and horror (genres which the studios were then largely ignoring).

This was the beginning of the age of the straight-to-video action movie. The studios had to forfeit at least some control of how their films were being marketed and sold. Their philosophy changed. When it came to which movies they greenlit, they were thinking as much about potential home entertainment value as how the pictures would perform in cinemas. In what really did seem like a case of the tail wagging the dog, video was beginning to drive the industry. No longer was it seen as an afterthought. Even the most prestigious British costume dramas were financed through video deals. Michael Radford's *White Mischief* (1987), set in the aristocratic expat English world of Happy Valley in Kenya in the early 1940s, had a budget of $7.5 million, sizeable enough for the time. Its cast included Sarah Miles, Trevor Howard and Greta Scacchi. The money was put together in what its producer Simon Perry calls the usual 'patchwork' fashion, with contributions from Goldcrest and Columbia, and even some money from Kenya.[40] However, $2.5 million came from Nelson Entertainment, a US video company run by former EMI executive Barry Spikings. This was an advance only against North American video rights and yet it accounted for a third of the budget – evidence of how lucrative video had become.

With so much product flooding the market, a cinema release wasn't seen by some distributors as an end in itself but as a way of proving the respectability of their titles. Palace was one company which quickly moved from video only to theatrical releasing.

As 'home entertainment' grew, the way film companies were managed changed too. This was now turning into a retail business, not a marketing and advertising one. Films were regarded by home entertainment divisions and video companies as 'consumer goods', which wasn't at all how the studios had originally conceived them.

The rise of VHS revolutionised the viewing habits of the public. For the first time, consumers could watch films at home whenever they wanted. They could rent them and then, later, when the sell-through market matured, they could own them too. They made up their own minds. No longer were their viewing choices controlled by film distributors or TV schedulers. Video stores had huge selections of titles which could be browsed at leisure in the same way as books or records.

The main video distributors published magazines to which their customers contributed. They would arrange midnight openings for some of their bigger titles. (Fans would turn out by dead of night, dressed in costumes from the films that were about to be released on VHS.) Video stores tended to be found on high streets, alongside the supermarkets. They became an absolutely fundamental part of everyday life for British shoppers.

Video store owners listened to their customers' feedback about what films they should license and stock – and sometimes what films they should produce as well. 'We got feedback and we needed that feedback because we needed to know what rights to buy,' Palace's Powell says of the company (which had three stores in London).[41] At the same time as they were listening to the customers, the distributors also had close relationships with the film-makers whose work they licensed – and, in some cases, produced as well.

The video boom happened at the same time that the first multi-screen cinemas were being built. As mentioned, The Point at Milton Keynes, the UK's first multiplex, opened in 1985. The venue's operator, AMC, refused to hire anyone who had worked in cinema exhibition before. Terry Ilott remembers:

> They didn't want to be infected by the same mentality, the same culture. They specifically said in their recruitment advertising for The Point, previous experience definitely not required. Don't bother applying if you have previous experience. They didn't want anything to do with the culture of defeatism and underinvestment that plagued the UK.[42]

The executives of AMC chose Milton Keynes as the site for a multiplex after studying the map and doing a demographic analysis. They worked out 'drive times' for reaching the venue – something exhibitors had never bothered with before because British cinemas had traditionally been on the high street, not out of town. They realised that Milton Keynes was a short hop from other towns like Stevenage, Luton, Hatfield and Hitchin. The new site was straightforward to reach by road and AMC ensured there was easy, plentiful parking and plenty of places at which to eat. As Terry Ilott notes,

> It was an instant success. They showed the same films as every-body else, the difference being that in a multiplex, you could have a much more varied programme, which audiences liked.

Sky Movies was launched in 1989 – the UK's first pay-TV channel for cinema. The new channel may not have shown many British films or have attracted big audiences in the early years but it was part of the regeneration of the British industry alongside the multiplexes and the gleaming new video stores. After years of underinvestment, when many British cinemas had justifiably been called fleapits, the film business was managing to connect with a new audience. With more potential sources of income, independent distributors were prepared to take greater risks. From the low point of 54 million in 1984, cinema audiences began to rise – and there was no sense that video was eating away at box-office receipts. Nonetheless, the old cinema exhibitors remained suspicious of the upstart new film format. 'I always felt it [video] was competition to cinema,' says Stan Fishman, Odeon's chief booker in this period. 'They [the video distributors] were the other side of the fence.'[43]

Ironically, the money that came from video enabled more and more films to be given a theatrical release. Distributors wanted the movies in the cinemas because that would enhance their visibility and value on VHS. Films like David Cronenberg's *Scanners* (1981), released by New Realm, or Palace's *The Evil Dead* itself, found their way into cinemas.

'The great thing about video was that as it became a mass market, the actual production costs [for videos] became less and less. The discs were virtually nothing. The margins were huge, absolutely enormous,' recalls Muspratt. Videos and discs could be manufactured and pressed very cheaply at a time when prints for cinemas still cost thousands of pounds. 'Our experience was that our customers went to the cinema more because of video than they would have done otherwise.'[44] The video companies would use their customers and their staff as 'information gatherers'. They'd always ask what the customers thought about new cinema releases.

In the mid-1980s, the sell-through market began to develop in tandem with the rental business. At first, sell-through videos had been far too expensive for all but the most affluent customers. If you wanted to buy a film and own it, it would cost you £30 or more. However, a far-sighted executive called Paddy Toomey, entertainment buyer at convenience store Woolworths, saw the possibility in selling videos at cut-rate prices. The initial Woolworth collection, licensed from K-Tel, was branded 'The Video Collection'. It was promoted as 'a video for the price of a blank tape', the idea being that the customers could buy and watch the film and then tape over it. The leading video stores began to include sell-through sections in their shops and even experimented with the mail-order business. Where Woolworths led, others followed. Soon, supermarkets began selling videos alongside groceries. Newsagents stocked them too. Sales would spike at Christmas and Easter and in advance of Mother's Day. On a wet bank holiday, rentals and sales would shoot up.

'We used to hate hot weather and we liked the school summer holidays being wet,' Muspratt recalls. When the sun did shine, the video companies could at least console themselves with the thought that the cinemas had been so slow to introduce air conditioning. Film lovers wanting to escape a heatwave were better advised to close the curtains, pull down the shades and watch the films at home.

When the Eady Levy (the tax on cinema tickets which aided production) was abolished, there was serious talk of a new levy on video. Producer David Puttnam was pushing for the new levy and almost managed to persuade the Labour Party to include the proposal in its manifesto for the 1992 general election. He recalls:

> It was going to be tiny, 1p. The advantage of the tax was very real. If you put a tax on something, you put a stamp on it. If you put a stamp on it, it was legal. If you bought something which didn't have a stamp on it, it was illegal.[45]

When one of the tabloids heard about the proposal and ran a story warning readers that Labour was planning a tax on their weekly video, the idea was quietly dropped.

One of the US majors had carried out research to discover how many employees in its distribution offices around Europe were graduates. The answer was... precisely one. Alan Pritchard himself rose to become senior executive vice president and European general manager for Columbia TriStar Home Entertainment. He was one of the five most senior figures involved in running Columbia's worldwide operations. The other four were all Ivy League – from Harvard, Yale or Cornell – while he was a Welshman from a humble academic background: 'Aberystwyth on a wet day', as he joked.[46]

In the new era, executives in the home entertainment divisions of the studios tended to be far better educated. It was no longer enough to have worked in a cinema or to have started as an office junior. Tensions became apparent between those on the theatrical side of the business, who dealt directly with the film-makers and felt they were part of the fabric of the industry, and those who were busy renting out video cassettes.

'The theatrical people, because they were closer to the production process, felt they were the gods,' remembers former Sony Pictures executive Brian Robertson.

> If you looked at the way they treated themselves in those days, they all had chauffeurs, they all had two secretaries and all of that type of thing. The people on the home entertainment side didn't have any of those trappings of luxury at all. They were just people who sold to significant retailers.[47]

Those on the theatrical side referred to their home entertainment colleagues as being in 'the dry goods business'. As if to live down to such a name, the home entertainment divisions sometimes treated films with a conspicuous lack of respect. Widescreen epics were 'panned and scanned' so they fitted the shape of the TV screen. The action on the left- or right-hand sides of the frame would be lopped off. Films were also sometimes speeded up. If you had a David Lean movie that lasted over three hours, it simply wouldn't fit on the cassette. The home entertainment companies would therefore 'cut out the pauses' or speed up the film slightly.

In Europe, a mini trade war broke out as the video boom began in earnest. European Economic Community (EEC) countries were worried about just how much Japanese hardware their citizens were buying. Their own manufacturers of video machines and cassettes, companies like Grundig in Germany and Philips in the Netherlands, wanted protection and claimed that their Japanese rivals were under-cutting their prices. 'The recorders are subjected to time-consuming checks, and this bottleneck has virtually choked off the flow of record-ers into France,' the *New York Times* reported.[48]

The French took draconian action to protect their own market. In November 1982, they came up with a system that all foreign-made recorders entering the country had to be vetted by a customs depot in Poitiers. This was deliberately understaffed to make the process as slow as possible.

As the home entertainment business grew, new trading conditions were put in place. The British Video Association (BVA) was established in 1980 as a representative body for the industry. The Video Recordings Act was passed in Britain in 1984. The Video Standards Council was set up in 1988.

'When I arrived at the BVA, there were a lot of members of Parliament, particularly elderly peers, for whom video meant something rather salacious,' remembers Lavinia Carey, director general of the association, of how the video industry cleaned up its image in this period. Her own appointment was (she believes) part of the process.

> One of the reasons I was hired was not only because of my marketing background and time in advertising but also because I was female. I think they thought that might be an asset – to have somebody who looked as if they might not be involved in that rather sordid side of the industry.[49]

The Federation Against Copyright Theft (FACT) was founded in 1983 to combat piracy. Copy-protection systems, notably Macrovision, were set up to prevent the illegal duplication of first video cassettes and then DVDs. The videos themselves carried warning messages, stickers and holograms testifying to their authenticity.

Once the studios entered the video market, they quickly took a dominant position. Companies like Fox, Warner Bros., CIC (Universal and Paramount) and, later, MGM began to put the squeeze on the independents. They demanded extra shelf space for their titles in the stores. That meant less space for the independents. This was a very lucrative business. The major players weren't just renting and selling the films – they were providing the machines on which these films were played. Sony, which had bought Columbia Pictures from Coca-Cola in 1989, produced video players. Warner Home Video worked very closely with Japanese partners Toshiba.

Even after the studios came into the business in earnest, the home entertainment market was still lucrative. In 1999, the UK video industry was worth £1.3 billion.[50] In the US, consumers spent $18 billion on home video products in 1997, of which $9.5 billion was rental expenditure.[51]

The figures for even some of the smaller players were astounding. Choices Video was a Peterborough-based chain that had over 236 stores in the UK at its height and where Muspratt became managing director. By his calculations, the company was renting out 500,000 titles each weekend during the peak video years. Each film was being watched by an average of four people. That's an annual weekend audience of well over 100 million for one company alone. Bigger video specialists like Blockbuster, which had over 800 stores in the UK at its peak, would be reaching around 400 million viewers each year. There were many other players in the market too.

The hitch, at least as far as Palace was concerned, was that so many of them were chasing the same movies. Whereas Woolley had once had a free run at markets, naming his own price for video rights to titles no one else in the UK market wanted, there was now fearsome competition. Prices rocketed. That was one reason why Palace set up its theatrical releasing business and then moved into production. Woolley recalls:

In our first year [1982], I was very fortunate. I bought *Diva*, I bought *The Evil Dead*, I bought *Merry Christmas, Mr Lawrence*. We became victims of our own success. When Palace in its first year of trading was so successful, and we had a very high public and industry profile, suddenly if I was going to Cannes or I was going to the AFM [American Film Market] or if we were going to any of the markets, our interest in any titles would whet the appetite of the competitors who had started coming in very quickly.[52]

Companies like Virgin – which had set up its own video label, VCL – Guild, Entertainment and various others would compete against

Palace in bidding wars. Woolley had acquired Wes Craven's cult classic *A Nightmare on Elm Street* at script stage. The project had come to him because Bob Shaye of US indie outfit New Line, who had already sold to Palace various of John Waters' kitsch comedies, was looking for money to finance it. He saw Palace as a potential partner. The film was a huge hit. Now, with so many competitors bidding to acquire rights, Woolley began to think that the easiest way to differentiate Palace from its rivals, and to get to the talent first, would be to make its own films. That was how Palace came to make Neil Jordan's *The Company of Wolves*, a lurid and playful slice of Gothic horror with a flavour of Jean Cocteau about it that was adapted from a werewolf story by feminist writer Angela Carter. The film was heavily influenced by Woolley's knowledge of the marketplace. He knew that (as he puts it) 'an elevated genre horror fantasy film was exactly what the VHS market was looking for'. The idea was to appeal to the same cinemagoers who had been lapping up John Landis' *An American Werewolf in London* (1981), a massive hit on film and on video. *The Company of Wolves* was at once very British and a film with an obvious international appeal. This was an example of a British movie made without subsidy or tax credits (soon to become essential crutches for British film-makers) that owed its existence to the power of the video market.

Palace Pictures may eventually have overextended itself, crashed and burned (as detailed in Finney's book *The Egos Have Landed*), but it provided a model that not just British but US companies too were keen to imitate. The company was a source of particular fascination for Harvey Weinstein, who had founded Miramax with his brother Bob in 1979. 'He was fascinated by how Palace could have made a film like *Absolute Beginners* and still have released films like *A Nightmare on Elm Street* and the Ken Loach movies,' Woolley recalls of the American executive who was to have a major influence on British cinema until his career came crashing down in late 2017 amid multiple accusations of bullying and sexual impropriety. At the time of writing, Weinstein continued to deny the accusations, which had been very widely reported in the US and UK press. 'We had a wide range of films and that was his [Weinstein's] aim for Miramax – to be able to keep the music side, and, at the same time, go into the art world and more intellectual foreign-language films.'

Woolley recalls a breakfast meeting with Weinstein that went on all day as they shared ideas about their respective philosophies for their companies. He came away from the meeting convinced that Miramax would buy the project Palace was then developing, Michael Caton-Jones' *Scandal*, about the Profumo affair (the fling between British cabinet minister John Profumo and the young model and showgirl Christine Keeler).

'He [Weinstein] took a big risk on *Scandal* and it was a very important film for him. It was incredibly successful in the States,' Woolley recalls. The film began a working relationship between Palace and Miramax that would culminate in *The Crying Game*, which Weinstein bought after it was completed and then became an Oscar winner. Palace and Miramax also acquired films together, among them *My Left Foot* and *Cinema Paradiso*. These were both companies that wouldn't have prospered in quite the same way if there hadn't been a booming video market.

Miramax's fascination with the British industry (and with newly available British sources of film financing) was underlined in 1997 when the Weinsteins financed a new UK-based production company, HAL, run by David Aukin (former head of film at Channel 4), Colin Leventhal, another former Channel 4 executive, and Trea Hoving. The company made a handful of films, among them Patricia Rozema's adaptation of Jane Austen's *Mansfield Park* and Jez Butterworth's *Birthday Girl* starring Nicole Kidman, before HAL dissolved amid tensions between the UK executives and their overbearing American bosses.

Once the majors moved in, Palace found itself squeezed. The company had released David Lynch's *Eraserhead* and Woolley was desperate for Palace to handle Lynch's *Blue Velvet*, but Fox did the job. 'I tried to buy it from them but the more money I offered them, the more it dawned on them: "why don't we release it ourselves?"'

The transition to DVD in the late 1990s gave that market an extra fillip. The DVD format offered quality, seemingly greater security from piracy and vastly increased marketing opportunities. There was space for extras: directors' commentaries, trailers, making-of documentaries, shorts, alternative endings, photo galleries, and so on. The discs were inexpensive to press and could be sold at enormous profits.

The video business was shunned initially by the majors because it was perceived as being somehow shady and illicit. The irony was that once it had earned respectability and video/DVD had begun to provide far more revenue for Hollywood than cinema, organised crime moved in. Piracy was arguably to play a significant part in the demise of the industry. Iain Muspratt claims that 'it reached the stage where, if you filled a 44-foot trunk with [pirate] DVDs, you would make more money than if you filled it with cocaine.'

'It [piracy] was terribly well organised and it was a massive business,' Muspratt continues. 'There was no question that it was organised crime.'[53] The police didn't want to intervene, arguing that this was the responsibility of Trading Standards. Politicians weren't minded to help much either.

At the time of writing, in 2018, the video days of the 1980s and 1990s already seem a very distant memory. The stores have long since closed. Woolworths has gone. So has Blockbuster and Our Price. Video on Demand (VoD) is on the upswing, DVDs and Blu-rays are still bought online and some of the popular titles are available in supermarket checkout lanes, but if you didn't know better, you might believe the video boom had never happened. Woolley, for one, argues that its part in the resurgence of the British film industry can't be overstated:

> A lot of companies still don't realise how much video did to spark the notion that there is a way of pulling people into the cinemas. It was not just [about] renting videos but [the idea] let's do something fresh and different and get the young audience and the old audience as well to come back into cinemas.
>
> We are constantly as producers being thwarted by the idea that somebody somewhere is saying yes or no to our projects because they think they know what the public wants. But what happened with that first video explosion is that we interacted directly with the public.

Woolley says of the period in which Palace was born, independent companies briefly eclipsed the majors and VHS gave British cinema the shock treatment it needed in order to survive:

> It was a very unique time [...] people had given up. Companies like Cannon, Brent Walker and to a certain degree Palace were given a free hand because nobody really cared any more. Those big hulking [cinema] buildings were either bingo halls or they were going to be closed or scrapped and used as car parks. It was only the video boom that made everybody come alive again and rethink [that] there may not be money to be made in theatrical but there is money to be made in video and we can use that money wisely to reinvest back into production.[54]

CASE STUDY

SHAUN THE SHEEP MOVIE (2015 – ANIMATION)

The British have long dreamed of creating their own Disney-style animation studio. This was the dream of J. Arthur Rank in the 1940s when he recruited David Hand (director of Snow White and the Seven Dwarfs) to come to Britain. Animation, though, is an expensive and labour-intensive business.

Without deep pockets, patience and guaranteed access to international distribution, any attempt at emulating Disney is almost certainly bound to fail. That is why the achievements of Bristol-based Aardman Studios are so startling. They began as a small company in the mid-1970s, founded by old school friends, Peter Lord and David Sproxton, who had been drawn together as kids by their shared love of Hanna-Barbera's Top Cat cartoons. The name Aardman ('hard man') was first registered in 1972 and the company was officially formed four years later.

Sproxton was fascinated by puppetry, marionettes and what he calls the 'illusion of film and theatre'. Lord, meanwhile, was superb at drawing. What was to distinguish the company was Aardman's discovery of plasticine as a material in which to mould their characters and its use of stop-frame animation. A decade or so after Aardman was founded, a new recruit, Nick Park, joined the company. He was to go on to create clay animation characters, Wallace and Gromit, who, thanks to shorts like *A Grand Day Out*, *The Wrong Trousers* and *A Close Shave*, were to become household names. Over time, the eccentric and homely British company began to delve into the world of features.

The economics were still daunting. The company was tiny by comparison with the US studios. It worked with DreamWorks SKG and Sony on some of its projects but then turned back to Europe to finance its films.

Shaun the Sheep Movie (2015) was a spin-off from a character first featured in *A Close Shave* (1985) and who had subsequently featured in a long-running TV series. Directed by animator Richard Starzak and screenwriter Mark Burton, it was financed by French company StudioCanal. Its genius was that it appealed both to young children and to their parents. It was a dialogue-free movie. In its use of music, sound and incredibly complex visual gags, it evoked memories of Chaplin and of Jacques Tati films. The closest the film comes to words is the belching and snoring of the Farmer, who loses his memory and, through a bizarre plot twist, ends up as a hairdresser in the big, bad city, a long way from his flock of sheep, who can't really cope without him.

In the UK alone, *Shaun the Sheep* took over $20 million at the box office, but it sold all over the world too. StudioCanal distributed it not just in Britain but in France, Germany, Australia and New Zealand. This was a European-made film with a $25 million budget – huge for a British film but tiny by comparison with the $175 million that, for example, Pixar invested in *Inside Out* in the same year. *Shaun* went on to gross over $100 million.

'We're all over the world,' Sean Clarke, Aardman's head of rights and brand development, told the *Daily Telegraph* of the success the company had in merchandising Shaun and in turning the sheep into a full-blown brand. A few years before, the Aardman bosses had been threatening to move the company abroad because UK animation wasn't receiving the same government support as live-action film. Aardman had been struggling to compete with foreign rivals. However, partly in response to their lobbying, a tax credit for animation was introduced in 2012. Aardman stayed in Britain. The company's history spans the period that is covered in this book.

By early 2017, pre-production work was under way on *Shaun the Sheep 2*. By 2018, Aardman's latest feature, *Early Man*, was ready for release and the company had long since become a name as recognisable to film lovers as that of Disney or Pixar.

CHAPTER 3

PolyGram Forever

The black Versace dress appeared to be held together by little more than safety pins. On a May evening in 1994, 29-year-old actress Liz Hurley arrived at the Odeon, Leicester Square, alongside her then boyfriend Hugh Grant for the British charity premiere of Grant's latest film, *Four Weddings and a Funeral*. Hurley wasn't even in the film and yet her appearance became inextricably linked in the public's mind with its success. Hurley was on the front page of almost every British

11. Without a hitch: Elizabeth Hurley and Hugh Grant at the post-premiere party for *Four Weddings and a Funeral*. This was the first film produced by Duncan Kenworthy, following a successful career at the Jim Henson Company. Grant would subsequently star in other popular romantic comedies, including *Notting Hill, About a Boy, Love Actually* and two *Bridget Jones* films, all produced under the Working Title banner.

Dave Benett/Getty Images

newspaper. She was the accidental figurehead as the film's backer, PolyGram Filmed Entertainment (PFE), made its play to become a rival to the Hollywood studios.

Owned by Dutch electronics company Philips, PolyGram was a music company formed in the early 1970s. It had had a very negative experience when it diversified into the film business in the 1980s under executives Peter Guber and Jon Peters. Nonetheless, PolyGram lawyer Michael Kuhn was made head of PFE in 1991 and given the chance by his boss Alain Levy to lead a second assault on Hollywood.

Kuhn was an owlish figure, very smart and, in his own self-effacing way, very driven. His great insight was that he could run PFE not as a traditional film business but as an extension of the PolyGram music empire that just happened to be dealing in movies. His strategy was to build up a number of 'labels' that operated under the PolyGram wing. There was US outfit Propaganda, behind David Lynch's *Wild at Heart*, UK production company Working Title (see below), Jodie Foster's Egg Productions, Interscope, ITC and Island Pictures.

'There were two models that I had in mind,' Kuhn recalled.

> One was the model Steve Ross devised for Warner Music where he set up labels and gave charismatic leaders lots of money, told them to make records and if they didn't do well, he'd fire them and get someone else in. Out of that came Atlantic, Geffen and Warner Bros. under Mo Ostin. The only thing that was done centrally was marketing and distribution. I thought it was a good model [...] it left creative stuff to the creative people – and you were backing people rather than projects.[1]

Kuhn's other great inspiration was Arthur Krim, the lawyer who had run United Artists from 1951 until 1978. 'He was one of the great heroes of mine [...] at the height of UA's production, they had about 50 movies a year from 50 producers.'

Under Kuhn, PFE had its own international sales company, Manifesto, which in 1991 struck a three-year output deal for PFE titles with Rank in the UK and Columbia in the US. PolyGram's intention was to focus on marketing and distribution as much as on production. As Kuhn still points out today, 'all the profits from film are made in the distribution side of the business, not in the production side. If you want [to build] a sustainable business, you had better have part of the distribution pie.'

'Our product is not schlock and it isn't big, mainstream studio [fare]. It's in between,' Kuhn told the trade press, identifying the niche which the new company wanted to fill.[2] One leading production executive wrote of the attraction of partnering with the new company:

> Kuhn was talking about PolyGram and its producers having control of their films on a global basis. The idea was to make sure distribution was linked closely with production from day one. Before then, we had been making films that we had been selling at markets to independent distributors. We were giving everything away on day one and then having no control over the marketing campaign, let alone the release date or release strategy.[3]

Marketing and distribution wasn't something that older companies like Rank then excelled in. As producer David Puttnam remembers, the system felt ossified: 'Distribution was 10 per cent of your production cost, totally standardised, cookie-cutter stuff and it was utterly primitive. To walk through the doors of Rank in those days was to walk into another century. It was quite incredible.'[4]

Rank already possessed almost everything that PolyGram wanted: a £100 million rolling fund for film production, its own studios (Pinewood), its own laboratories and its own cinema circuit (Odeon). It was a vertically integrated company that had been in existence for more than half a century and, in theory, should have been able to compete on equal terms with the Hollywood studios. Something, though, was rotten at the core of the company. That was how it seemed to young marketing executive Julia Short when she joined Rank in the early 1990s. 'I was going into an organisation where clearly nobody had a clue about films. It was absolutely shocking,' Short recalls of Rank in the early 1990s.[5]

The company's then chief executive Fred Turner had joined Rank as a tea boy in 1946 and then worked his way right up to the top. He was popular and well liked, 'a little old-school but very smart and an underestimated executive' as he was characterised, but he gave little sign of knowing or caring much about films.[6] He stayed with the company until 1997, when it was sold to Carlton.

In its pomp, the Rank Organisation had financed British films from directors like Michael Powell and Emeric Pressburger, David Lean and Alexander Mackendrick. By the early 1990s it was largely ignoring UK production in favour of American fare. When it did support local films, they tended to be determinedly old-fashioned affairs like *Defence of the Realm* or *The Fourth Protocol.* Thanks to its output deal with Orion, Rank distributed some of the best movies of the period, among them *Hannah and Her Sisters* (1986) and *The Silence of the Lambs* (1991), but success was achieved more by accident than design. At a time when British producers were desperate for funding, Rank continued to pump money into or to distribute such ill-conceived US movies as *The Linguini Incident* (1991), *Pyrates* (1991) and *Lake Consequence* (1992).

The Linguini Incident, starring David Bowie and Rosanna Arquette, was the story of a waitress (Arquette) who dreams of becoming a Harry Houdini-like escape artist. It was 'an unbearably protracted dud' in the words of one British critic writing for *Empire.* It barely surfaced in cinemas. Nonetheless, as a romantic comedy with Bowie and Arquette in its cast, it had obvious appeal on VHS.

The same could be said for *Pyrates,* starring Kevin Bacon and Kyra Sedgwick as a couple who set off sparks (quite literally) while having sex (they have pyrokinetic powers). *Lake Consequence* was an erotic drama in the *9½ Weeks* mould. *Variety* described it as a 'feature-length display of fuzzy-focus sexual encounters too boring to qualify as soft-core porn'. Rank released it theatrically but its real appeal was on video.

Given its dominant position in the UK marketplace, it was only to be expected that Rank would release some decent films. Occasionally, the company still took bold decisions. Rank acquired Baz Luhrmann's romantic musical comedy *Strictly Ballroom* (1992) after one of its acquisition executives was at a screening in Cannes where it was given a rapturous reception. However, to outsiders (and to some of its own staff), it appeared that Rank distributed films by rote. 'At that time, it was very much "here's your poster, here's your trailer, here are your TV spots",' recalls Julia Short. There was no consideration of the nuances of the local market.'[7] The ingrained habit was to genuflect to the US and simply to copy the campaigns that had already been used in the American market. If there was a movie about, say, baseball, no steps would be taken to try to make the film accessible to British audiences.

By contrast, PolyGram was being run from the outset by executives from the music world and advertising who were brimful of energy and inventiveness. Its mantra was 'local knows best'. The company was also thinking beyond cinema. One of its first moves had been to bid (unsuccessfully) for the London Weekend independent TV franchise. Its idea was to produce its own news but to use the TV platform to broadcast films and drama from its producer partners.

At the beginning of 1992, Kuhn had brought Stewart Till on board to oversee the company's international operations. Till had been BSkyB's Head of Movies, overseeing the satellite operator's film channels.

PolyGram and Rank were partners, albeit very unlikely ones. Early on, PFE did all its sales and distribution through Rank. It used the Rank machine to make its cinema bookings and to oversee its cash collections but the marketing was done in-house. Kuhn's vision, again borrowed from the music business, allowed for failure. He wasn't so naive as to expect every film to strike box-office gold. 'Anyone who has done film production knows that to turn around things from zero activity to making meaningful films, you don't do that in five minutes. You have to assume there are going to be a lot of failures first,' he explained.[8]

The key idea was to back the talent. In the long run, he reasoned, if he had chosen correctly, that talent would come through for him. He didn't want to interfere or second-guess creative decisions. He also did his sums very carefully. Backing the Coen brothers to make *Fargo* at $10 million would have been a 'terrible decision' but at $7 million, he knew it could cover its costs and that even if it wasn't a big hit PFE wouldn't suffer.

This philosophy also applied on the business side. There was no question of the London bosses telling their colleagues in, say, France and Germany what to do once the company's international offshoots were established. 'From day one, I felt very strongly about that,' Stewart Till later remembered.

> I am a great believer in empowering executives in all roles. If you empower people, you get the best work out of them. If the person in Hamburg didn't know more about the German marketplace than anyone in London or LA, you've got the wrong person in Hamburg.[9]

Till had begun his career in advertising at Saatchi & Saatchi and he had noticed that the 'big brands in the world customised their advertising for different countries'. It therefore became a point of principle that the local PFE offices would take their own decisions about everything from posters and trailers to release dates.

> There were occasions when they [the local offices] ran campaigns that Head Office didn't think were particularly good campaigns and the film failed, maybe because of the campaign, but for every one of those, there were five where the film outperformed expectations in the marketplace.
>
> What PolyGram proved to the British film industry was that the real upside, and also the real risk, is in distribution, not in production. If you're a producer, you get your fee and some [sort of] profit position, which can be tenuous. In distribution, the money comes [from exhibitors] first to the distributor.

Till talks of how PolyGram made distribution 'sexy and interesting' at a time when it had been 'looked down on as a necessary evil', a process you had to go through to 'get the film out there' but without the 'glamour or prestige of production'.

It was lucky Kuhn had legislated in the business plan for failure as there was plenty of it. In the years leading up to *Four Weddings and a Funeral*, PFE's record was lamentable. Almost every film it supported flopped. Working Title came up with such titles as Ate de Jong's *Drop Dead Fred* (1991), starring Rik Mayall, Hanif Kureishi's *London Kills Me* (1991) and Peter Medak's gangster film *Romeo is Bleeding* (1993).

'When I got involved with Working Title, I assumed it would take them three or four years to get their development slate into proper shape – and indeed it did,' Kuhn later reflected on the teething pains the production company experienced, before developing into one of UK cinema's most successful film-making powerhouses.[10]

It helped that the company had two 'safety nets': the still-booming video market and its international sales arm, Manifesto. PolyGram would eventually open local distribution offices all around the world but in the early years it sold off rights to its films. This meant that with titles like *Drop Dead Fred* and *London Kills Me*, the foreign deals covered the budget. PolyGram didn't lose money, even when the films underperformed at the box office.

Variety reported on Kuhn's intention to 'sneak up on the Hollywood studios and give them a shock'.[11] The strategy was to base the company in London rather than Hollywood and then to build up a European distribution network. The tentacles of PFE stretched beyond Europe too. There were offices in Canada and Australia as well as in Paris, Brussels and Hamburg. In 1992, the company also set up its own US distribution company, Gramercy Pictures.

By 1994, PFE had two new films that it considered as potential winners. There was Iain Softley's *Backbeat*, about the Beatles' early years in Hamburg, and the mysterious, charismatic band member Stuart Sutcliffe, who died of a brain haemorrhage in 1962. The other was *Four Weddings and a Funeral*, a romantic comedy directed by the veteran Mike Newell, scripted by British comedy writer Richard Curtis and starring Andie MacDowell. She was a big American name who'd been in such successes as *Tarzan, Groundhog Day* and *Sex, Lies and Videotape*, and seemed to have far more box-office appeal than her co-star, the foppish British actor Hugh Grant.

Both films were taken to the Sundance Festival in January 1994. *Four Weddings* opened the festival and Kuhn then decided to buck conventional wisdom and open the film in the US first. It was released in Los Angeles and New York in March 1994. Kuhn's reasoning was that PFE couldn't compete with the marketing might of the studios nationwide but he could do so in two cities – and if the film worked there, it would be much easier to get it into other parts of the US. The marketing budget may have been small by comparison with that of the US studios – but it was still more than the cost of the film.

'Elegant, festive and very, very funny,' enthused the *New York Times*, not a publication generally especially well disposed toward modest British comedies. The initial release was on only a handful of screens but gradually it was shown in more and more cinemas nationwide – and six weeks after its launch, *Four Weddings* became a number one hit at the American box office.

Two months later, the film opened in the UK. PolyGram had been very bold in its American campaign, spending millions of dollars on marketing the film to US audiences. The company was then equally aggressive in the UK. It helped, of course, that the company could emblazon posters with messages telling audiences that the movie they were about to see was already a big US hit.

'We were very aware that the British press could be quite cruel,' Julia Short, who left Rank to head up marketing at PolyGram, recalls of the decision to open *Four Weddings* in America first.[12] To have already achieved success in the US was protection against the brickbats likely to come the film's way at home.

The review in the BFI's *Sight & Sound* magazine showed how vicious the British critics could be about locally made screen comedies:

> With a wealth of easy target caricatures to lean on (ghastly ex-girlfriends, drunken bores, senile old men – and this film doesn't miss one), a movie about a wedding can often feel like a wedding itself – two hours stuck in a crowded room with a lot of people you don't know very well and don't particularly like.

This, *Sight & Sound* concluded, was

> a smarmy little fable about the magic of true love […] lazy, *Sleepless in Seattle*-style romanticism, the kind that assumes that

if we are told often enough that the two dull protagonists are meant for each other, we'll eventually believe it.[13]

There wasn't 'a single spark of chemistry' between the two leads and the reviewer said that Hugh Grant looked like a chipmunk and had no sex appeal at all.

Such knocking had little effect, however. There were plenty of very positive American reviews and even most of the British critics came round in the end. Derek Malcolm wrote in the *Guardian*:

What the film proves beyond doubt, with its success in America, is that the more British the film, the more the non-British tend to like it. And I'll eat my hat, boiled with my shoes, if it isn't a success here, too. It certainly deserves to be.[14]

Even so, it still took luck and very hard work to make *Four Weddings and a Funeral* a success in Britain. 'Andy who? Who is he?' an Odeon booker is reported to have asked early on when told that the film starred Andie MacDowell.

Hugh Grant had co-starred as a nice but dim Englishman in Roman Polanski's erotic psycho-drama *Bitter Moon* (1992) and had played an upper-class journalist in Merchant Ivory's *The Remains of the Day* (1993), but wasn't exactly a household name in Britain. PolyGram hired publicists DDA to boost his image and sent him on the road to give as many interviews as possible.

There were unexpected factors which boosted *Four Weddings*. Originally, 20th Century Fox had been planning to release its thriller *The Good Son* in the UK in early 1994. This featured Macaulay Culkin, then the biggest child star in the world thanks to the *Home Alone* movies, cast (slightly) against type as a psychopath. According to Julia Short, Fox decided to delay the British release because of the ongoing controversy about the James Bulger murder the year before. This was the notorious incident in which two ten-year-old boys abducted a two-year-old in a shopping centre, tortured him and eventually killed him. In the wake of the murder, there was a prolonged debate in the British media about the possible effect that horror movies had

had on the two boys. As the debate raged, Fox postponed the release of *The Good Son*. The UK launch of *Four Weddings* had originally been planned for June but was brought forward by a month. 'Odeon came to us and said rather than doing 6 or 13 June, why don't you go in May [...] We can give you the Odeon, Leicester Square, and an entire circuit for representation – so we just moved the date,' Short recalls.[15]

It helped, too, that May 1994 was an unusually cool and wet month. 'Rainfall exceeded 10 mm on four occasions, with nearly 16 mm of rain falling on the 21st,' according to meteorological website London Weather.[16]

If there had been a heatwave, *Four Weddings* might have floundered. 'What could be cataclysmic with those spring/summer releases was if it was the first big hot day of the summer, the first hot weekend. You were petrified by the weather,' Stewart Till remembers.[17] If the sun had shone, all the ingenuity of the PolyGram marketing campaign would have counted for very little.

On the night of the *Four Weddings* premiere, John Smith, the leader of the Labour Party, died of a heart attack, but his death came too late to push the photographs of Liz Hurley off the front pages of the first editions of almost every British newspaper. Hurley had said to the film's publicists that she needed a dress for the premiere. Few of the designers knew who she was but Versace allowed her to choose something. The dress code for the premiere was 'wedding attire'.

There were differences in the UK and US marketing campaigns. Whereas the Americans foregrounded the romantic aspects of the film, the British placed far more of an emphasis on the comic elements. After all, the film featured several British comic actors, prime among them (as Father Gerald) Rowan Atkinson, an instantly recognisable figure to British audiences thanks to TV shows like *Not the Nine O'Clock News*, *Mr Bean* and *Blackadder*. The film's writer, Richard Curtis, who had worked on several of these TV shows, was becoming a recognisable name to British cinemagoers in his own right.

Another factor was the music. Scottish band Wet Wet Wet was signed to Mercury, a record label that was part of the PolyGram empire. Their cover of the Troggs' 1960s hit 'Love Is All Around', which featured in the film, topped the charts for 15 weeks. Thanks to the film, even book sales received a boost. W. H. Auden's poem 'Funeral Blues', which begins 'Stop all the clocks', was featured in the funeral scene of the movie, and was received with such enthusiasm that it quickly became a staple at real-life funerals. Many cinemagoers who didn't know how to get hold of the Auden poem approached the PolyGram press office, which would dutifully print it out and post it to them.

'You look back on it and you think we were really lucky, the gods were with us,' Short says of the circumstances surrounding the *Four Weddings* release that helped turn the movie into a hit.[18]

When I interviewed the film's director, Mike Newell, in 1997, he still seemed baffled by the size of the film's success.

> It was a light-hearted film with just enough seriousness to give it a rudder. I was dumbfounded by its success. I didn't think it was a bad film but I was completely amazed that it touched the nerves that it did. It can't be that widely loved unless it actually contains something completely other than we thought it contained. It wasn't just a clever script. It wasn't just a pretty film. It wasn't just that the actors were wonderful. There must have been a real nerve it hit. But I'm damned if I know what that nerve was.[19]

A film that cost under $10 million to make generated $250 million at the global box office – an astonishing result. *Four Weddings* not only made Grant 'a star of the highest order' overnight and turned Hurley into a tabloid obsession, it also launched PolyGram as a major player. By 1994, the time of the film's release, PolyGram had its own distribution offices in the UK, France and Benelux – and so was able to hold on to the profits from those territories.

'Nothing creates success like success,' Till reflects.

> I am sure it gave PolyGram Music confidence in us; it gave Philips confidence in us; it meant we could attract better

writers, directors and producers. The exhibitors in the UK realised we were a major force. The people who had bought the film in Germany, Italy and Spain bought a lot more product from us. It was incalculable, the benefits of it.[20]

Some believe that *Four Weddings* may even have saved PolyGram Filmed Entertainment. During the company's first three years its performance had been very patchy. There may have been strong titles in development but whether or not Alain Levy at PolyGram or his bosses at Philips would have given Kuhn more time remains open to conjecture. That is why this was the single most significant film in the history of the company. Its success also transformed the fortunes of Working Title.

'There was a certain type of film that was fundable. God forbid you try to do anything that was commercial,' remembered Working Title's co-chairman, Eric Fellner. 'It took *Four Weddings and a Funeral* to change everybody's attitude.'[21]

There were some other equally aggressive and memorable PolyGram campaigns, notably for Bryan Singer's thriller *The Usual Suspects* (1995) and for Danny Boyle's *Trainspotting* (1996), but *Four Weddings* was the first and most significant. PolyGram was ready to spend vast amounts on marketing for its films. The budget for releasing *Trainspotting* in the UK was bigger than the cost of producing the film. The company wanted to control what Kuhn calls the 'marketing levers' so it could ensure its movies were tailored to audiences in the countries in which they were released. He cites the example of *Bean* (1997). This was a big-screen spin-off from a slapstick British TV comedy which no one in the US knew. The original intention was to release it in Japan as an art-house title. Because PFE was able to tailor the release to local audiences in both territories it was rewarded with a huge hit. Till recalls:

I was taught at a very early stage of my career that the consumer has no inherent interest in the marketing. It's not as if they can't wait to see a trailer or a poster. The marketing has to be impactful, it has to catch the eye.[22]

PolyGram prided itself on its young, aggressive marketing executives, for example Julia Short and Christopher Bailey in the UK and David Livingstone and David Kosse internationally.

Another of the PFE's goals was to be able to green-light projects in London without having to defer to Hollywood paymasters. The company was competing for the same talent pool of directors and actors as the US studios. Its tastes were eclectic in the extreme. On the one hand, the company invested in literary adaptations, such as Michael Winterbottom's *Jude* (1996) and Jane Campion's *Portrait of a Lady* (1996), and upscale US indie fare, most notably the movies from the Coen brothers (*Fargo* and *The Big Lebowski* among them). But there were also such kitsch offerings as *Barb Wire* (1996), starring *Baywatch* beauty Pamela Anderson, and *Spice World* (1997), showcasing Britain's biggest girl band, the Spice Girls.

'It is true we tended to have a high proportion of people from the independent and specialised film sector,' Kuhn commented in the documentary inspired by his book, *100 Weddings and a Funeral*. 'It was really because they couldn't get their kind of films made by the mainstream studios who didn't really have specialised arms in those days. We tended to take risks other people wouldn't take.' *The Usual Suspects* won two Oscars and was a big box-office success, but its producers told Stewart Till that 50 companies had turned it down before PFE agreed to back it.

Twenty years on, the reasons for the closure of PolyGram Filmed Entertainment remain a matter of fierce debate. Kuhn argues that parent company, Philips, as a hardware manufacturer, 'never really felt comfortable with the software side of their business', run 'by people they didn't understand, paid far too much money, by Dutch standards, [who were] uncontrollable and didn't toe the corporate line'.[23] In the late 1990s, Philips was more interested in trying to break into the mobile phone market than in sustaining its movie and music businesses. When the company was offered over $10 billion for PolyGram by Canadian drinks and entertainment business Seagram, they wasted no time in taking it.

In the 1970s, PolyGram had been the world's biggest music company, releasing records from artists like Abba and the Bee

Gees. By the late 1990s, PFE was a credible competitor to the Hollywood studios – but that didn't affect Philips' thinking in the slightest. What made Philips' decision to sell PolyGram surprising was the fact that the Dutch company had invested so heavily in DVD technology, 'the hardware'. PolyGram seemed perfectly positioned to enable Philips to capitalise on the DVD boom. After all, it owned libraries of classic films and was producing some very commercial new ones.

Just when PolyGram was at its peak in 1996, Philips had appointed a new president of its board, Cor Boonstra, a former Unilever and Sara Lee executive who had no interest whatsoever in music and movies. Boonstra refused to approve Kuhn's bold plan to buy the MGM library. He also gave a notorious quote in which he announced: 'There are no taboos, no sacred cows, the bleeders must be turned around, sold, or closed.'[24]

Kuhn's extraordinary achievement in building a European film studio in the space of only a few years didn't count with Boonstra, who clearly saw PFE as one of the 'bleeders'. It didn't help that at precisely this moment in the late 1990s, PFE was tweaking its strategy. Instead of waging a stealth war against the US studios, releasing and marketing independent films in its own highly inventive fashion, it was now preparing to take them on head to head. David Fincher's *The Game* (1997) was a $50 million movie which PFE released in the US on thousands of screens to mediocre business. It was followed by Vincent Ward's *What Dreams May Come* (1998), a fantasy drama starring Robin Williams and made through Interscope, the company behind such hits as *Cocktail* and *Three Men and a Baby*. The film proved an embarrassing flop. The Hollywood studios didn't like the idea that a European interloper was gatecrashing their market. Back in Europe, Philips was increasingly uncomfortable about PFE's expansionist policies. 'It's not a business, it's a gamble,' Boonstra said in the documentary *100 Weddings and a Funeral* of the idea of PolyGram spending $60 or $70 million on a movie which might be released on a Friday and dead in the water by Sunday. In May 1998, Philips put PolyGram up for sale and quickly closed a deal with Seagram, who already owned Universal Pictures. There was talk of a management buyout but this eventually petered out. Universal kept the best bits of the company, including Working Title.

Exactly a year before, PolyGram had bid for one of the Arts Council film lottery production franchises, worth approximately £30 million over a six-year period. The bid was unsuccessful. It still rankles with Till that it wasn't taken more seriously. The £30 million was a tiny amount by comparison with the amount of money PFE had been spending. (At one stage, Kuhn had been looking to his bosses to allow him to bid over $1 billion for the MGM library.) Nonetheless, it would have been very useful money, especially at a time when the company was looking to break away from its parent business and to strike out on its own.

> The lottery bids was a completely flawed system and only in Britain, I'd argue. could you say, 'We won't give any money to PolyGram because they don't need it.' It's the British psyche to [think] let's give money to the underdog, even though they have none of the resources,

Till says of the franchise process.

> It was a hotch-potch of alliances that were never going to hold together. The Arts Council, in my opinion, didn't really know what they were doing. They said. 'You don't need it, PolyGram, we'll give it to people who do,' even though they've got a lot less chance of creating success on the back of it.[25]

The franchisees weren't successful (see Chapter 6). They never turned into 'mini studios', as the Arts Council had hoped they would. However, PFE already fitted that model. Till concedes that winning a franchise wouldn't have 'made a difference' to PolyGram, which had invested several billion dollars globally in its bid to set up a European 'major'. 'The bottom line was that Philips was desperate to offload both PolyGram music and film, even though previously the stock exchange value of PolyGram had been higher than that of Philips.'

It was a painful end to a bold experiment. 'We were a very riotous, badly behaved, uncontrollable management,' Kuhn says of the clash between PFE and its dour, Calvinist Dutch paymasters at Philips.[26] Film represented only around 10 per cent of the overall PolyGram business. It was tiny compared to the company's music division. Philips was in a rush to sell the latter – and if that meant including the former in the package, it didn't think twice about stopping the deal.

PolyGram's legacy, though, would be felt for years to come.

CHAPTER 4

The Working Title Magic

Working Title, which was to become the most successful British production company ever in box-office terms, began life in 1983 in decidedly modest circumstances. Three decades later, when the release of *Bridget Jones's Baby* (2016) added to the grosses already earned, Working Title became the first British company to earn $1 billion at the UK box office, but there was little sign of future glories when executive Sarah Radclyffe (who had been an associate producer on Derek Jarman's *The Tempest*) met bullish young New Zealand-born public schoolboy Tim Bevan in the early 1980s. They had set up a company to make music videos and that was how they met directors. (The third founding partner of the company was accountant turned producer Graham Bradstreet.)

As Radclyffe later remembered,

> We reckoned it was easier to ask them what they were doing if you were working with them, than ringing up someone like Stephen Frears and asking if you could work with them on a movie, when you have zero credits. Film was always the end goal.[1]

Working Title began slowly. Its first significant credit was a film made for television, *My Beautiful Laundrette* (1985), which was backed by Channel 4 and directed by Stephen Frears, who had met Radclyffe and Bevan when working on pop promos for them. The story of a gay love affair between a Pakistani teenager and a white punk who once had fascist leanings, the film (as critic Alexander Walker wrote in *Icons in the Fire*) offered 'a porthole into the swirling dirty linen of contemporary Britain'.[2] It was scripted by Hanif Kureishi.

'I was rung up and told this boy wanted to get a script to me,' Frears (then a leading director in television drama) remembered. 'A script came through the letterbox. I read the script and my heart sank because I realised it was about Pakistanis and then I started to laugh.' Kureishi turned up to visit him. 'I can remember saying [to Kureishi], "You think that people like me are just ridiculous old liberals." And he said, "I like ridiculous old liberals."'[3]

It was the start of a beautiful friendship – and one that helped establish Working Title as an exciting and risk-taking company. The film was shot on 16 mm and intended for TV. However, after its rapturous reception at the Edinburgh Film Festival, there was a clamour for it to be released theatrically.

Working Title's early films, such as *Wish You Were Here*, *Sammy and Rosie Get Laid* and *A World Apart*, were a very long way removed from the hugely successful romcoms the company started making in the 1990s. They were all films with grit and a political dimension to them. Whether they were stories about growing up in a small English seaside town in the repressive 1950s, or in apartheid-era South Africa (*A World Apart*), they confronted hypocrisy and racism. They were made on relatively modest budgets, often with Channel 4 support. It was possible, though, to see hints of how the company would later evolve in some of these earlier works. For example, you can trace a direct line from *Wish You Were Here*, with its rebellious teenage heroine (played with youthful charisma and bad attitude by Emily Lloyd) growing up in a post-war seaside town to the foppish hero played by Hugh Grant in *Four Weddings and a Funeral*. The former's catchphrase was 'up your bum.' The latter liked to say 'fuck fuck fuckity fuck.' The idea of swearing for comic effect was shared by both titles.

'The punkish side came far more from Sarah than from Tim,' remembers Ate de Jong, who directed *Drop Dead Fred* for Working Title. 'For Tim, the whole punkish side was a fun thing he did in his video clips but it wasn't so deeply felt. For Sarah, it was much more deeply felt. It was much more her culture.'

According to de Jong, Radclyffe regretted the way the company was moving toward the mainstream.

Sarah didn't mind the success – not at all – but she wanted to keep on making films that she thought were important. She knew that there was a limitation to their commercial success but she nevertheless thought those were the films that were important for her to make – the commercial success was a benefit and a bonus. That wasn't exactly the direction Tim wanted to go […] there was ultimately a division in the type of films they both wanted to do.[4]

In the early 1990s, Working Title's box-office glories were some way in the future but it was already, by default, the pre-eminent British production company. Palace was in its death throes. PolyGram, Working Title's future parent, was just about to start up.

Working Title had offices at Water Lane in Camden. There was a television arm run by Antony Root, which was busy developing such titles as *Tales of the City* (adapted from Armistead Maupin's novels). Comedy producer Simon Wright was developing *U.F.O.*, a saucy and very crude sci-fi comedy starring end-of-the-pier comedian Roy 'Chubby' Brown.' *Hear My Song* producer Alison Owen had also recently joined the company. Other key executives included Debra Hayward, Dixie Linder, Grainne Marmion and Jane Frazer. Jon Finn, later to produce runaway box-office hit *Billy Elliot*, had been the company receptionist, although some remember visitors struggling to understand his Geordie accent. Caroline Hewitt, later to become producer of such titles as Jane Campion's *Bright Star* and *The Two Faces of January*, was a line producer on *A World Apart*. Fiona Morham, later to become head of BFI Production, had been a production runner and coordinator at Working Title at the start of her career. There was a huge amount of talent in the company and this was already one of the only British production companies with its own development, as well as TV, department – but that didn't mean Working Title was yet anywhere near profitable.

'As you walked up the stairs, the posters you would walk past would be a litany of everything that was going wrong with the company but everything that promised a future,' remembers one executive.[5] The posters included Mel Smith's *The Tall Guy* (important as the film that brought writer Richard Curtis into the Working Title stable), Derek Jarman's *Caravaggio*, Nick Broomfield's *Diamond Skulls*, Bernard Rose's *Paperhouse*, Frears' *My Beautiful Laundrette* and *Sammy and Rosie Get Laid*, and Kureishi's own directorial debut, *London Kills Me*. It was a very creditable list of productions for a company less than a decade old, but the proviso was that very few of these films were remotely commercial. The company was heavily in debt. Its financial plight was such that its chief financial officer would only allow the runners to replace 'every other' light bulb.

Working Title needed PolyGram's patronage every bit as much as PolyGram needed Working Title (see Chapter 4). With PFE backing, Working Title could plan ahead. It was soon to move base to new offices in Oxford Street. Bevan told the *Guardian* in a 2005 interview:

> Before that, we had been independent producers, but it was very hand to mouth. We would develop a script, that would take about 5% of our time; we'd find a director, that'd take about 5% of the time and then we'd spend 90% of the time trying to juggle together deals from different sources to finance those films. The films were suffering because there was no real structure and, speaking for myself, my company was always virtually bankrupt.[6]

While giving evidence in Parliament, Bevan also pointed out that when the company started, £3 million gross on one of their films was considered 'huge' but, 20 years on, their titles were regularly making £16 to £20 million at the British box office alone.

Movies in development in the early 1990s included *Loch Ness*, *French Kiss* and *Film Stars Don't Die in Liverpool* (which wouldn't be made for another 20 years). Those working at the company have vivid recollections of the arrival of the Richard Curtis screenplay for *Four Weddings and a Funeral*. Everybody realised it was an exceptional piece of work: 'It leapt off the page. It was an unbelievable piece of writing, unbelievable!' remembers Laurence Gornall, later to be managing director of distribution company the Works, but then a junior assistant at Working Title.[7] The first draft contained a long scene involving two intellectuals discussing media theory (then very much a buzz topic) but this was wisely taken out. Casting suggestions were thrown around. Hugh Laurie was talked about as a potential lead. The role eventually went to Hugh Grant.

Even before the overwhelming success of *Four Weddings*, the company was already beginning to change. As contemporaries acknowledge, Bevan was a force of nature. 'He was an amazing guy. The risks he used to take…' one fellow executive recalls. 'He would press the button on a film before he had closed the money. That's the sort of thing you have to do if you're going to be that sort of producer.' Still only in his twenties, Bevan had forged relationships with directors like Frears and Mel Smith. The leading agents in the period, figures like Jenne Casarotto and Anthony Jones, were already steering clients toward Working Title.

One of Working Title's first projects with PolyGram as a parent was the Rik Mayall and Carrie Fisher comedy *Drop Dead Fred*, directed by de Jong. It may not have done great business in the UK or been liked by the critics, but it was a solid success internationally, especially in Australia. Bevan began to realise that comedy might work in the international market in a way that dramas like *London Kills Me* and *A World Apart* didn't.

After PolyGram fully acquired Working Title in 1992/3, Radclyffe left the company. 'It cost me a fortune to start this company and it has cost me a fortune to get out of it,' a colleague remembers her saying at the time of her exit.

Eric Fellner came in. There was a very obvious culture change. Radclyffe had been associated with the socially relevant dramas and comedies the company had been making in the late 1980s and early 1990s. Now, it became much more ambitious and commercially oriented. PolyGram was looking to it to supply films for its international distribution operation, not for it to make a handful of low-budget art-house dramas with British Screen and Channel 4 support that struggled to travel beyond their home shores.

The new partner, whose credits included Alex Cox's *Sid & Nancy* (1986) and *Straight to Hell* (1987) and Ken Loach's *Hidden Agenda* (1990), had come to Working Title from Initial Pictures, the company he founded in the mid-1980s after a stint at Island Pictures. In Cox's words, he was 'an upper-class lad, confident and enthusiastic'.[8] He was also a man in a hurry. Whereas other Working Title executives arrived for work in Citroën 2CV dollies or other relatively modest vehicles, in March 1992 Fellner roared up in a black BMW coupé ('a muscle car') with a picture of a slavering bulldog (the Initial logo) on the back windscreen. He blithely parked in someone else's space and marched into the office.

Fellner's arrival (in the words of one insider) 'frightened the life out of the Laura Ashley lot in the office'. 'Be in absolutely no doubt about it, he had an aura about him,' a former colleague recalls.

The company at this stage was in a parlous state. It didn't have any films going into production and so wasn't receiving production fees. It was sinking further and further into debt. These were the less than auspicious beginnings of what was to become Britain's most prestigious and successful production company. *Four Weddings* transformed its fortunes.

Over the last three decades, Working Title has achieved a level of continuity of production that no other British company has matched. At any given time, it will have dozens of projects in development. Its overheads are huge. There have been misfires (*Captain Corelli's Mandolin, The Boat that Rocked, Thunderbirds*), but these have been easily counterbalanced by the successes. First with PolyGram's patronage, and then with the support of Universal and StudioCanal, Working Title turned into a powerhouse, working not just with Hugh Grant and Richard Curtis, but with the Coen brothers too.

The company was (as Bevan told the politicians) 'integral to the British film industry'. It may have been American-owned but it was British-based and the principals still had 'creative autonomy'. Bevan and Fellner remained as intimately involved in every aspect of the business as they had been since the early 1990s.

Our role encompasses everything from putting the finance in place to making sure that the dailies are right, that the budget is being adhered to, that the schedule is being run properly and that we are delivering the film we intended to make. We work very closely on the editing and on the marketing campaign. We strategise about potential dates for release around the world; we work with the marketing team; we make sure that the TV

12. Raising their game: producers Paul Webster, Tim Bevan and Eric Fellner celebrate with director Joe Wright (second left) as their British film *Atonement* scooped the Best Film BAFTA award in 2008. *Atonement* had been adapted by Christopher Hampton from the 2001 novel by Ian McEwan, whose other books brought to the big screen include *Enduring Love*, *The Cement Garden* and, in 2018, *On Chesil Beach*.

Leon Neal/Getty Images

13. Just Wright: after his debut feature film, *Pride & Prejudice* (2005), garnered four Oscar nominations, Joe Wright was reunited with its leading lady, Keira Knightley, for *Atonement* and *Anna Karenina*. When *Atonement* opened the 2007 Venice Film Festival, 35-year-old Wright was the youngest director ever to have a film selected for that prestigious slot. In 2017 he directed Working Title's production *Darkest Hour*, starring Gary Oldman as Winston Churchill.

Adrian Dennis/Getty Images

spots, the trailer and the online materials are correct. Every single aspect of everything, we are all over it [...] It's not that Tim and I are so brilliant. We are not. We have just worked really hard, we're halfway intelligent and we had some luck with a few films. That's all it is. It's like going to the casino. You get the luck if you keep turning up. Occasionally, you'll win. Then it's a case of building on those winnings. You don't want to wager them all on one movie and lose everything. The winnings aren't necessarily just cash. They are the expertise you develop, the ability to attract bigger talent – all of those things.[9]

As Working Title continued to prosper, the rest of the UK production industry was becoming ever more dependent on what producer Simon Perry quipped was the film industry equivalent of pure heroin, namely National Lottery Funding.

CASE STUDY
BRIDGET JONES'S DIARY (2001)

The Americans had been very upset when David O. Selznick cast a British actress, Vivien Leigh, in the plum role of Scarlett O'Hara in *Gone with the Wind* (1939). In Britain, 60 years later, there was the same consternation when an American actress, Renée Zellweger, was cast in the leading role in Working Title's production of *Bridget Jones's Diary* (2001).

This was because Jones was very British indeed. The character had been created by journalist Helen Fielding, who had been asked to write a column about single life for a woman over 30 in London for the *Independent* newspaper in 1995. She agreed, with the proviso that the column was anonymous and was about a fictional character rather than herself. That is how, in February 1995, Fielding started chronicling the alcohol Bridget consumed in units and the 'fuckwits' she shagged. The column very quickly caught on and spawned a book which became a bestseller.

Five years on from its runaway success with *Four Weddings and a Funeral*, Britain's most successful production company, Working Title, found itself, in early 1999, in a period of transition. Its parent company PolyGram Filmed Entertainment had closed. The company had now been taken over by Universal Pictures. Its principals and co-chairmen Tim Bevan and Eric Fellner had just signed a five-year deal with Universal. One of the first projects for the Hollywood studio was a film version of Bridget Jones.

The film was to be directed by a newcomer, Sharon Maguire, a friend of the writer who had provided the inspiration for Bridget Jones' friend, Shazzer. Early on, the film was conceived on a fairly modest scale. Fielding herself had written an early draft of the screenplay, which had been completed by Richard Curtis (of *Four Weddings* fame) and renowned British TV writer Andrew Davies (who had also scripted the mildly risqué BBC version of *Pride and Prejudice* starring Colin Firth as Darcy). Firth had been recruited to play Bridget's love interest. With the casting of Hugh Grant, the budget crept up. Then came the decision for Texan actress Renée Zellweger, best known for *Jerry Maguire* and *Nurse Betty*, to take on the role of the British singleton heroine in the movie.

'There was an enormous amount of backlash and UK actresses were up in arms. At that point, it became quite scary,' Eric Fellner later told the *LA Times* of the decision to snub every British actress and cast the American instead. It turned out to be an inspired choice.

Romantic comedies tend not to be taken as seriously as dramas but Zellweger's preparation for playing Bridget Jones was just as intense as that of Robert De Niro when he was preparing to portray boxer Jake LaMotta in Martin Scorsese's *Raging Bull* (1980). Like De Niro, she had to put on weight for the role (Bridget is in a constant battle with her calorie count). She also needed to learn how to speak with a middle-class British Home Counties accent. The producers sent her to work incognito at the publisher Picador, where she made the tea and no one seemed to recognise she was a movie star; they gave her hundreds of hours of elocution lessons. By the time shooting began, the makeover was complete: few could actually begin to guess that she was actually from Texas and wasn't a Chardonnay-quaffing, chain-smoking single British woman, working in publishing and yearning to get married.

Bridget Jones's Diary didn't just star a Hollywood actress. It was marketed with all the fanfare of the biggest US studio releases. The film went on to gross over $280 million worldwide at the box office on a production budget of $25 million. Released in the US by Disney-owned Miramax, it took $71.5 million. It sold 1.8 million copies on VHS and DVD in the UK alone. There were to be sequels, first with *The Edge of Reason* in 2004 and then, after a lengthy hiatus, *Bridget Jones's Baby* (2016). This was an example of a quintessentially British property that, largely thanks to the boldness of the casting, was transformed into a global hit.

CHAPTER 5

The Great British Lotto Bonanza

In the wake of the Downing Street summit of 1990, radical changes were being made in British arts funding and how it was administered. The Department of National Heritage (DNH) was created in 1992, to amalgamate a number of functions related to the arts, broadcasting, film, sport, architecture and historic sites, royal parks, and tourism.

Then, in 1993, the National Lottery Act was passed, with the aim of raising extra money for the arts, sports, 'millennium' initiatives and good causes through the creation of a weekly national gambling game whose proceeds would feed into those areas. The first lottery draws started in November 1994. Prime Minister John Major, who championed the Act, later wrote that the 'genesis of the Lottery' lay in his belief that

> the lives of millions of people are enhanced by their love of the arts, sport and our National Heritage. I saw that a Lottery could raise funds – free from the grasping hand of the Treasury – that could be used to improve the enjoyment and, in some cases, the lifestyle of many millions of people.[1]

Major had been Chancellor at the time of the Downing Street summit. There were no indications, though, that film was at the front of his mind. In theory, lottery money was supposed to support 'capital' projects and not revenue-generating ones, which is what films were. Intense lobbying led to a relaxation and fudging of the rules. Through some clever finessing, films were therefore defined as 'capital

14. Having been Foreign Secretary and Chancellor of the Exchequer in Margaret Thatcher's Government, John Major served as British Prime Minister from November 1990 until May 1997, when Tony Blair won the first of his three successive general election victories. Major launched ticket sales for the inaugural National Lottery draw a week before it took place in November 1994. The game gripped the public imagination as 48.9 million tickets were bought in that week alone. In its first year, £267 million of lottery money went to the 'good causes' – the arts (including film), heritage, millennium and sport – while £154 million was given to charity.

Wikipedia / public domain

expenditure' as if they were the equivalent of arts buildings or equipment. This was where Richard Attenborough's intervention had been so useful. As Major later recalled, he and Attenborough had been discussing the benefits that access to the lottery resources would give to the film industry. As Major revealed shortly before Attenborough's death in 2014, when launching a National Film and Television School fund for young film-makers that was to be named after the great actor and director,

> The underlying problem as it related to the film industry was really rather a simple one. We saw grants in the first instance as being for capital expenditure only, and not for funding revenue [...] Richard Attenborough pointed out to me that film production, under that definition, was classed as revenue rather than capital and hence would be excluded as the Bill was initially drafted. That certainly wasn't our intention, but film might have been inadvertently excluded had Dickie not pointed out the drawback in the draft legislation.[2]

Attenborough's intervention ensured the National Lottery Bill was tweaked and opened the gates for what would be hundreds of millions of pounds of funding over the next 20 years.

The Arts Council began funding film production in April 1995. The pilot scheme for funding lasted for two years, until April 1997. Jeremy Newton, National Lottery director at Arts Council England (ACE) from 1994 to 1998, remembers that the government was keen to be seen to be doing something to help the British film industry 'and the lottery was the only new game in town with the only prospect of any new money'.[3] This was a time of strict government spending restrictions. There was little chance that money was going to be found anywhere else to support film production. Newton speaks of interest from the Department of Trade and Industry (DTI) in supporting the film industry.

As for ACE overseeing the lottery money for film, Newton says that 'there was no real discussion of who else might distribute it because there was no one else entitled to distribute it'. Other bodies such as the British Film Institute or British Screen weren't considered. This is confirmed by Virginia Bottomley, DNH Secretary of State at the time: 'Going through the Arts Council was as independent and detached as the government was willing to go. To hand lottery money to an entirely autonomous group would have led to precedents all across the waterfront.'[4]

The very idea of lottery money coming into the industry infuriated Alexander Walker, the influential and irascible *Evening Standard* critic, who both chronicled the debates of the time in his newspaper columns and books and was one of the most belligerent and outspoken participants in those debates. He wrote an angry letter to the then Culture Minister, Stephen Dorrell, pointing out that

> a film is a wager, a bet or a gamble, and to refer, as you do, to 'the generally supportive views of a wide range of very different people in the industry' is akin to saying that a convention of croupiers thought it a good thing to build more casinos.[5]

Some felt that Walker's angry broadsides against the use of lottery money were prompted by his dislike of gambling. He took issue with the idea that the DNH was staking 'film people's creative bets' and financing 'their dreams' when this money by rights should have been devoted to the public good. He was proud of the headline that ran above one of his stories stating in bold capitals: 'LOTTERY MONEY WILL BE WASTED ON FILMS'. In 2003, when he reflected on the introduction of the lottery money in his book *Icons in the Fire* (published posthumously), he described these words as among 'the truest' he ever wrote.[6] That is how it might have seemed to him then, although many would dispute that assertion now.

The combative Walker, who died in 2003, relished being at the centre of any debate going. He had several pet bugbears. Smoking was one of them. (His answerphone message said, without irony, 'I can't come to the phone right now so please leave me a message [...] and remember, smoking is a slow way to suicide.') Lottery funding for film was another.

Walker wasn't alone in his dismay at this new source of funding for British cinema. Terry Ilott, author, producer, academic and former editor of *Screen International*, said of money he felt should have been used for good causes:

> I thought it was unconscionable, completely indefensible to use the little spare cash that lottery punters had to support film. I thought it was just ridiculous. I was not alone. I think a lot of people were embarrassed by it [...] Nobody said that if you buy lottery tickets, we will give money to these film producers [...] film is just a commercial venture.'[7]

There were obvious and very considerable teething pains with the introduction of the lottery funding for film production. 'What they're doing is releasing pure heroin onto the streets rather than the diluted methadone that everyone is used to,' producer Simon Perry, then the chief executive of British Screen Finance, told *Variety* after the subsidy first came on tap.[8]

Speaking in 2017, Perry recalls that he initially felt the arrival of the lottery funding was 'great'. 'Our budget [at British Screen] was so small, and the only other sources of funding were FilmFour, the BBC, which had very little money, and the BFI Production Board. Another source of money seemed like extremely good news.'[9]

There was a very warped logic about the way the money was allocated by the Arts Council. Lottery awards were supposed to uphold the concept of 'additionality' by funding activities which would not otherwise take place. This money was therefore effectively for films that the market had shunned – that would not have been made otherwise. There was often still a strong case for supporting them on cultural grounds but it was naive to expect commercial success. 'You'd get scripts that had been rolling around the industry for ten years,' notes one former ACE executive of the orphan projects which ended up asking for lottery funding.[10]

What was also very curious, and stemmed back to the trip to Downing Street, was the government's tendency to see the British film industry only in terms of production. A lot of ingenuity had gone into securing the lottery financing for film, but little attention had been paid to how the movies that were then made were to be distributed and marketed. As Simon Perry noted, 'The idea of the money seemed great but the worry set in quite early when we saw the Arts Council was going to award it in a slightly odd way.'

The lottery money changed

the whole game. I thought we were working in a register where we understood the clever thing to do with the public money was to make it go as far as possible and to use it strategically to trigger more money, whereas suddenly there were lashings of cash coming into the industry which didn't seem to be connected to any measurable outcome.[11]

An initial £10 million in production finance through the lottery for 1995 was announced in April of that year.

The haphazard approach to choosing which films to support very quickly became evident. Mainstream feature projects were pored over by an Arts Council advisory panel, overseen and chaired by producer Marc Samuelson, and including such figures as Stewart Till (PolyGram), Lyndsey Posner (Chrysalis), Mark Shivas (BBC), Colin Leventhal (Channel 4) and Romaine Hart (Mainline Pictures). They were all respected figures, representatives of the most active companies in the industry, who had been chosen in an attempt to weave the lottery finance into the existing structures as intelligently as possible. Nonetheless, it became obvious that the committee system was not only unwieldy but actually downright absurd. The advisory panel members were put in an invidious position, often finding themselves obliged to give substantial amounts of money to projects that they had little faith in and hadn't actually been given the chance to read properly.

Samuelson, an energetic young producer then in his mid-thirties, recalls that he had been approached by Richard Attenborough, who wanted him to chair the panel. Samuelson was flattered but also wary about the job he was taking on. He put together the rest of the group. 'It would have worked brilliantly were it not for the fact that the Arts Council had inflicted on themselves the most insane rules,' Samuelson remembers.[12]

The panel members were required by ACE to consider the question of 'public good' and of creating 'lasting benefit for the public'. 'We constantly asked ACE to define what they wanted (by which I mean at virtually every meeting) and they swerved the answer time and again,' Samuelson remembers of what constituted the 'public good'. He adds that the panel members knew from the outset they were picking up 'a bit of a poisoned chalice but the alternative was letting ACE handle all of it without even an attempt at involvement by the industry.'[13] (In theory, the lottery money was for projects 'not intended primarily for private gain', but there was never a film producer then or now who didn't at least hope his or her film would set the box-office tills ringing.)

There were instances when they would reject films on the grounds that 'the creative quality of the project was not sufficiently strong to meet the public benefit criterion', but the means by which they measured 'creative quality' were invisible to everyone but ACE.[14] An insider on the panel remembers that projects which were clearly completely amateur and inappropriate would be rejected. The problem came with projects from experienced people with nothing clearly terrible about them, but that just weren't 'interesting or exciting'. 'ACE made it pretty much impossible for us to recommend rejection of those, particularly if they had somehow arranged a distribution deal,' he recalls.[15]

Any projects ACE supported needed to be 'accessible'. They were supposed to have 50 per cent of funding already in place. This meant producers would often strike disadvantageous deals with distributors simply to be in a position to secure the lottery money. If the panellists didn't have any strong reason to say 'no', they were required to say 'yes'. One reason they weren't allowed to read scripts was that they weren't supposed to be 'inflicting our own taste' (as one panellist puts it) in their judgements. Instead, they had to rely on second-hand reports on the projects put together by readers appointed by the Arts Council. The specialist script readers, who were recruited on the advice of the European Script Fund, had little direct experience of film writing or production. They asked to remain anonymous. Alongside the script readers were 'assessors' from the British Screen Advisory Council (BSAC) and the BFI. In their reports, you can see the contradictory pressures they were under. If they received an application from a film that seemed mainstream, they were immediately suspicious. Why, they wondered, hadn't other investors supported it? However, if the project was too esoteric, that would worry them just as much.

A one-to-ten 'scoring standards' scheme was agreed for assessing projects. One with a 'ten' rating was 'exceptional' and 'should be supported as a top priority' while 'one' meant 'this project is likely to be damaging to the development of film production and merits no support'. There were occasions when the panel members knew that the projects they were being asked to back had little artistic or commercial potential – but they had to support them anyway because there weren't any grounds on which to reject them. They had no powers to initiate films or to develop scripts, but had to respond to the projects that came across their desks.

The first wave of films to get the lottery backing included a Thomas Hardy adaptation, *The Woodlanders*, which received £1.4 million, and Dutch director George Sluizer's thriller *Crimetime*, which received £300,000.

Almost all the films supported through the lottery received distribution – but that didn't mean anyone actually saw them. Box office was often lamentable. Simon Donald's *The Life of Stuff*, adapted from his own play involving Glasgow gangsters, scraped around 300 admissions in British cinemas, grossing under £5,000, a pitiful return given its £1 million lottery grant. Other early lottery-backed films, like *Food of Love*, *The Sixth Happiness* and *Glastonbury: The Movie*, did equally badly. Several of them had big names attached. *Food of Love*, for example, starred Richard E. Grant and Nathalie Baye. It had been released by FilmFour.

The panellists did their work but complained bitterly about it, hampered by the government's policy of 'additionality'. After the first rounds of funding, the same British producers who had been so keen to access the lottery funding began to attack the system under which it was dispensed. 'It's not so much the eight films awarded the $6 million to date that are attracting the criticism; it's the ramshackle system by which the choices are made, and the inexperience of the people who are making them,' *Variety* reported in late October 1995.[16]

No one seemed to like the system. The Arts Council of England, which had fought hard to be allowed to administer the new lottery funding, tied itself in knots, creating a structure which made it almost impossible to green-light decent movies. The lottery panel members may have been forbidden from expressing their own opinions regarding the projects submitted, but the ACE executives themselves were surprisingly outspoken about these projects' shortcomings.

'The downside of the British film industry was glimpsed yesterday when the people in charge of giving lottery money to new British films revealed that most of the scripts they are sent are sub-standard,' reported the *Independent*.

> Carolyn Lambert, director of the Arts Council's National Lottery Film Unit, said many of the scripts sent in by production companies have 'weak characterisation, poor dialogue and poor plotting [...] Some films that we have put money into are pretty weak. British scripts go into production too soon. The typical four drafts – if you're very lucky – are simply not enough for a polished product.[17]

Speaking in 2017, former ACE National Lottery Director Jeremy Newton still makes the same point. 'It would have to be said that this was not a golden era for British film-making in terms of scriptwriting, development, the delivery and the making of films,' Newton says.[18] The best directors (Ridley and Tony Scott, Anthony Minghella, Alan Parker and others) had migrated to Hollywood; or, at least, were making films there. This was one period in which there was seemingly more money than there were decent projects. Films rejected by ACE for lottery support were often made anyway – and tended to sink without trace.

The problems that ACE faced were exacerbated by the introduction of the Wednesday Lottery. This meant there was yet more money flowing through its coffers – and even less idea about how to spend it effectively.

Few of the early films were successful either commercially or critically and outsiders were baffled as to how they were chosen. Perry's remarks about the lottery funding being like 'pure heroin' turned out to be depressingly accurate. The pilot lottery film finding

15. The talented Mr Minghella: scripted and directed by Anthony Minghella (1954–2008), *The English Patient* won six BAFTAs and nine Oscars. He went on to direct *The Talented Mr Ripley, Cold Mountain* and *Breaking and Entering,* all of which starred Jude Law. He had only recently completed a five-year stint as chair of the BFI when he died, aged 54, having suffered complications after tonsil cancer surgery.

Fiona Hanson/PA Images

scheme was launched by the Arts Council in April 1995. By the end of 1996, £32,849,639 had been awarded to 62 projects. This was a huge influx of cash. 'British film producers were not used to being able to get public money to the tune of £1 million into one film,' Perry remembers.[19]

At least some of the first wave of lottery-backed films made their way into official selection at Cannes in 1997, among them Udayan Prasad's *My Son the Fanatic* (scripted by Hanif Kureishi), Sean Mathias' *Bent* and Richard Kwietniowski's *Love and Death on Long Island*. However, even these films struggled to make any impact at the box office and there were others which didn't make it to Cannes.

Once or twice, decent ideas were spurned. Newton talks of his regret that ACE turned down a film called *Sliding Doors* from a director, Peter Howitt, who used to co-star in the long-running Liverpool-based BBC comedy *Bread*. The proposal mentioned that Gwyneth Paltrow, then one of the most sought-after young actresses in Hollywood, was interested in starring in the film (about a recently fired London PR agent who exists in two parallel universes). 'The script readers said it was unbelievable which, when you think about the film, of course it is!' Newton looks back on the romantic fantasy drama. 'I well remember that the application said there had been interest from Gwyneth Paltrow in starring in it. This was widely ridiculed by the Film Panel.' The assumption was that Howitt had met Paltrow at a party and that she had said she would read his screenplay without ever meaning it. 'It was actually a really good and very successful film. If we had put money into it, that would have changed the climate of thinking about lottery films,' Newton suggests.[20] *Sliding Doors* (which ended up being financed by British Screen and released in the UK by UIP) could have been the 'conspicuous success' early in the history of lottery film funding that would have disarmed the critics and softened the public's attitude. (One panellist has a different memory of why the project was rejected. He suggests it was 'too commercial' and that, with Paltrow's involvement, it was likely to get made anyway and so didn't need lottery support.[21])

Alexander Walker was quick to ridicule these films and he took to listing the amount of lottery money they had received at the end of his reviews (and sometimes even further up). 'The front runner, to date, for Worst British Film of the year: how did something so bad get into rehearsal, never mind production?' Walker wrote in typical fashion of 1999 feature, *Janice Beard: 45 WPM*.

> Predictably, National Lottery money funded such a catastrophe: £868,000 (out of £2,535,000) plus £12,000 in script development and £210,000 toward the cost of prints and publicity. What a week to launch such a film, as Chris Smith, committing £150 million of public money to fund the film industry, promises we shall make better movies by spending even more on them. With the £98 million that Janice Beard and her even more tawdry predecessors have cost (and not earned back) since 1995, the Lottery could have contributed to hospital beds, schoolbooks and playing fields. What makes film-makers so special that public money foots their bills?[22]

This was very jaundiced criticism of a film that other reviewers actually quite liked, but Walker's were the only words that anyone remembered. Thanks to his invective, the public began to think that lottery-funded movies were duds as a matter of course.

'Alex was just sitting chucking stones every week,' Marc Samuelson recalls. 'I had a lot of time for Alex and I liked him very much, but I felt he was essentially dishonest because he would never credit the lottery money on the good films.'[23]

For example, Walker was very enthusiastic about the Oscar Wilde biopic *Wilde* (1997), starring Stephen Fry as the Irish dandy, which Samuelson had produced. Walker reviewed it in positive fashion but when Samuelson pointed out to him that the film couldn't have been made without its lottery support (which amounted to £1.5 million out of its £5.6 million budget), the critic simply ignored the insight.

Jeremy Newton met Walker regularly and was on reasonably cordial terms with him, but that didn't stop the *Evening Standard* critic's 'waspish' criticism. Newton argues that ACE deserves some credit for helping to 'build capacity'. At least, he argues, the lottery money was enabling films to be made – and their directors and crews were learning through their failures. There was a 'quantitative jump' which he felt to be to the long-term benefit of the film industry. In 1995, there were a total of 81 film starts in the UK or with some UK production input. That was a major spike in production levels from 1989, when only 30 were produced. One of the Arts Council panel's main objectives had been to increase the number of British films made. At least in this it was definitely successful.

'With any industry at different stages of development, there is a stage that is about capacity building,' Newton argued.

That was what was going on in the mid-1990s. The number of films being made did take a jump thanks to lottery money and to the general climate that lottery money encouraged. I think it was genuinely good for the industry. It paved the way for people of talent getting involved.

Newton concedes, though, that he and his colleagues

probably could have and should have fought against the constrictions that were placed on us earlier and more vehemently. We could have mustered better arguments for why a more flexible type of support that did include script development and training.[24]

In hindsight, one panel member argues that an eventual return of maybe £30 million on the £99 million from a brand-new arts subsidy scheme 'wasn't actually that disastrous – most film subsidy schemes around the world return around 50 per cent'. He points out that 'ACE were used to funding organisations like the National Theatre or Whitworth Art Gallery where the returns were, obviously, zero. I guess that's the heart of why they were institutionally so ill equipped to run the scheme.'[25]

Amid the box-office duds from those early lottery years, there were one or two films that the critics cherished. John Maybury's *Love Is the Devil* (1998), a biopic about artist Francis Bacon and his love affair with petty crook George Dyer, was a critical success and gave a first important cinema role to Daniel Craig (then best known for TV's *Our Friends in the North*, but later to be cast highly successfully as James Bond). Many directors were able to make their first feature films, among them novelist William Boyd with *The Trench*, documentary maker Phil Agland with *The Woodlanders*, poet Tony Harrison with *Prometheus* and the brilliant young Scottish director Lynne Ramsay with *Ratcatcher*.

The arrival of soft money in the form of lottery funding wasn't matched by 'hard' equity investment from city financiers. In the summer of 1995, DNH Secretary Stephen Dorrell had given a state-ment on the British film industry in which he had floated the idea of setting up an advisory committee involving financial institutions and producers to improve film-makers' access to capital markets, but he didn't mention tax breaks, which the industry had long claimed it desperately needed.[26]

There had been a tax break in the 1992 Budget, Section 42, which allowed for the write-off of 'production expenditure over a three-year period for a qualifying film once the film has been completed'. This had been expected to allow producers to 'generate an immediate cash sum of between four and eight per cent of a film's budget', but, as the Advisory Committee on Film Finance, chaired by Sir Peter Middleton, reported in 1996, this wasn't enough to have any meaningful impact on investment decisions.[27]

For all the positive attitude toward the film business shown at the Downing Street summit, there was still sometimes a sense that film policy was being made up on the hoof. This was certainly the case with the UK withdrawal from Eurimages, the Council of Europe's co-production fund which existed to encourage its members to make films together. They all paid an annual membership and then, out of their contributions, the fund supported selected projects on which two or more member states were collaborating.

The British had joined Eurimages (founded in 1988) amid much fanfare in 1992 but then promptly withdrew just under three years later, in November 1995, for reasons that still remain foggy today. There was a perception later among the British that too much horse-trading and politicking went on at the fund and that its decision-making processes weren't always transparent. The emphasis at Eurimages has always been on 'quality European art-house films' – not necessarily the type of movies that the British were most interested in making. It didn't help either that the application process was so cumbersome. Film producers reportedly had to send in 15 copies of every document because the Council of Europe had only one Xerox machine. However, at the time, Britain's decision to leave took almost everybody by surprise, apart from the then Secretary of State for National Heritage, Virginia Bottomley. The Labour MP Mark Fisher asked Bottomley:

> Will the Secretary of State now account to the House for one of the most damaging and self-destructive actions that she has taken – the Government's withdrawal last November from the Council of Europe's Eurimages scheme? Does she appreciate that the £2 million subscription leveraged between £45 million and £50 million a year of European co-production money to the advantage of our industry?[28]

She dismissed the question with the usual government line – 'the responsibility of the Government is to make difficult choices and to set priorities' – and pointed out that film had benefited from plenty of lottery funding. It was clear, though, that this wasn't a decision she had thought through in any depth.

Simon Perry recalls visiting Bottomley, together with producer Richard Attenborough, to ask the Secretary of State what on earth she had done in quitting Eurimages without even consulting the industry. Attenborough banged his fist on the table. A little taken aback by such indignation, Bottomley struck a vaguely apologetic air. Perry recalls Bottomley saying:

> We just didn't think it was that important. I asked my civil servants what is this 'your images' thing and they didn't seem to know. They said we have to send money to this fund in Strasbourg and apparently our producers get some of it back, but we don't really know if it is value for money.

Britain, Bottomley pointed out, already had a European Co-Production Fund administered by British Screen. That, Bottomley clearly thought, was quite enough of Europe to be getting on with.

Interviewed 20 years on, Bottomley has little recollection of the circumstances in which Britain left Eurimages. 'I would only have done it on the basis of evidence that it really wasn't delivering the necessary results. I've been scratching my head in trying to think what was behind [the decision].'[29]

Bottomley insists that all the ministers at the DNH, whether herself or her predecessors such as Stephen Dorrell, Peter Brooke and David Mellor, believed in the capacity of the British film industry to reinvent itself. They felt that film industry matters should be in their in-tray and not left to junior 'Parliamentary secretaries'. Bottomley herself went on a fact-finding trip to Hollywood, meeting studio bosses and figures like Motion Picture Association of America (MPAA) president Jack Valenti. 'We were relentlessly and charmingly lobbied by the likes of David Puttnam, Dickie Attenborough, Wilf Stevenson and many others,' Bottomley recalled. 'Being able to invest lottery money in the film industry was transformational.'

In the meantime, British Screen under Simon Perry was given some of the lottery money in late 1995 to set up the so-called Greenlight Fund, which had a budget of £5 million a year for two years. This would invest up to £2 million per production in big, prestigious films from directors who might otherwise have been lost to Hollywood – or those who had been working in Hollywood but wanted to come back to Britain to make films. The projects it supported included David Leland's *The Land Girls* (1998), Mike Leigh's *Topsy-Turvy* (1999), Thaddeus O'Sullivan's *Ordinary Decent Criminal* (2000), Beeban Kidron's *Swept from the Sea* (1997) and Brian Gilbert's *Wilde* (1997), so admired by Alexander Walker.

Asked in Parliament in late 1996 about the impact of the National Lottery on the British Film Industry, Bottomley blithely replied:

The National Lottery has had a good impact on the British film industry, which is currently enjoying an excellent year. Already, more than £60 million has been awarded to 150 projects, which includes more than £35 million for 96 film productions. That is a tremendous achievement in so short a time, and it has been welcomed by the film industry.[30]

Her remarks didn't pay attention to whether or not the films had reached an audience. Success was seemingly measured in disbursing funds, not in what the films funded actually achieved. The Arts Council didn't want to sit on the money.

Eventually, Charles Denton (former head of BBC Drama) was drafted in to chair the lottery panel. The Arts Council's awards for single projects were considered to be an abject failure. The rhetoric now changed as the government, prompted by producers' association the Producers' Alliance for Cinema and Television (PACT), began to talk about using the lottery funds to create vertically integrated UK studios that could sit alongside Rank and PolyGram Filmed Entertainment and compete with the US majors. Rather than award lottery money on a 'fund any film' basis, PACT was calling for the creation of British mini majors which could use their public funding to attract private risk capital.

In the autumn of 1996, ACE announced that companies were to be invited to apply for four commercial 'lottery franchises'. This prompted a mini stampede which involved almost every player in the British film industry – and quite a few from abroad, too. New alliances were formed between producers, distributors, bankers, broadcasters and sales agents. 'An astonishing 170 preliminary applications have been submitted to the Arts Council of England for the four film production franchises which will be funded by the National Lottery,' *Variety* reported in December 1996.[31] By the next application deadline, there were still 37 applicants in the running. The four lucky winners stood to receive $64 million each. The guidelines for applying stated that the winning companies 'would have to demonstrate an ability to raise private sector partnership funding and plan for exploitation, recoupment and their own growth within the sector'.[32] The aim behind the franchise system, easy enough to state but very difficult to achieve, was to 'increase the production of British films for widespread cinema release, and so strengthen the independent production sector'.

The awards were finally announced during the Cannes Film Festival in May 1997, a few days after the election of Tony Blair's Labour government. It was a slightly surreal occasion. The great and the good of the British film industry crammed into the Star, a dingy backstreet cinema on the Rue d'Antibes, to hear the new Culture Minister Chris Smith and ACE chief executive Mary Allen read out the results. Alexander Walker was there in his familiar spectre-at-the-feast guise, ready to lambast whoever won.

The first surprise was that three awards were given rather than four. In advance of the event, almost everyone was sure that the bid submitted by Oscar-winning British producer Jeremy Thomas, together with leading independent UK distributor Entertainment and sales outfit J&M, was bound to be awarded one of the franchises. Thomas was one of Britain's most distinguished producers. As the chairman of the British Film Institute at the time, he was at the very heart of the UK film establishment.

'It was a mystery to me, I'd love to understand. It is something I will never know the truth about,' Thomas later reflected on why his bid was overlooked.

> We were arguably the three most successful companies in the jobs we were doing at that time. We applied for the maximum award. We had the best UK distributor, our production company with all skills and films behind it and J&M as a sales company, who were riding high. It was a very good idea, if we had put our heart and soul behind this operation.

Thomas likens being passed over, after everyone had tipped their bid as a definite winner, to being like 'losing a horse race'.[33]

The gossip suggested that Alexander Walker may have frightened the government out of the idea of giving the franchise to Thomas and his team. But in *Icons in the Fire*, Walker writes of waiting with the rest of the audience to see how 'the promised fourth franchise' would be awarded. He didn't appear to realise in advance that only three awards would be given.

However, it was exactly a year since David Cronenberg's *Crash* (his J. G. Ballard adaptation based around sex, death and automobile crashes) had premiered in Cannes. With his usual flair for understatement, Walker had described it then in his *Evening Standard* review as 'a movie beyond the bounds of depravity'. Walker's fellow reviewer Christopher Tookey at the *Daily Mail* considered it 'sick and immoral' and called for it to be banned. Jeremy Thomas had produced the film. If his consortium had won the fourth lottery franchise, the *Mail* and *Evening Standard* would have made a deafening din about public money being given to pornographers. That wasn't a noise that the Arts Council or government was keen to hear.

It was said that the timing of the announcement of the franchises had deliberately been postponed to the late afternoon as a way of spiting Walker. He was writing for the *Evening Standard*. By the time the announcement was made, his deadline for that day's edition had long passed. All the other newspapers would have the details of the franchises in their morning editions, but Walker would have to wait until the following afternoon to get anything into print, by which time his thundering was bound to seem a little late. He was still able to rile the organisers, though, by asking a question about why the Film Consortium, which had ex-Palace execs aboard, 'filmmakers of unquestioned talent but dubious business sense', had been given public money. As for the failure to award the fourth franchise to Jeremy Thomas and his team, that was still a mystery.

'*Crash* was a great movie. It is shown on TV now but it was used as a political pawn by Virginia Bottomley and Councillor John Bull [who tried to have the film banned in Westminster],' Thomas recalls of the controversy surrounding Cronenberg's film the year before the lottery franchises were announced.

It didn't help, either, some felt, that so many of Thomas' films, from *The Last Emperor* to *Merry Christmas, Mr Lawrence*, had been shot abroad. He was an internationalist and that grated with some of his colleagues. There was feverish speculation as to just why his bid didn't win a franchise. One well-placed source suggests that the Thomas/J&M/Entertainment application 'lost out on a technicality' which had 'fucked up their bid'.[34]

There were other surprising losers too. Merchant Ivory, one of the UK's most successful and upmarket production companies, had joined with sales company Capitol Films, bank Guinness Mahon, UK distributor First Independent and a small posse of independent producers in a bid called Partners in Film, which had TV support from Yorkshire–Tyne Tees TV, backing from leading Japanese production company NDF and American and British equity too. It was passed over. So was Double Negative, a bid backed by PolyGram Filmed Entertainment (the one vertically integrated British-based company that looked as if it had the production and distribution reach of a Hollywood major). This bid also included Working Title, the production company behind *Four Weddings and a Funeral* and *Notting Hill*. In subsequent years (see Chapter 3), PFE executives lamented, after the company folded, that if they had received the lottery franchise they might have had a chance of surviving.

The three winners were Pathé Pictures, DNA and the Film Consortium. What was startling to outside observers was the failure of all of them to adhere to the promises they made in order to access the lottery money. Charles Denton (then head of the Arts Council's advisory panel on film) told the audience that the three winners would make 90 features, with total budgets running into hundreds of millions, over the six-year period of their franchises, lasting from 1997 to 2003. This forecast proved to be wildly optimistic and wide of the mark. Critics who had been complaining that the Arts Council backed too many films in the early days of the lottery soon became equally indignant that the franchises backed too few.

'You might as well set fire to the fucking lot,' distributor Mick Southworth quipped at the time about what the £92 million of lottery money set aside for the franchises was likely to achieve. Speaking 20 years later, he still feels it was an opportunity lost. The funders were only looking at one part of the industry, namely production, 'rather than considering its needs and problems as a whole'.

'If someone who understood about progressive business had looked at it and said, "Where do we need to fill the gaps?" [they would have realised] it was not just about propping up production,' Southworth states.[35] 'Why not put money into distribution?' he asks.

No one thought about that. What was happening was we were creating more product, a lot of which was almost immediately bankrupt stock. The distributors were still struggling with P&As [prints and advertising costs] and staffing levels. Why not invest in the business? If you invest in the business, then the business will grow, the quality of the production will grow and it [the film business] will become more responsive to the commercial coalface. My real problem with it was that no one really cared if the users wanted these films.

He likens the process to a manufacturer spending millions and millions of pounds producing sausages and then turning up at the supermarket to discover that none of the customers liked them.

Only the film industry can make the wrong sausage. There was no thought that went into it [...] it [the lottery invest-ment] should have been about everything – about training and development. Production? Yes, sure, but production in a way where you award the commerce of production, not the fact that it exists.

On paper, though, the three mini studios looked impressive enough – and they all seemed to have robust distribution arrangements in place.

The DNA ('Duncan and Andrew') consortium combined the two most prominent British producers of the moment, Duncan Kenworthy (who had produced 1994 runaway hit *Four Weddings and a Funeral*) and Andrew Macdonald (the man behind 1996's *Trainspotting*). They had been promised $47 million over six years. They announced plans to make 16 films in that period, a dozen with budgets of up to $6.4 million, three that would cost up to $9.6 million and one bigger project that would cost to $12.8 million. There would be one film in the first year of the franchise and three films per year for the following five years. Either Macdonald or Kenworthy would produce one of the three films each year. They aimed to be material-led, not producer-led, and had guaranteed distribution through PolyGram.

'We're going to make low-budget films with energy, taste and style for British audiences,' Kenworthy declared at the outset... and then nothing happened. The DNA mantra was that script development was sacred. An Arts Council executive from the period said:

> That was their main pitch, that scripts weren't good enough and they were going to be script-led and that was it. That was the be-all and end-all of their thinking. Then, they got into the problem that none of the scripts were good enough. They would write and then they would rewrite and rewrite and rewrite. After the first three years, they had made two films – and one of them was unwatchable.[36]

The beleaguered head of development at DNA was said to be reading between 20 and 30 scripts a week – and not finding anything worth pursuing further. A few months after being awarded the franchise, Macdonald told *Time Out* magazine that DNA had received 500 scripts already... and not a single one they wanted to make. It didn't help the new company's momentum that both of its principals had other major projects to distract them. Kenworthy was beginning to prepare the *Four Weddings* follow-up, *Notting Hill*. Macdonald was still working with *Trainspotting* director Danny Boyle. They were soon to embark on their most ambitious project yet, *The Beach*, which would shoot in far-away Thailand with US studio backing and would star Leonardo DiCaprio.

The Film Consortium's winning of a franchise had greatly infuriated Alexander Walker. Producers Nik Powell and Stephen Woolley were part of the consortium – and, as Walker tried to remind the audience in Cannes, they had run Palace Pictures together. Palace had eventually gone bankrupt, leaving creditors in the lurch, and it chafed against Walker's sense of natural justice that they should now receive public support.

Powell described the Film Consortium as 'the REM' of the lottery franchise applications. By that, he meant that it encompassed 'the radicals, the establishment and the mavericks'. Alongside Scala (the company run by Woolley and Powell) were three other production companies: Simon Relph and Ann Skinner's Skreba, Sally Hibbin's Parallax and Ann Scott's Greenpoint. Virgin Cinemas was on board. Carlton Film Distributors, which had taken over Rank Film Distribution, was to handle the UK distribution of the films. The Sales Company would handle their foreign sales. The new company was committed to making 30 features over the six years of the franchise with budgets ranging from £1.5 million to £6 million. The day-to-day running of the new business was to be overseen by chief executive Kate Wilson, together with head of production and development Colin Vaines. There were plans to invest in animation and children's fare. In its bid, the consortium declared that it was 'essential' the franchise would be a 'conduit for the development of fresh talent and skills at all levels of the industry'. The consortium was going to be 'self-sustaining' and aimed to be profitable within three years.

What looked promising on paper was undermined by the harsh realities of Wardour Street. The Film Consortium had an exhaustive business plan, but it wasn't one which anticipated that its distributor partner Carlton would withdraw from film distribution only a few weeks after the franchise was awarded.

At least the Film Consortium was quickly into its stride, the first to sign its contract with the Arts Council of England. By the early autumn, it actually had a movie shooting. Gillies MacKinnon's *Hideous Kinky*, starring Kate Winslet, went into production in Morocco.

At DNA, it took a small eternity for any films to be made. The producer–founders of the company, Macdonald and Kenworthy, were used to working with key creative collaborators they knew well – director Danny Boyle in Macdonald's case and writer Richard Curtis in Kenworthy's. They didn't adjust easily to having to make films with outsiders.

Macdonald had always fully acknowledged the role that distributors PolyGram had played in his early successes, with both low-budget thriller *Shallow Grave* (1994) and then *Trainspotting* (1996). 'I've felt from the beginning that the reason *Shallow Grave* was a success and I have a career is that it was distributed properly by PolyGram,' Macdonald later told the *Guardian*.[37]

16. The joy of creativity: having worked in theatre and television, Danny Boyle was approached to direct the feature film *Shallow Grave*, which became the springboard for a remarkably eclectic and energetic film-making career. Famously, he was the highly acclaimed artistic director of the London 2012 Olympics Opening Ceremony.

Alamy

Unfortunately, by the late 1990s, when DNA finally began to develop such ill-starred films as Pat Harkins' debut feature *Final Curtain* (2000), Bill Eagles' Glasgow-set *Beautiful Creatures* (2000) and Peter Capaldi's comedy-drama *Strictly Sinatra* (2001), PolyGram was in the throes of being sold off by its corporate owner, Philips, to Seagram, owners of Universal. It was effectively being shut down (see Chapter 3). PolyGram had agreed in principle to distribute DNA's films but this agreement didn't mean much if there weren't any films to distribute and its own existence was coming to an end.

Pathé also struggled to live up to its commitments. Even before the announcement of the lottery franchise award winners in May 1997 in

Cannes, the French-based Pathé group (one of the oldest companies in world cinema) had been looking to become involved in British production. Now, it had its bridgehead. Pathé Pictures UK was run by Alexis Lloyd, a smoothly spoken former civil servant from an elite French background who had previously run independent distribution company Guild Entertainment. The head of production was Timothy Burrill, an internationalist who had made such films as *Bitter Moon* with Roman Polanski and *The Lover* with Jean-Jacques Annaud.

The Pathé franchise bid was structured very differently from those of the Film Consortium and DNA. Its strategy was to use the international strength of the Pathé group to help to attract other partners. There were plenty of those. Producers linked to the Pathé bid included Norma Heyman's NFH Productions, Thin Man (behind the Mike Leigh movies), Sarah Radclyffe Productions and Fragile Films (producers of Spice Girls film *Spice World*). Its financial backers included StudioCanal, BZW and Coutts. Its distribution partners included Guild, BSkyB, Canal+ in France and German outfit Tobis. Pathé announced it would make 35 films over the six years of the franchise. The outfit's advantage over the other two rivals was that it could fully finance films on its own, without outside help, simply by tapping 'minimum guarantees' put up by its distribution partners and financing from its equity partners. Through these partners, it also offered access to European markets.

In an interview just before Pathé signed its deal, Lloyd made the predictable bullish noises about developing the best possible projects.

> As far as we are concerned, commercial potential resides first of all in the script. It is not the stars that create the commercial profile of a film. The kind of projects we are looking for are more in the category of *Shallow Grave*, rather than films with very established stars and directors attached.[38]

Lloyd blithely declared that focusing on films with commercial potential in the UK made the best strategic sense. These were the films that would work in Europe and the rest of the world as well. Development, Lloyd declared, was the priority. The idea was to invest in around a dozen projects each year, of which half would go into production. There would be an open-door policy with at least a third of films coming from producers not officially affiliated to the bid.

In the event, Pathé did make some very fine films (most notably Lynne Ramsay's *Ratcatcher*), but there were a lot of disappointments too. Its movies neither really worked at the box office nor became critics' favourites – and there weren't that many of them.

'What nobody took into account was how long it takes to build up a production operation,' Andrea Calderwood, ex-head of production at Pathé Pictures later reflected on what went wrong with the franchises.

> None of the franchisees acknowledged how long it takes to go from idea to screen. They all should have said they might not make anything for the first two years [...] the way the applications were set out, there was an expectation of immediate activity.[39]

By the time they'd finished *The Beach* and *Notting Hill* and were ready to devote their attentions to DNA, Macdonald and Kenworthy were in danger of losing their golden halos. They had promised they would make 16 films over six years, but quickly discovered that unearthing new talent wasn't that easy.

As the *Guardian* reported,

> By 1999, DNA had finally assembled a development slate of ten films ranging from a Busby Berkeley-style musical comedy written by novelist Jonathan Coe to a teen pic about first love, *How to Get a Boyfriend*, scripted by Amy Jenkins. Few went into production. Amazingly, by early 2000, when the mid-term franchise reviews were being held, the company hadn't released a single feature in British cinemas.[40]

The triplets, as the franchises were nicknamed disparagingly, became regarded in some quarters as an embarrassment. Plans for five additional low-budget franchises were later scrapped as the lottery funds available had reduced.

Some home truths were gradually being recognised. While the lottery franchisees were accused of sitting on their money for too long, it had become apparent that, elsewhere, films were being rushed into production without proper development because their producers needed money and couldn't afford lengthy delays. These producers received their fees when films began shooting, and so had an obvious incentive to get their movies in front of the cameras quickly.

The figures weren't impressive. According to internal documents, film commitments made by ACE between September 1995 and September 1999 amounted to £99.244 million. Total revenues from investments in this period were £5.021 million. In other words, there was an absolutely glaring chasm when it came to the lottery money spent on film production and the money recouped. Southworth's throwaway remark about 'setting fire to the fucking lot' didn't seem so flippant after all.

CHAPTER 6

The Life and Death of the Film Council

Chris Smith was an unlikely figure to revolutionise the British film industry. The Labour MP for Islington South and Finsbury was a Cambridge University English graduate who had written his PhD thesis on the Romantic poets. He was Britain's first openly gay politician and was seen as a rising star in Tony Blair's Labour Party of the mid-1990s. The high regard in which he was held was underlined by the positions he occupied in the run-up to Blair's election as prime minister. He served stints both as Shadow Secretary of State for Social Security and Shadow Secretary of State for Health.

More relevant for the future of British cinema was the year he spent in an arguably less prestigious role as Shadow Secretary of State for National Heritage from 1994 to 1995. His areas of responsibility here included arts, broadcasting, sport, architecture and historic sites, royal parks, tourism... and film. Smith had no specialist knowledge of the industry but, almost inevitably, in his time as Shadow Heritage Secretary he was wooed by David Puttnam and Richard Attenborough. They were British cinema's lobbyists-in-chief. Both were firm Labour Party supporters. Both were hoping for strong public support for the industry from a new Labour government if one was to be elected.

Smith first met Puttnam through his work on a policy forum on the 'information superhighway', as the internet was called in the mid-1990s. The two quickly became friends and Smith was briefed in passing about some of the challenges then facing British cinema. By then, Attenborough, made a life peer in 1993, was as grand a figure in Parliament as he had been for many years in British cinema. He was also very close to the then Shadow Chancellor, Gordon Brown. He, too, cultivated Smith's acquaintance.

In 1995, Smith had gone on a fact-finding mission to California to meet representatives from the tech companies. He also took the opportunity while there to pay visits to Disney and Sony and to speak with Jack Valenti, the president of the Motion Picture Association of America (MPAA, the trade association representing the interests of the Hollywood majors).

Valenti, a flamboyant, fast-talking Texan who had been a press officer in John F. Kennedy's White House and was on the motorcade in Dallas at the time of Kennedy's assassination in 1963, was very forthright in what he told Smith about Hollywood and the British film industry. He made it clear to the Shadow Minister that, in a globally competitive environment for film production facilities, the US studios wanted 'efficient' tax incentives to lure them back to shoot in Britain. Film may have been only a minor part of Smith's portfolio but, during his short time as Shadow National Heritage Secretary, he established high-level movie industry contacts on both sides of the Atlantic.

When the Labour Party swept back into power in May 1997, Smith was made Secretary of State for Culture, Media and Sport. That gave him full cabinet responsibility for the film industry. The years that Puttnam, Attenborough, BFI director Wilf Stevenson and others had spent assiduously lobbying the Labour Party paid immediate dividends. Labour's Chancellor Gordon Brown provided tax breaks for the industry in his first mini budget in July 1997, declaring:

Despite our film industry's outstanding record of creative and critical success, too many British films that could be made in Britain are being made abroad, or not at all. The talents of British filmmakers can and should, wherever possible, be employed to the benefit of the British economy. So, after today, production and acquisition costs on British films with budgets of £15 million or less will qualify for 100 per cent write-off for tax purposes when the film is completed. That is a three-year measure at a cost of £30 million, and it should boost not only the number of British films, but the British economy by increasing our exports.[1]

Film, after all, was part of the creative economy and Brown was keen to support it. A few months before, *Vanity Fair* magazine had published a special edition on 'Cool Britannia' with the cover headline 'London Swings Again!' Just as in the swinging sixties, the magazine proclaimed, London was a 'cultural trailblazer'. British culture seemed hip again. Alongside the music, art world and fashion coverage, even British film seemed to have a new appeal. Admittedly, the movie everyone cited as an example of cinema's resurgence was Danny Boyle's *Trainspotting* (1996), a tale of heroin addicts in Leith (a long, long way from London), but, alongside its grimmer elements, the film had madcap energy and lots of Britpop music on its soundtrack. Brown was giving cinema special treatment. He didn't offer tax write-offs to other creative industries.

Smith recalls that Brown introduced the incentives in the face of ferocious opposition from his own civil servants in the Treasury. 'They [the Treasury officials] were absolutely adamant that this was something over their dead body. They saw it as tailor-made for tax evasion.'[2] The officials weren't altogether wrong. There were plenty of chancers keen to exploit loopholes in the original legislation (see Chapter 10). Nonetheless, this was an important symbolic moment. Twelve years after the abolition of the Eady Levy, the government was again providing the UK industry with significant support.

By the time of Brown's intervention, Smith had already commissioned *A Bigger Picture*, 'the most comprehensive review of film policy for many years', as it was billed. Smith explains the rationale behind the report, which was to pave the way for the announcement of a new public body to oversee the industry, as follows:

> One of the things everyone had been saying to me was that there was a huge amount of talent, a huge amount of promise, in the British film industry. We have brief moments of huge success when we get a *Four Weddings and a Funeral* or whatever, but then it all subsides again and we go back to watching American

movies. We really needed to think about what could be done
to get more sustained success.[3]

The report was announced at the Cannes Festival in May 1997 at the
urging of David Puttnam, who later recalled:

I worked with Chris Smith devising the Film Council. We even
had a conversation with [Prime Minister] Blair. We talked about
the film industry probably the year before the election and Blair
said, 'Oh, it's not a problem. David is sorting all of that out.' I
thought oh yeah, really, that's a hospital pass. Chris had assumed
that, as I had done the work, I would chair it [the review].[4]

For over two decades, the *Chariots of Fire* producer and former
Columbia Pictures studio boss had been, alongside Attenborough,
the British film industry's most prominent and formidable lobbyist
and champion. Now, with a Labour government finally in office,
his career was about to take a different turn. In the days after
Blair's election, in short succession, he was approached by new
Education Secretary David Blunkett to work for the Department
of Education on improving standards in teaching (he was to be the
first chair of the General Teaching Council) and then by Tony
Blair's chief of staff, Jonathan Powell, who wanted to see if he
would join the House of Lords as a Labour peer. Puttnam saw a
chance to move away from the film industry after 30 years and to
embrace a new career.

'People imagine that being a film producer is just about reading a
book or having a great idea,' he later explained to the *Independent* in
early summer 2000.

That's only a bit of it – it soon degenerates into a choice
between two actors, neither of whom you admire, dealing with
their agent over the size of their Winnebago and whether or
not their wife is going to have three first-class return tickets to
the location. My tolerance level for that stuff has evaporated: it
takes from you as a human being. I could bullshit with the best

of them, but I don't want to do that any more, having dinners
with people I don't want to have dinner with.[5]

Smith, normally a well-prepared and meticulous politician, was
obliged to work on the hoof. He arrived at the 1997 Cannes Film
Festival ready to announce the Film Policy Review Group but without
a chair to oversee its activities. That was the role originally envisaged for Puttnam, but he was no longer available. Puttnam suggested
that Smith should appoint Stewart Till, president of international
at PolyGram Filmed Entertainment, instead. Smith had never met
Till. However, he contacted him the night he arrived in Cannes and
arranged to meet him for breakfast the next day.

> I wrote out overnight the four or five things that I wanted the
> review to have a look at. We had a press conference at lunch-
> time the following day to announce we were doing it. I was
> setting up the working party, Stewart Till was going to be in
> charge and here was its remit.[6]

The film-loving Scottish politician Tom Clarke MP, the Minister of
State for Film and Tourism at the Department for Culture, Media
and Sport (DCMS), was the co-chair but, according to Smith, 'didn't
play a big part in it'.

The review, *A Bigger Picture*, published in March the following year,
represented a major shift in government film policy. On its very first
page, it noted that 'encouraging production will not by itself deliver
the outcome we want. The market needs better capitalised, broader-
based companies, able to integrate the processes of development,
production and distribution.'[7]

Much of the rhetoric had a familiar ring, though. The philosophy
espoused by *A Bigger Picture* chimed with that of PolyGram Filmed
Entertainment. Its emphasis was on marketing and distribution as
much as on production.

'Up to that point, most [government] attempts to provide impetus to the film industry had been about pushing rather than pulling,'
Smith later noted, using a metaphor which would continue to find

favour once the Film Council had been established. 'It had all been about putting money in at the creation end but hadn't been about audiences, about distribution, about marketing – about the other end of the chain.'[8]

'Until PolyGram came along, the British industry was obsessed with production,' Till agreed.

> We said no, it is a business. You can make the most cultur-ally impactful film in the world and if no one watches it, it is irrelevant. It is all about making powerful films and finding an audience. Obviously, distribution isn't the be-all and end-all either, but we tried in *A Bigger Picture* to focus on both sectors.[9]

A Bigger Picture was an exercise in self-criticism, an example of the British film industry putting on its hair shirt. The exercise, though, was felt to be bracing, worthwhile and cathartic. It highlighted the fact that the industry was 'fragmented', undercapitalised, structurally weak and in such 'precarious' health that it was in no position to take advantage of its own successes or to attract city or foreign investment. This was also the most thoroughgoing film industry report since the Monopolies Commission report of the mid-1960s, which, in the words of the *Spectator*, had

> condemned the film industry as monopolistic, restrictive and rigid in structure, dominated by Rank and Associated British Pictures, and operating in numerous ways against the public interest. Yet this is the industry which Parliament has been asked to subsidise, keeping alive producers who ought to be dead and restrictive practices which ought to be abolished.[10]

One of the new report's most welcome aspects was its efforts to pull together meaningful statistics. At this stage, in the late 1990s, the British film industry's attempts at keeping meaningful records on its activities were (as producer–distributor Chris Auty, chair of *A Bigger Picture*'s inward investment subgroup remembered) 'woefully inadequate'.[11]

There wasn't much data available but *A Bigger Picture* was able to make the case that huge opportunities could beckon if the industry did more to court the US studios and to persuade them to shoot in Britain. *A Bigger Picture* also called for the setting-up of an all-industry fund for supporting development, production and promotion of British films and for the creation of a private sector 'Film Marketing Agency'. The FMA concept emphasised the need to 'create an environment that is attractive to foreign investors and supporters of British exporters'.[12] In the event, the FMA was folded into the pre-existing generic All Industry Marketing (AIM) committee.

An all-industry fund wasn't something that the UK television companies were remotely interested in supporting. The US studios didn't oppose the idea but the ITV companies did. They didn't want to pay a levy toward British cinema, and came up with a vague alternative promise to invest £100 million in British film at some future date. The money never materialised.[13] Till suggests that the BBC and Sky might have been talked into supporting the fund but were swayed by the vehemence of the ITV opposition.

In the event, one insider remembers that the report had to be hurriedly rewritten 'very late in the day' when it became apparent that the ITV companies weren't going to support the all-industry fund on anything other than a voluntary basis. This ultimately meant that the final document didn't have much in the way of 'concrete, substantive money items in it' (in the words of Chris Auty) and that it turned out to be a 'policy document' rather than the 'costed and financed plan for an integrated British film industry' that it might have been if an all-industry fund had been established.

The Film Policy Review Group, which put together the report, featured an impressive array of the UK industry's leading producers, distributors, sales agents and publicists. John Woodward, the influential former chief executive of PACT, was on the inward investment subgroup. Woodward had masterminded PACT's '25 per cent campaign', obliging the BBC and ITV to acquire 25 per cent of their programmes from independent producers. In 1998 he was appointed director of the British Film Institute, refocusing it as an educational body under the chairmanship of Alan Parker.

As Chris Smith digested the report's findings, he began to think how best to overcome the many problems it highlighted. The UK industry was undercapitalised and unstable. Local distributors didn't have the 'critical mass' to compete with their Hollywood rivals. Production was a 'cottage industry' and most local producers didn't have meaningful relationships with their distributor partners. Smith felt there was an absence of central leadership. He later explained how the germ of the idea for the Film Council grew:

> I didn't have a concept at the outset that what we needed was an all-encompassing and more commercially minded body, but that [idea] did emerge out of the discussions that were being had. There were about four or five different agencies, all dealing with some aspect of the film industry and film-making, as well as some residual work being done through the Arts Council. I felt there was a need for two things. One was much greater coherence – hence the idea of bringing everything under one roof. Second, I wanted to make sure that we brought what one might call the artistic side of British film-making together with the more commercial side, so that each could usefully feed off the other.[14]

Even before the report was published, David Puttnam and Richard Attenborough had been 'blueprinting' plans for what became the Film Council and were advising Smith behind the scenes. The Labour politician wanted 'a body with real clout' that could fund film-making and film initiatives while also pressing the government on the issues that mattered most for the film industry.[15]

There were indeed many agencies administering different parts of the industry. The cultural side was overseen by the British Film Institute, which had been set up in 1933 and had a Royal Charter. The BFI had its own production arm. There was also the British Film Commission, busy trying to lure foreign production to the UK. British Screen Finance (privately owned but with some public backing) was investing in production. The Arts Council was still backing single projects from film-makers and had committed £96 million to the three lottery franchises. The idea was to bring the separate bodies together in a 'super-quango'.

In July 1998, the DCMS formally announced plans to set up the Film Council. Smith appointed Alan Parker as the first chair of the organisation.

> I wanted someone who had made movies and who was a respected figure in the industry; who knew where all the bodies were buried and was brilliantly networked around the world; and who was a no-nonsense figure and would roll his sleeves up and get on and do something.[16]

In the late 1990s, Parker had served for two years as chair of the BFI, an appointment which itself caused consternation in some circles. After all, the *Midnight Express* and *Bugsy Malone* director had often been withering in his remarks about the BFI, calling it an 'ivory

17. Action! Alan Parker prepares a scene with Kate Winslet, playing an investigative reporter, in *The Life of David Gale* (2003). Parker was nominated for a Golden Bear at that year's Berlin Film Festival for his direction of the movie. Earlier in his distinguished career he had received Oscar nominations for *Midnight Express* (1978) and *Mississippi Burning* (1988).

David Appleby/Universal Pictures

tower' and 'twenty-eight intellectuals in a library'.[17] He was a self-proclaimed 'hooligan from Islington' who was very belligerent in his public pronouncements about the shortcomings of the British film industry and the snobbery of the cultural elites.[18] The highly respected Jeremy Isaacs, the founding chief executive of Channel 4, had been mooted for the position at the BFI but the job went to Parker.

'It was an odd appointment as previously I'd only ever criticised the BFI – for being a rather snobby academic backwater with very little relevance to the bigger audience,' Parker says himself.

> But I wanted to change that. Its cultural remit appealed to me and when I was asked to be chairman I was living in LA, so I thought it gave me a legitimate reason to return home. I enjoyed my time at the BFI, brief as it was.[19]

The Culture Secretary then approached Stewart Till (who had over-seen the *Bigger Picture* report) to become Parker's vice chair. Till immediately agreed. Their first step was to try to appoint the strongest board possible, with some of the biggest-name producers in the UK industry sitting on it. The next move was to find a chief executive. Parker, Till and a high-ranking civil servant from the DCMS conducted the interviews. They weren't impressed at all with the quality of the candidates who came forward.

'John [Woodward] was the stand-out candidate, at least 100 per cent better than anyone else,' Till recalls.

> A few people who applied weren't even from the film industry but had senior positions in the public sector [...] I don't think people at the time realised the impact the Film Council was going to have and we didn't attract many high-profile names. People didn't realise it was as good a job as it was. John had worked at PACT and the BFI, which was a huge advantage, and he was very articulate about the good the Film Council could do. There were very few people who could straddle both the private and public sector. People in the film industry didn't get

how government worked (and vice versa). It was a no-brainer [to appoint Woodward].[20]

The prospect of the arrival of the Film Council, this new 'super-quango', caused excitement, anxiety and resentment in equal measure. There was a clear sense that the BFI was about to have its wings clipped.

'What I did do was very specifically say that the BFI should remain a semi-independent cost centre within the overall Film Council,' Smith says, speaking in the kind of language that was to exasperate the critics of New Labour. He describes the BFI at the time as 'doing a good but fairly limited job'.[21]

Right from the outset, the friction between the BFI and the new organisation from which it was going to receive its grant-in-aid was obvious. Stewart Till acknowledges feeling 'some frustration' toward the BFI and suggests that it was 'a little stuck in its ways'.[22] Parker concurs:

[When we worked there,] John Woodward and I tried to modernise the place, but it was hard work with a stubborn staff entrenched in their own views of how they saw the place. It did change eventually, that was inevitable, but by then John and I had moved on to the Film Council.[23]

The Film Council bosses noticed how protective the BFI's chairs, first broadcaster and journalist Joan Bakewell and then film-maker Anthony Minghella, were of the organisation. They were determined not to let it be bullied by the Film Council. Figures brought in from outside tended to 'go native' as soon as they began to work at the BFI. Minghella, for example, proved far less pliable than those who appointed him had anticipated. 'He worked his guts out at the BFI,' Puttnam later said of the *Cold Mountain* director.[24]

The National Audit Office had demanded that the BFI's objectives 'fell into line' with those of the Film Council but rather than simply kowtow to its new parent, Minghella oversaw a strategic review of the organisation.[25] The aim was to move the BFI from being an 'inward-looking organisation' to one that was 'engaged and outward-facing'.[26]

This review, which emphasised the safeguarding of the National Film Archive and encouraged the BFI to embrace a digital future, had a symbolic significance. It was a chance for the BFI to express its independence. Alan Parker had famously travelled all the way to the set of *Cold Mountain* in Romania to persuade Minghella to become chair of the BFI. Minghella agreed. He was coming into a dysfunctional organisation but was determined to ensure that the institute wasn't squeezed out of existence. There was also already tension between the BFI and the Arts Council, which still controlled the lottery purse strings for film.

'With the creation of the Film Council, the question as to who leads and who speaks for film can now be resolved,' an internal Film Council memo suggested. That resolution, though, was to come at the cost of both these organisations – the Arts Council and the BFI – being summarily bypassed. The internal memo also pointed to the bad feeling between the BFI and the Regional Arts Boards: 'From an RAB perspective, there is exasperation with what they see as excessive BFI bureaucracy, especially in relation to the low level of BFI investment on offer.'[27]

Again, the Film Council felt it could overcome the bad feeling simply by taking on the responsibility for the regions itself. 'The Film Council has the will to oversee a step change in the fortunes and potential for film in the English regions,' the memo suggested.

> While the BFI has done much over the last two years to improve its service position role effectively across the UK, it still finds it difficult to give adequate attention to its role as a funder of regional organisations. On balance, therefore, the Film Council believes that the existing conflict of interest between the BFI's current role as regional funder and film service provider is not sustainable. The Film Council therefore recommends that the BFI's planning and funding functions should be carried out directly by the Film Council.[28]

Even before its official launch in the summer of 2000, the Film Council's influence was being felt all across the industry. To some, it seemed like a new broom sweeping away the dust. John Woodward

said in an interview in the months leading up to the launch of the
new body:

> Helping build a sustainable British film industry is half the
> mission. The other half is to help improve access to culture and
> education around film and the moving image. That's a function
> which is equally complicated in its own way [...] You have to
> ask how much you can do in a multi-billion pound industry,
> a cultural and educational industry, with £50 million a year.
> What we're not going to be able to do is to use our money to
> fix all our problems [...] what we know and what our board
> identifies as the real endemic long-term problems of the British
> film industry are never going to be solved by chucking £50
> million at it [...] it's just not possible.

Woodward flagged up the problems the new organisation was hoping
to address. One was the 'very, very large number of tiny little production companies, basically one-man bands operating round Soho'.
These companies tended to have 'no capitalisation' and would 'stagger
from project to project', rushing their films into production too early
because they needed the money to support their overheads and keep
themselves in business.[29]

The Film Council was determined to improve the quality of
scripts. It wanted to train up a new generation of business executives
who understood 'managing and growing businesses'. The new Film
Council boss had a withering description of what the typical British
producer then tended to be like. He (and it almost invariably was a
he) was 'a guy in a leather jacket with a Filofax, a mobile phone and
a great idea, who is interested in all sorts of things but not necessarily
growing a company'.[30]

Another key issue was what Woodward called the 'almost complete disconnection across the UK between the production sector
and the distribution sector which has been the core of the success
of industry'. The new body wanted to set up 'large companies with
clout and market capitalisation who are in there for the long term
and want to build businesses around film production and distribution'.

In other words, there was the desire to create new equivalents to PolyGram Film Entertainment, the pain of whose closure was still keenly felt.

The principals at the Film Council didn't have a high opinion of the films then being turned out by British Screen Finance. The new body was planning to take a commercial tack in its production choices and was dismissive of the overly 'arty' films British Screen was making under its chief executive Simon Perry. Giving someone 'a million pounds to make a movie when you're certain in your heart that you are kissing goodbye to it and [only] the director and his family and a few hundred people of the intelligentsia of north London are going to watch it' was no longer justified, Woodward suggested in typically forthright language.[31] He also warned against British taxpayer money being spent on enabling British producers to be minority partners on foreign art-house movies that wouldn't be seen outside the BFI's London Film Festival or the National Film Theatre.

There was what, in hindsight, appeared to be a conscious attempt to sideline British Screen. Simon Perry was kept on for a few months to shepherd the films that had already been green-lit toward completion, but was then let go, and British Screen was closed down, as was the European Co-Production Fund it administered. The loss of British Screen was lamented by some but it was clear that, in the new order, there wasn't room for both organisations.

'The Film Council was immeasurably bigger and with a much bigger remit,' Till says.

> We were just a much, much more aggressive organisation. In the areas where we were doing the same function as Simon Perry's British Screen, I think we were measurably more successful than British Screen were. We had a much bigger overhead but a much bigger role. We had a whole slew of films much more successful than British Screen.[32]

In an internal memo, 'A new strategy for film', circulated as the Film Council was being formed, British Screen's role and strategy were questioned:

The company's original (DTI) remit was to help new entrant producers start a career in the industry through investment in films expected to be commercially successful. In fact, cultural considerations have, for the most part, taken precedence over commercial ones in British Screen's investment decisions. This approach was confirmed when, on the creation of DNH, the original remit was changed so that it became one of supporting new creative talent. This was perhaps an unfortunate change of approach as it is new producers who stand to gain most from the hands-on editorial interventions of British Screen.

The DTI decision that the Chief Executive alone should determine which films should be financed by British Screen has, in the view of many, left the Chief Executive of British Screen free to pursue a rather personal vision of the nature of British film. The low level of accountability required of the company, the personal authority of the Chief Executive and its autonomous board of directors, may make it difficult for British Screen to integrate itself within the overall author-ity of any Film Council. It may, however, prove politically unacceptable to wind up the company. An alternative would be to tighten up the company's contractual obligations, includ-ing reporting requirements, to the Film Council in order to ensure that British Screen's investments visibly contribute towards achieving the government's objective of developing a sustainable film industry.[33]

In the event, British Screen was outmanoeuvred. Accountants were commissioned to pore over its books. Its funding decisions were criti-cised. Its achievements, which were considerable, were conveniently ignored. While it was true that British Screen was characterised as pursuing only 'arty' projects with no audience and that the organisa-tion was less accountable than it should have been, prioritising cul-tural over commercial concerns, much of this was demonstrably not borne out by what British Screen actually did. Films like *Sliding Doors*, *Richard III*, *Wilde*, *Hilary and Jackie* and *Bend It Like Beckham* reached size-able audiences at home; *The Crying Game* (still an all-time top-grossing independent release in North America), *Orlando*, *Naked*, *Butterfly Kiss*, *Land and Freedom*, *Beautiful People*, *No Man's Land* and others sold and performed very well all over the world. Every investment decision the organisation made had to be reported in detail to the board (and ultimately the department) and assessed for additionality, Britishness, the involvement of new talent and commercial prospects – and a balance of these elements achieved over time (although additionality was generally a *sine qua non*). The European emphasis, and minority co-production ventures, had to be justified on strategic grounds and in the context of the volume of British-originated work the organisation supported. The 'foreign language' films attracted attention, and sometimes criticism, because a number of them (*Before the Rain*, *Antonia's Line*, and so on) attained prominence by winning major awards. Overall, its principals claim, British Screen's rate of recoupment was far higher than that of any other public film fund in the world at the time: the main fund consistently recouped 50 per cent of its output every year, as records attest – a level achieved only occasionally by the Film Council, and significantly only by the New Cinema Fund, never by the Premiere Fund. Perry's experience over ten years was that it was 'auteur cinema' that generated the best business, while 'commercial' projects underperformed with remarkable regularity. He argues that this was an inconvenient truth for the Film Council to acknowledge, given the remit it had devised for itself. He also felt British Screen was unjustly penalised for the perceived sins of the Arts Council. Perry says today:

> its levels of investment were far lower and more judicious than the Arts Council's, so that over ten years we supported 14 to 15 films each year with very limited resources and on an overhead of well under £1 million. The Film Council, with running costs of several times this amount, funded fewer films and at a poorer rate of return. So while it's accurate in some sense for Till to say that the Film Council was 'bigger', it is not accurate to claim that it was more 'successful'.[34]

Perry, although popular and well respected by film-makers, was regarded as a divisive figure who wasn't going to unify the industry.

There was also a sense that those behind the Film Council didn't like dissent or overly robust debate. Their rhetoric was about bringing rival factions together and about the industry speaking with a single voice.

'My view was that if the Film Council was going to be the body that I envisaged, it wasn't going to be something that Simon would particularly like,' Puttnam recalls.

> It was going to be very business-focused. That was not Simon's bag. Simon loved to hang out with film-makers. John Woodward's job was not going to be to hang out with film-makers. It would never have crossed my mind that Simon would have been the right person to run the Film Council. I don't think it crossed his mind. I felt Simon was far happier doing the things he did very well. They were European-focused. He was a film-maker's executive, not a business executive.[35]

Perry recalls that he was kept on as a consultant for three months. He had to go in and see Till at regular intervals to keep him up to speed on the final films that British Screen had backed.

The Film Council promised that it would have a 'comprehensive' European strategy and would spend 20 per cent of its money across all its funds on European projects, but this was not a promise that was ever fulfilled.

In the brave new world of the Film Council, there wasn't going to be as much space, either, for the style of cultural film-making associated with the BFI Production Board (which had supported films from British 'auteurs' like Terence Davies, Bill Douglas, Sally Potter and Derek Jarman). The Film Council hadn't hidden its desire to take a 'solidly commercial' approach to production funding. Woodward posed the rhetorical question

> are you going to put the money into art house films that you know are never going to get their money back and are going to attract very, very small audiences [...] or do you try, because it's public money, to put your money into films which people might actually want to go and see in large numbers?[36]

Woodward wanted to move away from what he perceived as the rashness and indulgence that had characterised some of the funding decisions made by the Arts Council and British Screen. That led him on occasion to speak rashly to the press, as in his conversation with the French journalist Agnes Poirier:

> Take for example a story about an English family that wins the Lottery, and one about a Croatian family that wins the Lottery and has to cope with the guilt problems. Only the first story will interest the Film Council [...] We are certainly not prepared, nowadays, to support small art films with a tough, social subject matter or European foreign-language films, which won't find a distributor in Britain. We have to accept the fact that the British public goes to see, 85% of the time, American films.[37]

To some, this seemed like craven defeatism and philistinism – an abandonment of the notion that cinema was a universal art and that British audiences might be interested in seeing stories from cultures other than their own.

The Film Council had three separate main funds: a 'Premiere Fund' which would have £10 million a year and would back eight to ten films a year in the £1 million to £8 million budget range; a 'New Cinema Fund' with £5 million a year to support adventurous and experimental low-budget film-making; and a 'Development Fund' with £5 million.

There was no question that the new body immediately provided much-needed leadership to a fractious and fragmented industry – although there were some within the industry who deeply resented the direction in which they were being led. As one senior producer of the Film Council says,

> the positive thing to anybody who had experienced the industry in the post-Puttnam nadir [of the 1980s and early 1990s] was to have one place that was speaking for the industry, that gathered statistics and could speak to the government and be listened to, that was a fantastic thing [...] That was a

genius move to have that as a body. We didn't have anything before that. It was just hopeless. Before that, all you could do was ring up Dickie Attenborough and hope he would wiggle himself into Downing Street and then hope that something would happen. Now we had a proper organisation with some resources.[38]

The Film Council (which quickly rebranded itself as the UK Film Council) had very rapidly entrenched itself at the heart of the British film industry.

'The British film industry is a broad church and so you know that you'll never please everyone,' Parker later said of the criticism that came the new organisation's way almost as soon as its doors opened.

There's always going to be someone snapping at your ankles. I had a very strong board of the UK's best film practitioners and we were determined to completely rethink all previous structures that had traditionally supported the industry. With so many different factions and interests there would be bound to be some moaners, but that was the main reason I took the job. Putting all of film support under one umbrella with a highly professional organisation seemed to me to be very necessary and the various disparate groups – the often amateur and ingenuous cottage industry – needed a dose of direction and professionalism, which the Film Council could provide.[39]

The dose of 'direction and professionalism' Parker refers to led to UKFC (as it became known) taking a prescriptive approach. The new body was intervening at every level of the film industry. This prompted resentment. The 'Ministry of Fear' was the nickname that Andi Engel, founder of leading art-house distributor Artificial Eye, gave the Film Council. Some well-known film-makers bristled with resentment about the extensive script notes they were given by Film Council executives who had only a fraction of their experience.

Producers grumbled about the way these executives micro-managed their productions. The Film Council was accused of extreme high-handedness. Some questioned Parker's role as chairman, pointing out that he had little experience of independent film-making and hadn't worked as an executive within the British industry. Critics claimed he encouraged a testosterone-driven atmosphere. 'Right idea, wrong people' was the verdict of some producers. It was claimed that UKFC 'killed' at least one of the lottery franchises by refusing to allow the franchisee to hold on to money recouped from its films.

'They [the Film Council] were amazingly presumptuous in terms of their ability to know. They did want film-makers basically to work for hire for them,' suggests former British Screen boss Simon Perry.

> The attitude was always this extremely arrogant attitude which everybody complained about. I don't know where it came from, this 'big willy' syndrome that was very strange. It was part of the 'it has all been rubbish before and we've got to put this right and we're the only people who can put it right and we know what is needed'.[40]

Oscar-winning producer Jeremy Thomas points out that the BFI Production Board made films 'very critical of the government' during the Thatcher era. No one at the BFI tried to stop them and there weren't complaints from government either. The Tory politicians simply weren't interested enough in the low-budget films being made at the BFI to bother getting upset about them.

> From the Film Council days onward, I don't believe that you could have got away with being as critical of the government of the time then because the Film Council was created in the mould of New Labour. It was created in their image by their employees or their missionaries.[41]

This wasn't (Thomas suggests) censorship as such. It was more that a 'form of thought' was internalised by the executives at UKFC. It's a contentious point of view but one that the Film Council's choices seems to back up: UKFC conspicuously failed to find and champion talents as offbeat, abrasive and as political as Derek Jarman, Bill Douglas or Sally Potter.

Thomas speaks with nostalgia of the era of Sir John Terry, for many years the managing director of the National Film Finance Corporation and credited with launching the careers of Karel Reisz, Ken Loach, Alan Parker, David Puttnam and many others. Terry was a patrician figure who would make decisions on what to back quickly and without fuss. With NFFC money, film-makers could then approach other backers (for example, Rank and EMI) to put together the rest of their budgets. The Terry approach was continued by his successor, Mamoun Hassan, who took over at the NFFC in 1979. British Screen Finance under Simon Relph and then Simon Perry in the 1980s and 1990s had a similar, film-maker-friendly style. Then came the UK Film Council. Thomas recalls:

> The idea of a national studio started with them [UKFC] want-ing to be very prominent in what they involved themselves in. That was at every level of the production, micro-managing every little area of the film business. It was very difficult for producers like me to interact with that because I had already made 30 movies.[42]

He likened dealing with the Film Council to 'having to go back to school on every film'. He was questioned about everything from casting to deciding to shoot David Mackenzie's *Young Adam* in colour rather than black and white. 'It's a different attitude toward what would be the idea of what independent cinema is.' The Film Council was seen by some as applying studio principles to what were often small art-house films. Film-makers were treated more as 'supplicants' than as talents to be nurtured.

Former Film Council board member Chris Auty acknowledges that executives working for the new organisation could be very prescrip-tive with the talent. The new body was like the curate's egg in the old *Punch* cartoon, good in parts.

> The intent [of the Film Council] was admirable. The desire
> to inject some level of order, information and structure was
> admirable. The wish to create a serious pot of development
> money was very, very sensible. The wish to create a central
> statistical unit was absolutely essential […] all those things
> were admirable. Over time, as the institution developed, it
> developed some very unfortunate habits, one of which was to
> treat public money as if the executive who was administer-
> ing it was working in a full-profit business. It got to the point
> where executives working for the Film Council behaved with
> a high-handedness one would not find at Warner Bros. or
> 20th Century Fox […] there's a way of saying no nicely and
> there's a way of saying fuck off and I think it is always best to
> say no nicely.[43]

Certain film-makers certainly bristled at the treatment meted out to
them by Film Council executives. Terence Davies, the brilliant and
very idiosyncratic director whose early work had been supported
by the British Film Institute, raged against the Film Council. In
a waspish interview with the *Guardian* after trying to develop his
adaptation of Lewis Grassic Gibbon's *Sunset Song* at the Film Council,
Davies said:

> 'There's a man there called Robert Jones [former head of the
> Film Council's Premiere Fund] who made us jump through
> all sorts of hoops, and we actually did everything he wanted,
> and he turned around after four months and said, "It won't
> travel." He pauses for effect. 'And that was somebody who
> had just put money into *Sex Lives of the Potato Men*! The way
> in which we were treated was absolutely shocking. If I can
> misquote Shaw, "Those who can, do, and those who can't
> become Robert Jones."'[44]

Ex-Palace and PolyGram executive Jones, who had worked in acquisitions and production, was an admirer of the director and had even
released some of his films. He recalls:

> To set the record straight about Terence Davies, he was furious
> with me because he felt that his film should have been funded
> blindly, with no regard to whether or not there was any chance
> of the fund seeing its money back.[45]

The Premiere Fund boss didn't give Davies script notes. However, he saw it as his responsibility to 'look at the combination of the creative package, the finance plan and the level of budget the film was being made at'. In this case, Jones' judgement was that the film wouldn't reach a big enough audience to justify the level of investment that Davies and his producers wanted. He wasn't there just to give grants blindly.

Given that UKFC had made one of its goals 'professionalising' the British film industry and was investing public money, its desire to intervene was understandable. The very idea of investing £4 or £5 million each year in a 'Development Fund' showed the new body was determined to nurture projects, not simply to hand over the money to make them to their producers. The Film Council didn't want to come in last to a project or to have the weakest recoupment position and least amount of influence.

'What we really want to do is come in first,' John Woodward said on the eve of the launch of the new body, clearly seeking to distance it from the strategies of the Arts Council's lottery board.

> What we are not going to do is have a panel. We are going to
> set up a number of funds run by the best creative people in the
> industry, delegate the responsibility for making and greenlight-
> ing to them, back them up with right personnel in business
> affairs, legal and financing skills, give them the budget, a clear
> frame of reference and then say off you go!

'I want the industry, when they are thinking about who they want to finance a film, to say, OK, we will go and talk to the Film Council,' Woodward continued, explaining the desire to put UKFC at the heart of British production.[46]

There was heightened sensitivity about the criticism that had poured down on lottery-funded films. Newspapers, Till notes, were 'hovering to point fingers' and the Film Council wanted to protect itself from the 'barrage of criticism' and 'chorus of derision' led by Alexander Walker, Christopher Tookey and their followers. 'You had to jump through an enormous amount of paperwork. That's the nature of public sector money,' Till acknowledges.

> I would defend us 100 per cent on that. We brought in very powerful people to run the funds. We paid them a reasonable amount of money, tried to get the best and they came in with an attitude. Sometimes they were too intrusive. But I would prefer to have someone intrusive who knew what they were doing rather than someone less intrusive and less knowledgeable.[47]

At PolyGram, the emphasis had always been on the 'empowerment' of writers, directors and producers. The Film Council also wanted to back the talent but within limits.

'The Film Council considered themselves as the ushers-in of a new way of approaching the use of public money, which was to pour money into films that were clearly for audiences,' former British Screen boss Simon Perry remembers.[48]

The Premiere Fund was designed to help 'more overtly commercial' films, while the New Cinema Fund was allowed to carry on in the vein of the old BFI Production Board and to support experimental work.

'You can't change the film industry overnight. What you can do is push it gently in the right direction.' Woodward stated, promising that the new body would not 'hack' money into

> dozens and dozens of £2–£3 million movies that are underdeveloped, their budgets are so small they never have a star in them, their production value is so low that when they have an explosion, the explosions are too small; they don't attract distribution, they don't go into market with enough welly behind them. They barely make it to the cinema and when they do it's on 20 prints, they last a long weekend and then they vanish.

The Film Council chief executive accepted that terms like 'commercial' and 'quality' were very slippery, but he had very firm notions about what the new body wouldn't support. No longer would public money be put into features like George Orwell adaptation *Keep the Aspidistra Flying*, starring Richard E. Grant and Helena Bonham Carter, about a penniless artist who leaves his job as a copywriter to become a 'poet and a free man'. The lottery-backed film received relatively positive reviews when it opened the 41st London Film Festival in October 1997 but the UKFC senior brass saw it as embodying all that was wrong with British cinema. In an interview with *Moving Pictures* in 1999, John Woodward commented:

> That is exactly what we want to get away from, that stolid notion of an English heritage film from a George Orwell novel but actually is made so cheaply that there are never wide shots because they can't afford to dress the set that much. It doesn't have a star in it and is dreadfully turgid. People say, 'Oh, it is going to a great bit of art, like a Merchant Ivory film.' You think, 'Oh no it's not, it's a fucking dog, nobody is going to see it.' There are many of those over the past two or three years.

As far as the Premiere Fund was concerned, the emphasis was going to be on supporting films the audiences actually wanted to see. If that meant taking fewer risks, so be it.

Woodward may not have wanted the Film Council to back heritage films but, ironically, one of its very first investments in UK production was in Robert Altman's country house drama/murder mystery *Gosford Park* (2001). The Kansas City-born director's first British feature was a troubled production. The £2 million put up by Robert Jones through the Film Council's Premiere Fund was the bedrock financing which enabled the £10 million feature to be made. Jones recalls reading the script in the bath. The film's screenwriter Julian Fellowes recalled in a BAFTA lecture in 2012:

> There was one really terrible moment when, just before we were about to start, literally about two or three weeks before

we were due to start shooting, suddenly we lost all the money. It just vanished, overnight.[49]

Other investors may have pulled out but the Film Council money was still there and its presence reassured Capitol Films, the British sales company which 'rescued' the film by coming on board as co-financier at a very late stage. Fellowes later told the *Daily Telegraph*:

> It is true that the council was crucial in providing the initial seed money for *Gosford Park*, but this was the result of a personal and very brave decision by Robert Jones, then head of the council's UK Premiere Fund, for which he was roundly criticised at the time, both in the press and, more to the point, by others serving on the council, because the project was 'commercial' and therefore, according to the philosophy prevailing, 'could find funding elsewhere'.[50]

In the event, *Gosford Park* turned into a critical and popular success. Fellowes, a genial, Micawber-like middle-aged actor from an aristocratic background, who was best known to the British public for a recurring role in Sunday night BBC series *Monarch of the Glen*, won a Best Original Screenplay Oscar and very successfully reinvented himself as a writer. *Gosford Park* paved the way for his later *Upstairs Downstairs*-style TV drama *Downton Abbey*, which also became a huge international hit. Nonetheless, the film offered early hints of just how much criticism the Film Council was likely to face, wherever it made its investments.

There was an initial outcry that so much British public money was being pumped into a film directed by an American. For Jones, though, part of the attraction was in having an outsider and maverick like Altman direct such quintessentially British material.

'I would go on the set and say to him, "Robert, how is it going?" and he would say, "I have no idea,"' Jones says of Altman's famously improvisatory working method, which he likened to organised chaos with multiple cameras and dialogue tracks.[51] At the time, Altman was in his mid-seventies. He had secretly had a heart transplant a few years before and no one would insure him to make the film. (British director Stephen Frears, who had recently directed *Dirty Pretty Things* with Jones as producer, had agreed to be on standby in case anything did happen to him.)

Altman himself was blithely unconcerned by all the fuss. 'My dear,' he told the *Guardian* during shooting,

> I think every dollar or pound that comes down the pike is tainted. I don't have the slightest problem whether it's drug money from Nicaragua, British lottery money, or from skim-off in Las Vegas. It doesn't make any difference. And what's lottery money supposed to be spent on – curing sheep or something?[52]

(The reference to sheep was prompted by the outbreak of foot-and-mouth-disease in 2001, which had already had a disastrous effect on British farming and tourism.)

At first, British distributors were singularly unenthusiastic about *Gosford Park*. Although it had been pre-sold all around the world, its British release was only sorted out very late on.[53] The trade press reported on the tepid response at trade screenings. Eventually, just a few weeks before its premiere at the London Film Festival, Entertainment Film Distributors picked it up. Only two distributors had bid for it seriously, Icon being the other. The response at the LFF was also low-key. To its detractors, the film seemed a little boring and old-fashioned. What some critics didn't notice was the continuing fascination among audiences on both sides of the Atlantic with the intricacies of the British class system and the allure of an ensemble cast of top British actors, Alan Bates, Maggie Smith, Helen Mirren, Michael Gambon and Derek Jacobi among them.

The other films backed by the Premiere Fund were in a different register – and had mixed success. *Mike Bassett: England Manager*, a laddish Steve Barron comedy starring Ricky Tomlinson; *Miranda*, a romantic comedy starring Christina Ricci; *The Importance of Being Earnest*; and *Sylvia*, a biopic of Sylvia Plath starring Gwyneth Paltrow (with future 007 Daniel Craig as Ted Hughes) were some of the early titles backed by the fund. It supported animation (*Valiant*, about a carrier pigeon in World War II), Shakespeare adaptations (*The Merchant of Venice*) and even a French-language film, Patrice Leconte's *L'homme du train*. There was a sense that the Film Council wanted to do a little bit of everything: to support as broad a range of films as possible.

The council was also clearly keen to avoid accusations of snobbery and pretentiousness. It was open to the idea of funding comedies, even those on the smutty side. Jones made the fateful decision to invest in *Sex Lives of the Potato Men* (2004), which gained instant notoriety as one of the worst-reviewed films in British cinema history since *No Orchids for Miss Blandish* (1948). The *Evening Standard*'s Alexander Walker had died in the summer of 2003 but his untimely passing did nothing to stem the brickbats which were hurled in the direction of the Potato Men. The *Daily Mail*'s Christopher Tookey called it 'the most shamefully inept, witless and repulsive British comedy that I have ever had the misfortune to see' – and that was one of the more forgiving reviews. It was called 'nauseous' and 'a masterclass in filmmaking ineptitude' by *The Times* and 'smut for morons, partly funded by your and my lottery money' by the *Financial Times*. The Film Council bunkered down and went into defence mode.

The 18-rated film, about the sexual antics of a group of vegetable delivery men, was indeed very vulgar. Starring popular comedians Johnny Vegas and Mackenzie Crook, it was in the tradition of saucy British comedy that stretched back to the sex films of the 1970s and to the risqué humour of end-of-the-pier comedians like Max Miller. This was as far removed from *Keep the Aspidistra Flying* and traditional British heritage cinema as it is possible to imagine.

As Film Council executives tried to point out, *Sex Lives of the Potato Men* did reasonable business, making over $1 million at the UK box office and then finding a sizeable audience on DVD. It was far from the most disastrous British film ever made and the argument that the Film Council had frittered away vast amounts of UK public money wasn't sustainable. Nonetheless, Robert Jones was startled to wake up one morning and find himself being doorstepped by *Daily Mail* journalists.

Jones acknowledges that the film 'didn't turn out creatively' as had been hoped when the script was delivered, but points out that

Entertainment, one of the UK's canniest independent distributors, also backed the project. 'It was an attempt to make a commercial film for a much broader audience, possibly a younger audience. If the creative team had pulled it off, it would have been a different story.' The hope had been that the film would turn into the '*Spinal Tap* of sex comedies'.[54]

'The quality of the criticism was very naive,' Stewart Till remembers. If the Film Council invested £1 million into a film with a budget of £5 million and that film made only £3 million at the UK box office, Till noticed that the critics would proclaim it a failure.

> Of course, [they were] ignoring what it might have done on DVD, ignoring what the foreign pre-sales might have been, as if there was a perfect one-on-one correlation between the cost of the film and the box office. People like Alexander Walker should have known better and did know better.[55]

Those within the industry had become inured to the attacks from Walker in the *Evening Standard*. Till recalled:

> Alan Parker used to say that because it [the *Standard*] was read in the main by people commuting home from London, the paper basically said everything in central London was wrong and bad and made the readers feel better about going home to the suburbs on their trains.

The editorial stance of the *Evening Standard* was, basically, one of anger and exasperation (reflecting the frustrations of the commuters).

The difference about *Sex Lives of the Potato Men* was that it provoked indignation in almost every newspaper. There was a certain malicious glee in the way it was reviewed – a sense that the journalists were enjoying themselves in skewering the film. It also became a very useful tool with which opponents could bash and lampoon the Film Council.

At the same time Robert Jones was having mixed success on the commercial side at the Premiere Fund, Paul Trijbits, the enthusiastic young Dutch-born producer in charge of the New Cinema Fund (with its £5 million a year) was also busy dividing opinion.

Walker's scattergun attacks continued apace. 'A more amateurish, misbegotten and badly made film it would be hard to find this year,' he proclaimed of *My Brother Tom*. Alex Cox's *Revengers Tragedy* was described as 'enjoyably exuberant' but Julien Temple's *Pandaemonium* (initiated before the Film Council came into existence) was much more harshly treated by the veteran critic:

> I don't know why the new Film Council wants to stick its name on the screen and claim any part in *Pandaemonium*. The council wasn't even in existence in 1999 when the Arts Council handed out £656,094 of public money from the National Lottery to help Temple make a film that's among the most vulgar travesties of English literature I've seen in years – certainly since Ken Russell gave up the ghost.[56]

Trijbits' manner sometimes exasperated film-makers, as Alex Cox later recalled in his book, *X Films*:

> The new head of the New Cinema Fund was twenty-five minutes late and couldn't stop talking on the phone. He had two phones, a mobile and a landline, and every time either rang, he jumped up and raced to answer it. His conversations seemed mainly domestic or about scheduling matters that his assistant could have dealt with.

'Numerous Film Council wallahs came up to Liverpool for the obligatory on-set visits,' Cox said of what happened when his film *Revengers Tragedy* started shooting.

Cox's complaint was that the Film Council executives had little practical experience of making feature films. They were 'naive at the business of film, in awe of the Americans. Yet they were drawing unheard-of six-figure salaries in an organisation that soon required a hundred full-time paid employees and hundreds of consultants more.' Cox advocated building 'small' and concentrating on the regions. He railed against the way that the Film Council was 'dismantling' the British film industry,' delivering 'certain profitable parts of it to the Americans and funnelling Lottery money to the Hollywood studios'.[57]

These criticisms were manifestly unfair. Trijbits may have had a short attention span but he threw Film Council support behind some remarkable films, among them Paul Greengrass' *Bloody Sunday* and Peter Mullan's Golden Lion-winning *The Magdalene Sisters*. Cox's charge that the Film Council executives lacked practical experience of the film business didn't really stack up either. The Film Council board consisted of many of the most seasoned executives from every sector of the film business, distributors like Entertainment's Nigel Green and exhibition veterans like Steve Knibbs among them. Alan Parker was nothing if not experienced. Nonetheless, Cox and others who attacked the Film Council exposed a tension at the heart of the British film industry, one that the new government body was never going to be able to resolve to everyone's satisfaction.

As Alan Parker noted, 'The UK has two industries: a) the indigenous film industry and b) the service industry, mostly at the service of giant American productions.' All the rhetoric about creating a sustainable UK film industry envisaged the British having the same access to distribution as its US rivals. Parker later remembered that

> our goal at the Film Council was to help create a dozen companies like Working Title (for 20 years a stand-out British production company of global significance, strongly financed firstly by PolyGram and then subsequently by Universal and Canal Plus). We had hoped this multiplicity of companies would create its own PolyGram. Whether we failed in this dream, or it was cut short by the summary execution of the Film Council, we will never know. The harsh reality of the film industry is that in the main, it is a distribution-dominated business and that's where the rewards and the rich pickings are.[58]

The dream for the British film industry, stretching back as far as Rank and Korda in the 1930s and 1940s, was to create its own equivalent of the US studio system. The British weren't greedy. They weren't asking for six major studios like in Hollywood. One studio would probably have done fine as long as it was vertically integrated, with an international marketing and distribution operation to take advantage of the films it actually produced. Parker noted that

> most major film producing countries have giant, vertically integrated companies (or at least one). Because we, as a country, have always been dominated by TV companies, we lost ours: Rank to incompetent myopic management and PolyGram (the best multifaceted company we ever had) to Philips' internal corporate politics.

Distribution was at the heart of the Film Council project right from the outset. 'We need a strong domestic distribution sector,' the report *A Bigger Picture* declared, as if creating such a sector would be straightforward enough. When Parker made a speech to the UK film industry in November 2002 on 'Building a Sustainable Film Industry', he talked about reinventing the UK as 'a film hub – a creative core [...] a natural destination for international production' and 'a natural supplier of skills and services to the global film market'. Parker also wanted this film hub to create 'British films that attract worldwide distribution and large audiences, while still using subsidy to support cultural production and new talent'. For this to happen, he suggested, the UK needed an industry 'led by distribution, not the other way round. Pull, not push. Robust, UK-based distributors and sales agents with a serious appetite for investing in British films and helping them to make a success all around the world.'[59]

Arguably, the British already had an industry led by distribution. There were several UK-based distribution companies in existence. The hitch, though, was that they were all American-owned. The independent British distributors lagged a very long way behind them.

Early in its existence, the Film Council consulted extensively with the UK distribution community as to what could best be done to help it. The independent companies bemoaned their low theatrical rentals and tried to draw attention to what they regarded as the very shoddy way they were treated by satellite broadcaster Sky. The pay-TV giant had generous output deals with the US studios but rarely bought or showed anything at all from the independents – and when it did so, its terms tended to be far less attractive than those offered to the American majors.

In February 2000, a few months before its official launch, the Film Council met with distributors, who were encouraged to air grievances and raise concerns. The distributors clearly enjoyed the novelty of actually being listened to. Veteran distributor Mick Southworth, then working for short-lived company Alchymie, wrote to Woodward after the meeting:

> The meeting stripped away all the usual bullshit and corporate posturing and engaged, face to face, the very real horrors that beset us all in this industry, be we large sharks (no slur intended on large sharks!) or we poor bottom-feeding minnows [...] One certainty [...] [is] the stark conclusion that even when the good and mighty have swallowed financial failure they can still remain standing, proof positive that whilst money doesn't always ensure success in distribution, it does give the big spender another day to live.[60]

The question of how best to help British distributors wasn't easy to answer. 'How do you achieve large companies with clout and market capitalisation who are in there for the long-term and want to build businesses around film production and distribution?' one senior Film Council executive asked early in the organisation's history. 'There are answers but we haven't worked them out in six board meetings.'

PolyGram was defunct. Other big British companies like Granada, Carlton and Pearson were involved in every aspect of the media business... except for film, which they dabbled in at best. The Film Council, a little reluctantly, had taken over the three lottery franchises. These were due to run for six years and had limped to the halfway points in their existence, but it was clear that neither DNA nor Pathé Pictures nor the Film Consortium were going to have any lasting or transformative effect on the industry.

To the surprise of many observers, all three sailed through their mid-term assessments, which were conducted by the Film Council in 2000. It was an open secret that the three franchisees weren't held in great regard by the new organisation. 'We very thoroughly checked whether we could terminate those agreements because we were not supportive of them,' Stewart Till remembers. 'Legal due diligence [showed] they were binding on us. If they had not been, we would have discontinued them or some of them.'[61] As it was, the three franchisees were all given green flags to continue until the end of the six-year period. Another consideration was that if their contracts had been terminated early, it might have caused a hiatus in British production.

What became apparent was that the Film Council simply didn't have access to enough capital with which to help the UK distributors to compete with their US counterparts or to build mini studios that had sufficient weight to make an impression in the marketplace.

In the infancy of the Film Council, there was discussion about reallocating some resources from production into distribution. The Film Policy Review Group had advocated the setting up of a P&A (Prints & Advertising) Fund of £10 million as part of the All Industry Fund it had recommended, and the *Bigger Picture* report had called for 'a substantial proportion of Lottery funds' to be used 'to support development and distribution'. 'A main criterion for selecting projects should be previous successful track record to encourage and reinforce commercial filmmaking,' the report stated.

In the event, the Film Council shied away from establishing a major fund to support distribution. Its emphasis was on development and production. A senior Film Council executive commented at the start of the Film Council's life:

What the hell can we do? We can throw the entire budget of the Film Council, £60 million, into the market, supporting distribution, and we can lose the whole lot in three weekends and it wouldn't make a blind fucking bit of difference to anything.

He claimed that the distributors themselves had questioned whether a P&A Fund would have any meaningful impact.

They [the distributors] basically said, if you're dumb enough to set up a fund which is going to give us access to subsidised prints and advertising, we'll take it, sure, but you shouldn't kid yourself that that is going to change anything. We've got access to money, we've got lines of credit to the bank. When we have a good British film, we've got the money to strike the prints and we've got money to buy the advertising. The problem we've got is that there aren't enough good British films around.[62]

The Film Council strategy, early on at least, was to put distribution on the back burner. Eventually, in 2002, a £1 million P&A Fund was announced (and launched officially in March 2003), but this was targeted at 'specialised' films rather than at commercial movies.

To qualify for 'matching' Film Council support, distributors were asked to commit to spending considerable amounts of their own money first. The smaller players in the UK distribution market complained that they couldn't afford to take advantage of the new fund.

'They [the Film Council] do nothing!' complained Andi Engel, co-founder of Artificial Eye, one of the UK's leading foreign-language distributors.

They pay themselves lovely salaries. You can only stand there with jaws open and say, 'Christ!' If you have a success, they will give you money. Who needs that? It's like the old joke about the banker. The banker is the person who asks for his umbrella back when it rains. That's the Film Council.[63]

Again, there was logic in the Film Council's position that its critics overlooked. Its intention wasn't to underwrite the bottom line of small distribution companies. The goal was to increase the chances for audiences to see what they defined as 'specialised' films. They didn't discriminate between big and little companies, US or UK ones, and weren't embarrassed about giving support to the US majors when they released foreign-language fare or critically acclaimed films that would otherwise receive only limited releases. The more the distributor invested, the bigger the contribution UKFC would make. In 2005, the P&A Fund was relaunched, now with a £2 million annual budget.

In January 2000, DCMS official Alan Sutherland wrote to Film Council chief executive John Woodward, calling on the Film Council to come up with

> a convincing package to put forward on distribution, even if this is one that does not involve a lot of direct subsidy. Political masters and the wider world will be looking for some sort of new departure and for a really concerted attack on the underlying weakness.

Sutherland acknowledged that it was 'a hell of a challenge' and that there was 'no quick solution' but pointed out that 'a strategy for exerting maximum influence is what people will want from FC'.

The Film Council failed to deliver such a strategy. It is hard to see what else it could have done given its resources. This was the paradox. A relatively small organisation had been set hugely ambitious strategic objectives that it couldn't hope entirely to fulfil. The UK Film Council was hoping to prompt the growth of vertically integrated studios – and, at the same time, it was behaving like a studio itself. The Film Council was (in Alan Parker's words) 'the best support organisation the British film industry had ever had and by some distance'. The decade of its existence witnessed 'unprecedented unity, stability and growth' and yet the organisation was still struggling to live up to its many commitments. Parker later summed matters up as follows:

> I think in the end the Film Council was possibly trying to do too much – involved as it became in every aspect of the industry, business and culture, thus usurping many roles, including some of government itself. By doing too much it became an expensive operation, which many saw as excessive and imperious. To some eyes, it had become more of a major film studio than a catalytic support organisation, and its growing influence and authority put a lot of people's noses out of joint, especially

freelance producers, who preferred the 'Wild West' days of the
Arts Council when they could get their hands on government
subsidies in a more ad hoc, less controlling way.[64]

This was a Janus-faced organisation, representing the industry to
government and government to the industry. It was so central to
every aspect of British film culture that it couldn't help but provoke
resentment.

'We sit between government and industry but we are not an industry body,' John Woodward told an industry audience at a 2005 debate.

> We are a government body. We are owned by the government.
> Our salaries are paid by the government. Our function is partly
> to translate government policy. That's a very difficult task some-
> times because people in the industry don't understand how
> government thinks. Our job is not to listen to the film industry
> and say is that what you want? OK, we're going to now go to the
> government and say this is what the film industry wants you to
> do. If anybody thinks that, they are totally and utterly wrong.
> Our job is to give the government impartial advice about what
> is sensible… and to try and mediate between the aspirations
> and ambitions of a rapacious film industry and what is achiev-
> able and realistic.[65]

It is instructive to read the Film Council's annual report for 2002–3.
This was early in the organisation's existence but it had already become
the first stop for every film-maker, regardless of age, experience or
talent. In 2002–3, the Development Fund received around 4,000
individual submissions and supported 117 of them (with a further
105 being funded through the slate deals it had established with
various production companies). In other words, over 96 per cent of
projects offered to it were turned down. The rate of rejection at the
other funds was just as high. By March 2003, the New Cinema Fund
had received around 950 applications for feature film funding and
had made 28 awards. Rejecting over 95 per cent of the applications
it received was a surefire way for the Film Council to make enemies.

As veteran producer/director Don Boyd told the trade press, 'I don't know one single person, if they're honest, in the film business who hasn't moaned about the Film Council.'[66]

Even the Film Council's boldest initiatives were attacked. In 2005, UKFC, under its head of distribution Peter Buckingham, launched the Digital Screen Network (DSN). This was a groundbreaking £12 million scheme through which an initial 240 screens in 210 cinemas were equipped with digital projectors. The idea had been conceived by Buckingham and Steve Perrin, an industry veteran, former Warner Bros. executive and strategist at the UK Film Council (where he was one of the key architects of the Digital Screen Network) and Rentrak Theatrical, where he held the post of senior vice president and head of international. It was taken to the Film Council board in early 2003. At first, chairman Alan Parker was fiercely resistant to the concept ('he was a 35 mm man – he hated the concept of digital'[67]).The UK Film Council awarded a contract worth £11.5m to Arts Alliance Digital Cinema (AADC), to establish the network of 250 screens.

In theory, the 2K Digital Screen Network was going to enable cinemas to show a broader range of films far more easily. It could cost distributors £1,500 or more to make a copy of a print for a specialised film but the DSN would take much of that cost away. It would enable a greater variety of films to be shown and would give these films a chance to stay in cinemas for longer. Exhibitors, though, quickly began to lobby to ensure that the new digital equipment wasn't just put at the disposal of the independent sector. The exhibitors' trade body the Cinema Exhibitors' Association (CEA) argued:

> The suggestion that financial assistance should be given to the subsidised cinema sector alone so that it can put itself in a position to project digital product is unfair to commercial exhibitors but, more importantly, will act as a restraint on producers. It will encourage them to produce product of limited audience appeal, for that is where the projectors are, and not to tackle the mass markets where their commercial future lies.[68]

The Film Council was attacked by the exhibitors for embracing 'specialised' film at the expense of the commercial sector and for being too producer-led. Richard Segal, chief executive of Odeon, wrote:

> I believe the Film Council has missed a golden opportunity to embrace UK exhibition and distribution. Odeon, therefore, recommends that the Film Council re-appraises the work undertaken to date and re-focuses its attention and resources on some of the more significant issues, like driving forward cinema visits per capita in the UK or reducing the financial burden of legislative red tape.[69]

In the end, major exhibitors such as Odeon and Cineworld 'participated' in the Digital Screen Network. That's to say that they took possession of digital projectors through the scheme on the understanding they would show a certain amount of 'specialised' films. Inevitably, some observers complained that big, mainstream operators were being subsidised to test out equipment that it was in their commercial interest to use anyway. The Film Council response was that if the range of films audiences could see was enhanced, it didn't matter which operators were showing them.

The 2K digital projectors used to equip the Digital Screen Network soon became out of date. The scheme, at the time, didn't seem like a big success. Nonetheless, in hindsight, the DSN is acknowledged as a pioneering, even visionary, initiative – one of the first of its kind anywhere. The fact that UK cinemas were 100 per cent digitised less than a decade later owed at least something to the Film Council's early intervention.

The Film Council lobbied hard to get Sky to change its policy toward independent UK distributors, but was roundly ignored. It didn't even help that Dawn Airey (Sky Networks' managing director) had sat on the Film Council's board. She still seemingly paid little attention to the Film Council's arguments as to why Sky should help.

The Film Council had very quickly become the most prominent organisation in British film culture. Even those who grumbled about the arrogance of its executives accepted that UKFC was providing leadership. It intervened at every level of the business, pumping money into training through Skillset and into production, distribution and exhibition. No one had any sense that it was under threat.

When Anthony Minghella stepped down as chair of the BFI in early 2008, he was replaced by former BBC director general Greg Dyke, a 'heavy hitter' in the parlance of the trade press. 'I wouldn't say I was a film buff,' Dyke told *The Times* in his first interview after his appointment. He was a 'television man', who watched movies on planes and had recently been to see *Sex and the City* with his daughter. Some were appalled to have this barbarian in their midst. Nonetheless, Dyke was a powerful presence in the BFI's corner at a time when its relations with the Film Council were still very strained.

Internal Film Council documents refer continually to the 'intransigence' of BFI senior management and to its 'stubborn' staff. Supporters of the BFI, meanwhile, railed against the way they felt the institute had been undermined by the Film Council. They pointed bitterly to the closure of its production arm and of various other of its functions. Their grant-in-aid was diminishing while the Film Council's operating costs were increasing. It didn't make them happy either that BFI staff were paid half or far less than what they claimed their Film Council colleagues received. They argued that the BFI's autonomy had been destroyed and that its reputation for excellence, built up over seven decades, had been severely tarnished.

This was the context in the wake of the economic downturn of 2008/9 as discussions began in earnest about 'merging' the two organisations. In August 2009, films minister Siôn Simon proposed that the BFI and the Film Council should be combined in 'a single streamlined body that represents the whole of the film sector [and that] will offer a better service for filmmakers and film lovers'.[70] From the BFI point of view, this wasn't going to be a marriage of equals. In effect, through the merger, they feared that the institute was going to be absorbed by the Film Council, thereby completing a process which had been under way since 2000.

Film Council chief executive John Woodward argued that the benefits of having a single film industry body were 'pretty obvious'.

> If it can be done well then we have the best chance of protecting film and the film industry from most of the pain that's heading in the direction of all publicly funded bodies in the next few years.[71]

It was estimated that savings of £10 million could be achieved by bringing the two organisations together.

Dyke, though, was not ready to give up the BFI's independence. 'We have got our own Royal Charter. We are a charitable organisation. We can't be steamrollered. The reason we're doing it is that we think there might be some real upside.'[72]

In late 2009, the Film Council was faced with very hefty cuts. It responded by announcing it would merge its three main funds, Premiere, New Cinema and Development, into a single Film Fund, and by drawing up a new three-year plan. This plan was never to be acted on. The Film Council went 'all out' to make the merger with the BFI happen but, a former Film Council insider recalls, the BFI refused even to engage with the plan.

> We used to tear our hair out that the BFI just wouldn't respond to it. What was gut-wrenching was that it felt that somehow the Film Council was under attack and being criticised and no one questioned the BFI. No one asked the same strong questions of the BFI as they did of the Film Council. The default position was that the Film Council has got this wrong.[73]

In the UK general election in the early summer of 2010, Gordon Brown's Labour government was toppled, replaced by a new coalition Conservative/Liberal Democrat administration. To the general astonishment of the film industry, as part of his 'bonfire of the quangos', the new Secretary of State for Culture, Olympics, Media and Sport, Jeremy Hunt, took the decision two months later to abolish the UK Film Council. This, he blandly declared, was part of the new government's campaign to 'cut waste and inefficiency and to stop lower-priority projects'.

'It is simply not acceptable in these times to fund an organisation like the UK Film Council, where no fewer than eight of the top executives are paid more than £100,000,' Hunt wrote in the *Observer*, claiming that he wanted to 'focus resources on supporting frontline filmmakers rather than expensive bureaucracy'.[74]

As with the closure of PolyGram just over a decade before, the decision blindsided the industry. No one had seen it coming.

'He [Hunt] needed a Medusa's head to be able to wave in front of the Prime Minister and the public,' is how Chris Smith saw the decision to shut down the Film Council in such a sudden way.

> There had been quite a bit of newspaper coverage about John Woodward's salary, the level of remuneration the Film Council was paying, and there also had, of course, inevitably been coverage about some of the turkeys that had been invested in. A combination of that adverse coverage and the need for a scalp (made) it an obvious thing for him to go for.[75]

When Hunt told Smith the body he had ushered into existence a decade before was to be abolished, he tried to reassure him by suggesting that the BBC and Channel 4 would be able to pick up the slack. Smith replied, 'I don't think so.' In the event, Hunt 'alighted' on the BFI as the organisation best placed to take over the Film Council's leadership and funding role. To many, Hunt's decision looked to have been made on ideological grounds. The Film Council had been an invention of New Labour – and that in itself was justification enough to close it down.

'Political malice: pure and simple,' is how Alan Parker saw Hunt's decision.

> It was seen by Conservatives as a dreaded quango created by New Labour and so newly appointed Conservative Secretary of State at the DCMS, Jeremy Hunt – with no knowledge of, or consultation with, the film industry – shocked his own civil servants by deleting the UKFC with the stroke of a pen.[76]

He also described Hunt's decision as 'a hasty, petulant act of political vandalism executed by an arrogant and ignorant, right-wing ideologue'.[77] He was dismayed at the infighting and chaos that UKFC's disappearance left in its wake. Parker wrote on his website:

> At the news of the Film Council's demise, the grabby producers' organisation, PACT, rubbed their hands together and the directors' groups, the DGGB and DUK, shamefully rolled over and let the moron Hunt piss all over them and the film industry. The garroting of the UKFC has led to a miserable void: impotent, lacklustre and far from golden, as each self-interested group scrambles – grabbing at their ten quid's worth of lottery pie. It's so reminiscent of the dark ages that preceded the UKFC, with the BFI acting just as the inept Arts Council did before them: a bunch of spineless, clueless amateurs overseeing an interminable cycle of seminars, conferences and gas-bag posturing, as the gabby periphery talk the core filmmakers into an early grave. The ability to shape and guide an industry has been lost.[78]

Puttnam called the closure 'one of the great political disgraces' of his lifetime.[79] 'The rundown was appallingly handled. It cost them a lot of money. There were leases on buildings put in place [by the Film Council] in good faith. It was a classic [case of] a politician searching for a headline,' Stewart Till suggests.[80] Hunt responded to general criticism of his decision to close UKFC in the *Observer*, claiming that this was simply a case of sensible cost-cutting.[81]

To some, it appeared that the BFI had outmanoeuvred the Film Council. It had survived, even as the rival organisation which had acted as its overseer and funder for a decade was killed off. To others, the foolhardiness of Hunt's decision was underlined by the way the BFI began very quickly to look and behave just like the Film Council. Many of the figures in its business affairs and Film Fund teams simply (and necessarily) moved over to the new organisation and carried on doing the same jobs but under a different roof.

Ironies abounded. During the decade of its existence, the Film Council had been roundly criticised and attacked by every section of the industry. At the moment of its demise, almost everyone's attitude shifted. Film directors from Mike Leigh to Clint Eastwood praised its achievements and lamented its passing. The BFI was being made the lead body for film but many within the organisation fretted that its new industry responsibilities would distract from what they felt was its core cultural task.

In the late 1990s, Chris Smith had commissioned the *Bigger Picture* report which had paved the way for the Film Council's creation. Now, as the new government tacitly acknowledged that destroying the Film Council may have been hasty and rash, he himself was commissioned to undertake a new report looking at where the industry should head now. Its conclusions were remarkably similar to those reached a decade before. Puttnam suggested:

> I'd say that the closure of the Film Council caused more of a political stir than either [films minister] Ed [Vaizey] or Jeremy Hunt had imagined [...] there were certainly people who felt, on balance, it was rather a hasty thing to do. Now, if you've got yourself in that situation, you seek correctives, political correctives [...] Chris [Smith] is trusted. Chris has a remarkable track record.[82]

The Film Council's legacy is still a matter of ferocious debate. To some, the organisation had never been bold enough. One senior producer, still wary about speaking on the record years after UKFC's closure, suggests that

> the money they had year after year after year could have been leveraged up with private sector money to create a big enough fund to build at least one central marketing and distribution and funding operation that could help [create] a sustainable industry for independent producers that work in the UK [...] But there was never any interest in that because that requires effort, risk, political risk and danger whereas if someone says, 'Why did you give £1 million to host a school film club?' nobody is going to criticise you for that or for training DOPs – nobody is going to criticise you for that or for supporting

art film distribution in the UK, nobody is going to criticise you for that. It was always the easier option, to do the easier thing that everybody agrees to and that you won't [then] be blamed for.[83]

The Film Council may not have led British cinema to the promised land of a 'sustainable film industry' or have created a new British studio to rival Rank in its prime or PolyGram. At the end of its existence, independent British producers were still grumbling, just as they had been when it was first formed. There was still factionalism. Distributors and exhibitors were still often at loggerheads. The industry remained fragmented. Nonetheless, the Film Council had played an absolutely crucial role in what was one of the most transformative decades in British cinema history. It had provided a degree of leadership that the industry had never seen before. No longer did British film-makers have to rely on the heroic efforts of Attenborough and Puttnam to get governments to pay attention to them. Now, film was seen by both left and right as a 'key economic driver', in the jargon of politicians. It was driving inward investment and creating jobs. The momentum it created has continued. Leading producer Iain Smith says:

I do believe that the benefits we've seen since the demise of the Film Council were down to the Film Council. It was a fantastic board, ego-free, altruistic in the best sense. I think we were really on to something.[84]

Not the least of its achievements was, after considerable trial and error, putting in place a tax relief system that would act as a magnet pulling the Hollywood studios to make their movies in Britain.

Perhaps, those disbursing the lottery money began to think, it would make sense to invest money in development as well as production, so that scripts could be polished.

CASE STUDY
RED ROAD (2006)

A persistent criticism of the UK Film Council throughout its ten-year existence was of its failure to support low-budget auteur film-making. In a period when Danish cinema was thriving thanks to the maverick Lars von Trier and younger followers of the Dogme creed like Thomas Vinterberg and Lone Scherfig, the British were struggling to uncover distinctive new talent.

Eyebrows were raised when the Film Council's New Cinema Fund backed *The Wind That Shakes the Barley* (2006) from director Ken Loach. Few begrudged Loach's entitlement to the support. His film was a triumph, winning the Palme d'Or in Cannes, but whatever Loach represented, it wasn't 'New Cinema'. He had been making movies since the late 1960s and was already one of British cinema's most venerated figures.

The British may not have had their own equivalent to Denmark's Dogme directors, but the New Cinema Fund's record in supporting emerging film-makers was more impressive than critics allowed. The fund had already backed Peter Mullan's *The Magdalene Sisters* (2002), which won the Golden Lion in Venice, and David Mackenzie's *Young Adam* (2003), which screened in official selection in Cannes. The film-makers and their producers may have complained about creative interference from Film Council executives but at least they were able to make their movies.

When it came to Andrea Arnold's debut feature *Red Road* (2006), which was to win the Cannes jury prize, its Scottish producers at Sigma Films worked directly with the Danes. This was the first part of an envisaged trilogy called *Advance Party*, an attempt to revive the Dogme spirit. Sigma combined with Lars von Trier's company, Zentropa. The idea was that the films would be shot on a tight schedule (six weeks each) with the same characters. Two other directors were aboard, Morag McKinnon and Danish newcomer Mikkel Nørgaard, but Arnold's feature was the only one to make an impact. McKinnon completed her film, *Donkeys*, but Nørgaard's wasn't shot at all.

Red Road was an intriguing hybrid: a revenge drama in social-realist guise but with an undertow of gritty lyricism too. Kate Dickie starred as a security guard whose job entailed watching CCTV cameras trained on the 'Red Road Flats', a housing estate in Glasgow. She is peering into other people's lives, an early twenty-first-century equivalent to James Stewart in *Rear Window*. She spots a man on the camera and then begins to follow him obsessively. He is in some way involved in traumatic events in her life and she is prepared to go to extreme lengths to secure revenge.

Former kids' TV presenter Arnold had won an Oscar for her short film *Wasp* (2004). *Red Road* was an astonishing debut feature, received in the main competition in Cannes as if it was directed by some long-established art-house favourite, not the first full-length film by a newcomer. It had a claustrophobic intensity and a warped eroticism about it but Arnold also showed an eye for the pathos, humour and brutality of the street life that the CCTV operator observes and then enters into.

Supported by BBC Films as well as by the Film Council, *Red Road* sold to many well-known art-house distributors all around the world but it was 18-rated and too dark in its themes to find a big audience anywhere. This, though, was an example of auteur film-making from a director with an utterly distinctive style – the type of film it was feared that the British had forgotten how to make.

CHAPTER 7

Potter Gold

The gossip was that Warner Bros. wasn't going to renew the two-year deal it had struck with young British producer David Heyman's Heyday Films. In 1996, the US studio had hired Heyman, recently returned from working in the US, on a development deal as their 'eyes and ears' in Britain. He was supposed to be identifying talent and British projects which could be sold on to Warner Bros. The studio was looking for a hot property that it could get hold of before anyone else; one that would be easy to market and that could turn into a long-running franchise like James Bond. This was another way of saying that Heyday execs were in search of a needle in a haystack – and they hadn't come close to finding it.

Tanya Seghatchian, a young Cambridge University graduate who was then working in development with Heyday Films, knew what she was supposed to be looking for. One day, by chance, she read an article about a novel by a first-time author called J. K. Rowling.

'It was about a little boy who went to wizard school, which was a form of boarding school, and discovered he was a wizard. There were magical components and it was going to be the first of seven books,' Seghatchian remembered in an interview years later.[1] She had been told by Ken Loach's old producer Tony Garnett just what Warner Bros. was likely to be after. This novel seemed to tick all the boxes. It was the first in a series. It had magic and wizardry. It was also 'uniquely British', which was an essential part of the appeal. The author, soon to achieve worldwide fame, was still relatively unknown, a single mother living in Edinburgh. Rowling had told a journalist in one of her first interviews:

> This book saved my sanity. Apart from my sister, I knew nobody.
> I've never been more broke and the little I had saved went on
> baby gear. In the wake of my marriage, having worked all my
> life, I was suddenly an unemployed single parent in a grotty
> little flat. The manuscript was the only thing I had going for me.[2]

Seghatchian later recalled:

> I thought I should get in touch with the agent and see whether
> or not it was something that was available. Interestingly enough,
> nobody at that point had picked up on it. I think the agent had
> submitted it to a number of places where it had been rejected.
> The agent [Christopher Little] had no idea who we were and
> no intention at all of submitting it to us. He was looking for a
> studio buyer.

She met Little, got on well with him and was able to explain the link
between Heyday and Warner Bros.

> It was one of those things. If I hadn't read that article that
> day, there is absolutely no way we as a company or I or David
> [Heyman] or any of us would have become involved because
> it was pure chance [...] we were very lucky because we got
> there much earlier than anyone else did.[3]

Seghatchian's curiosity about Harry Potter mirrored that of Bryony
Evans, the office manager at Christopher Little's literary agency. In
1995, she had been sifting through the pile of unsolicited manuscripts
and *Harry Potter and the Philosopher's Stone* was one she saved from
rejection. 'What I was supposed to do was to send it back because
we didn't really handle children's books from new authors,' she told
the BBC in a 2017 interview.[4] She only noticed because 'it was in an
unusual clamp folder'. She started reading and immediately found
herself drawn in. She put the three chapters of the manuscript aside
to read in her lunch hour ('It wasn't something I was supposed to be
working on'). The publisher's reader also liked the book. Evans asked

to be allowed to read the rest of the book just so she could find out what happened next.

'It came to us in July 1995. It came into our unsolicited manuscripts [pile],' Little remembers. 'It was three chapters. I don't think I had read anything like it since Tolkien really.' Even when Little took the book on, publishers remained resistant. 'I couldn't sell it to anybody. It had been turned down twice before by two major publishers,' the agent recalls.[5] Over the following year, several others decided they didn't want it either. Little later told the BBC:

> I asked many people later what the reason was and one of the reasons was that it was a big book. Looking back into the mid-1990s, it was considered by the children's publishers that parents would not be prepared to pay more than £2.49 for a children's book, so the school of thought was that anything over 30,000 words was going to be too costly to produce.[6]

Another negative factor in publishers' eyes was that Harry Potter went away to boarding school. This was felt not to be politically correct. Publishers were suspicious of the whiff of privilege and elitism. Little, though, was persistent. He says that when he is working on behalf of a book he admires, he is like 'a dog with a bone': he won't let go.

Thanks to his efforts, Bloomsbury eventually took the book on in 1996, yet they were still uncertain about what they had. *Harry Potter and the Philosopher's Stone* ran to well over 90,000 words – a *War and Peace*-like length for a children's book. Little suggested that the reason Barry Cunningham, heading up Bloomsbury's new children's department, was ready to take a risk on Rowling's little wizard was that he 'came from a marketing background, not necessarily an editorial background'. He wasn't constrained by the usual rules about length or approach. The book was finally published in June 1997 on a print run of only 2,500 paperbacks and largely ignored. 'I think we got about one review at the time,' Little recalls. He talks of everyone 'pushing very hard' to promote Harry Potter but 'getting nowhere at all'.

Even so, Potter was casting a spell on its young readers. The media may have been ignoring the book but Bloomsbury was receiving orders for it in ever increasing amounts. Schoolkids were spreading the word to each other and to their parents. 'It was a momentum really started purely by word of mouth among the children,' Little says.[7] The book's growing popularity in the UK enabled Little to launch it elsewhere. There was an auction for US rights and for the book to be published in Europe and the Far East.

At David Heyman's office, in the summer of 1997, it goes without saying that no one realised that Seghatchian had just stumbled on the elixir which was going to help cure many of the British film industry's woes, provide employment for half of Britain's acting fraternity, revolutionise UK distribution patterns and generate hundreds of millions in inward investment to the UK.

At first, the Harry Potter novel was just another manuscript on the bottom shelf in the Heyday offices, not a priority at all, as Heyman made clear in several later interviews. 'Next to the Bible, Harry Potter is probably the most famous book in the world,' actor Gary Oldman, who joined the series in the third film, later observed.[8] That wasn't how it appeared to the staff at Heyday Films as they took their time even to read the manuscript. When they finally did so, their enthusiasm was immediate. Nisha Parti, production consultant at Heyday Films, later told the *Guardian*:

> I read the first Harry Potter at home on a Saturday morning. It was brilliant – a huge, original story which felt so visual and filmic. I came in raving about it on Monday morning. David asked what it was called and I told him: *Harry Potter and the Philosopher's Stone*.[9]

She encouraged Heyman to read the book and his response was equally fervent. 'He was completely enchanted,' one source remembers.

The story of how Heyday discovered Harry Potter sounds like the perfect movie-world fable. It chimes with the equally magical accounts of how Rowling herself, the impoverished single mother, wrote the first novel longhand in Edinburgh cafes, a pram beside her, and of how she was rejected by a dozen agents before one took her on, and publisher Bloomsbury waved its magic wand on behalf of her and her book.

Of course, it wasn't quite as simple as that. When Heyman had approached Little, the agent responded positively enough but told the producer that if he had a deal with Warner Bros., 'then I should be hearing from Warner Bros'.[10] He wanted to make sure that the film would actually be made and wasn't sure that an independent British producer would be able to pull it off.

At the time Warner Bros. was negotiating the rights to Harry Potter, Hollywood's most celebrated director Steven Spielberg was also 'sniffing around' the novel.

It took Warner Bros. a year and a half to negotiate their acquisition of Potter. Heyman had approached high-ranking London-based studio executive Rick Senat, senior vice president for business and legal affairs in Europe, Middle East and Africa. The avuncular Senat was a family friend who had known Heyman through his father, agent and producer John Heyman, since he was a child. Senat had then spoken to Lionel Wigram, a British executive working in a senior production role for the studio in the US. At this stage, neither Heyman nor Wigram had yet had any particular success in their endeavours for the studio and time might have been running out for them. Wigram was to serve a vital role as Heyman's key ally in LA.

As Warner Bros. continued negotiations with Little, it emerged that Spielberg had already called Rowling directly to express his interest in making a Harry Potter film. Predictably, this concentrated the mind of the Warner Bros. negotiators, who eventually managed to close the deal. The studio paid handsomely for the rights. 'I wasn't all that keen to do a deal unless the people [in Hollywood] were serious about it. I wasn't in a hurry. The whole process probably took about six months,' Little remembers.[11] He had told Rowling that the longer they held on, the better the deal they were likely to receive.

Warner Bros. agreed to buy the first book and also to take an option on the sequels 'at a specifically determined multiplier'; in other words, the price they paid for each subsequent novel went up and up. The advantage of this kind of deal to WB was that from the time of the making of the first film, they knew exactly what the cost of the rights for the entire series would be. The contract had what Little calls 'quite a lot of verbiage about consultation rights and so forth', but he wasn't under any illusions that this gave Rowling any legal rights to stop Warner Bros. if they took Potter in a direction she didn't like.

'The movie industry is notoriously keen to take hold of a very good property that has sold all around the world and has done very successfully and then change it into something it isn't,' Little says. This was why David Heyman was so important. The producer made it very clear right from the outset that he would protect Rowling and ensure that any film version remained faithful to her vision. This, Little quickly decided, wasn't just a negotiating ruse from a producer trying to charm an agent into giving him what he wanted.

> David is a very straightforward and honest person, a lovely person actually, and he was quite clear that his vision was the vision in the book. He didn't see any reason for changing it from what it was. Most of the people I've dealt with in the film world I wouldn't trust as far as I could throw them. David would be the one exception probably.

It helped that during Little's negotiations with Warner Bros., *Harry Potter and the Philosopher's Stone* had been published in the US. Just as in the UK, word of mouth from schoolchildren had helped to turn it into a phenomenon. By a happy coincidence, some of the kids who loved Harry Potter so fervently just happened to be the children of senior executives at Warner Bros. These executives were talking about Potter at work – and then coming home to discover it was the first subject of conversation there too. 'I think that did an awful lot to make Warner Bros. sit up and say, hang on, I think this could be something quite big,' remembers one insider.[12]

Even at this stage, there was still speculation that Spielberg might direct. That wasn't necessarily what Warner Bros. wanted. Spielberg at the time was the most successful film-maker in the world but working with him was sometimes a mixed blessing. A deal with him would effectively mean the studio having to cede a major portion of the profits to the director. Little and Rowling, meanwhile, were worried that he would Americanise the novel and possibly even base the film adaptation in the US which, as Little puts it, would 'change the whole character of the book'.

With Warner Bros.' permission, Spielberg had a 'creative' conversation with Rowling in which he explained just how he planned to go about adapting the first novel. He told the author that he had already worked with a brilliant American child actor called Haley Joel Osment in *A.I. Artificial Intelligence*, the movie he inherited from Stanley Kubrick. Spielberg thought Osment would make the perfect Harry Potter. Rowling had no approval rights but instantly made it clear she didn't like the idea at all. To her mind, Harry had to be British and the film needed to be shot in the UK. Spielberg didn't pull rank. He accepted that his vision for Potter wasn't quite the same as that of the original author and ended his interest.

Warner Bros. had been looking to Heyday to come up with a British property. The question was how British Harry Potter would remain once it went before the cameras. Heyman was determined that it would reflect Rowling's vision and have creative integrity in her eyes. He sent her each draft of the script. She was introduced to the screenwriter Steve Kloves before he was hired. Heyman also realised that the Harry Potter novels were a work in progress. Rowling was still hard at work finishing the series. If the film-makers took liberties, they would risk hindering the author and forcing her to mould her creative vision to fit their own.

Prior to the film deal, with Rowling's blessing, Little had taken it upon himself to trademark every aspect of Harry Potter, from the characters to the titles of the books. This gave him control of merchandising. 'When they [Warner Bros.] acquired the rights to the first book they actually took over that and refunded all the trademarking costs.'[13]

It was crucial to appoint the right director. There were obvious candidates. *Four Weddings and a Funeral* director Mike Newell was considered and there was talk of a Richard Curtis script. Newell turned the project down (although he did eventually direct the fourth feature in the series, *Harry Potter and the Goblet of Fire*, in 2005).

Alan Parker was a British director who had the confidence and belligerence to be able to helm a project on this scale. He had directed *Evita* and *Birdy*. He'd worked with very young children on *Bugsy Malone* and with teenagers and young adults on *Fame* and *The Commitments*. Parker, though, wasn't a Potter fan. He said in a 2013 interview at Cannes Lions (the festival for advertising and the creative industries):

> I helped the producer, David Heyman, just general advice really, on setting up the first one. And he kept saying to me, why don't you do it? And I said to him, it's not really my thing [...] I had been sent the book previously, which I really truly didn't get. A lot of people didn't.[14]

Parker had a conference call with the Warner Bros. top brass from his kitchen in north London, which ended abruptly when they told him many other directors were desperate to direct Potter and Parker responded with typical bluntness, 'Why don't you go and talk to them then?' Terry Gilliam and Tim Robbins were other names considered, before Chris Columbus landed the job.

Early on in the preparation for the first film, *Harry Potter and the Philosopher's Stone*, the studio suggested that the main female character, Hermione, should be American. There was talk of cheerleaders at Hogwarts. Heyman and Columbus, the director of *Home Alone* and *Mrs Doubtfire*, who agreed to direct the first two Potter movies back-to-back, balked at the idea.

'My first instinct was "'no". We did not want to change the spirit of the [Harry Potter] world,' Columbus later recalled.

> That was always Jo's philosophy and it was our philosophy. Whenever something was against the grain of what the world was, we felt as fans (as well as film-makers) that we shouldn't do it. At the same time, we were all given a tremendous amount of freedom to make the movie [...] J. K. Rowling has always been an invaluable collaborator, incredibly open, and she has never once looked over a production and said, 'You must do

this.' Whatever we wanted to do we could do, with the exception of rewriting the world.[15]

Columbus was an American, but he was a fan of the book and bought in entirely to an idealised vision of Britain that Rowling's writing seemed to support. 'These are quintessentially British novels and have to be treated with the respect a British director would bring,' he declared.[16] He and Heyman insisted to the studio that the films would have an all-British cast.

Rowling may have been a first-time author with no contractual rights over the direction of the film, but Warner Bros. very quickly learned to defer to her. If Heyman and his collaborators were worried that they might have been straying from her creative vision, they would call her up. She was remarkably forthright in telling them what she wanted. An insider says of the novelist:

> What makes her extraordinary is her instant knowledge of this world, this universe she has created in the books. One moment, she's a perfectly normal person walking down the street, going shopping, but when she is talking about the books, she can snap into that world, rather as I suspect Dickens did.[17]

Rowling would be able to give exhaustive details about every character in her universe, from the colour of the clothes they should be wearing to where they should be standing. 'Her mind is like that.' Rowling had crates of notes covering the world of Harry Potter. The producers realised that she was an invaluable resource and certainly not the type of author to pay off and keep in the background.

Heyman's brilliance as the producer of the Potter series lay in his making sure that Rowling's influence was all-pervasive. He was also insistent on working with the very best technicians available. Hiring production designer Stuart Craig was another crucial and complementary decision. Just as 'Phiz', the nineteenth-century artist and illustrator Hablot Knight Browne, was able to bring Charles Dickens' fiction to life in his drawings, Craig knew precisely how to depict Rowling's world on film. He took responsibility for everything that was shown on screen except the actors. 'On the Harry Potter films I start six months before the beginning of shooting, so if each film takes around a year, that entails six months of preparation and six of shooting,' he told *Sight & Sound*, likening the art department to an architect's office with 'teams of draftsmen' following his instructions. He paid attention to every detail, however small. His approach on the Potter films was as painstaking as it had been on Richard Attenborough's modestly budgeted love story *Shadowlands*, in which he considered everything from the cup that the main character C. S. Lewis (played by Anthony Hopkins) used to his pipe, pipe rack and slippers.[18]

Rowling herself has testified that when she visited the set at Leavesden Studios in Hertfordshire, she would often be startled by the detail of the design and the uncanny way it conformed to what she had pictured in her imagination. The secret that made the books so appealing was also what made the films so successful. They provide an all-enveloping world into which readers and viewers can escape.

Thanks to Heyman and Rowling, the Harry Potter movies were as British as could be imagined. The paradox, at least as far as the British film industry was concerned, was that they were financed in Hollywood and the immense profits from what they made at the box office – the exhibitors' shares aside – went back to Burbank.

Even so, the boost that Potter gave to the British industry can't be overstated. It can be measured in many different ways: the tax receipts from the thousands of extras who worked on the films; the boost to the post-production and visual effects (VFX) sectors; the success in putting British actors young and old in the international shop window; the tourism brought in by Potter at locations all over Britain; and the 'soft power' of Potter promoting Britain abroad.

The film series was like a gigantic locomotive. Once it was in motion, it was very hard to stop. Eight features were to be made in the space of a decade. In that time, the actors went all the way through childhood and adolescence into young adulthood. Even before production began, Warner Bros. had exercised their option on the second novel so that they could shoot parts of it while making the first film. They knew that there were six more novels on the way and had an option on all of them. During the making of *The Philosopher's Stone*, they were already looking at the manuscript of the third book. Warner Bros. was beginning to put down roots at their facility in Leavesden, the site of the old de Havilland aircraft factory. These premises had been used for film-making before (initially on the 1995 James Bond film *GoldenEye*), but new sound stages were now being constructed and it was turned into a state-of-the-art complex on the scale of Pinewood or Shepperton. Eventually, the studio was rebranded Warner Bros. Studios Leavesden.

The Potter movies had to be made very quickly, otherwise the child actors, so well cast in the main roles – Daniel Radcliffe as Harry Potter, Emma Watson as Hermione and all the others – would become too old for their parts.

The books and the movies rapidly became intertwined in the public's mind. Both would appear at a time when they would have maximum impact, just before Christmas or at the start of a school holiday or half-term.

Warner Bros. suddenly found itself with a mini crisis over the merchandising. The studio was being flooded with enquiries for

18. Casting a spell over audiences: having appeared in a BBC adaptation of *David Copperfield*, and in John Boorman's *The Tailor of Panama* (2001), 11-year-old Daniel Radcliffe won the role of Harry Potter. Here he is in the media spotlight at the Leicester Square premiere of the second film, *Harry Potter and the Chamber of Secrets*, in November 2002. The eight films in the series conjured up worldwide cinema ticket sales of $7.7 billion.

PA

Harry Potter products. As one senior executive told Christopher Little,

> We haven't had this experience before. Usually, we have to bang on people's doors and twist their arms to get them to license anything at all. Now, we've got this huge queue of people who want to buy anything. We had a heck of a problem trying to maintain the integrity of the brand. There was a tendency to license whatever anybody wanted […] it's human nature, probably, but if somebody comes along and says I want to make underpants or ballpoint pens or T-shirts or sticker books [you'd say], 'Jolly good, yes, of course you can.' It wasn't being controlled.[19]

Little tried to stem the tide and to convince the studio that Harry Potter was a long-term brand, 'like a Tiffany or a Rolls-Royce', something that needed to be nurtured, not used as a cash cow or an excuse for 'mass-produced rubbish'.

It helped that the UK had tax incentives in place (see Chapter 10). Britain had always been one of the places where the US companies made their bigger films. It had long-established studios and top-notch technicians, and in addition the talent enjoyed coming to Britain. London was an international city and the American distributors had long used it as their international headquarters – the gateway to Europe, the Middle East and Africa.

For Warner Bros. in Britain, J. K. Rowling was to become every bit as important as the American-born but UK-based Stanley Kubrick had been a generation before.

'From early on, my colleague Neil Blair and I realized that she [Rowling] was a star and that she should be treated like a Spielberg, a Kubrick or a Clint Eastwood,' recalls Senat.[20] In time, the studio came to agree. The initial deal gave her limited rights, but gradually Warner Bros. realised she was 'more than just a writer'. Now, as was once the case with Kubrick, the studio will support her in almost anything she wants to do. In 2016 she scripted and executive-produced *Fantastic Beasts and Where to Find Them*, the first of an envisaged five-film spin-off from the Harry Potter franchise.

19. 'Wingardium Leviosa': the Making of Harry Potter studio tour, a permanent public attraction, opened in a section of the expansive Warner Bros. Leavesden lot in 2012. Visitors can explore Diagon Alley and the Hogwarts Great Hall, and discover how the special-effects wizards created much of their magic on screen. The innovative computer-generated effects developed for the Potter series helped to attract other post-production work into UK facilities houses.

Getty Images/Warner Bros.

Rowling keeps a very close eye on Potter as the franchise heads off in new directions. She doesn't want an animated version or a musical. She has written other things too, such as the Cormoran Strike crime novels and *The Casual Vacancy*, a story set in the Cotswolds and aimed at an adult readership.

There is at least a loose connection between the Harry Potter films and Kubrick's work. There are some technicians who worked on Kubrick's *2001: A Space Odyssey* and then, in the twilight of their careers, were also involved with the Potter films.

Harry Potter has ensured that Warner Bros. has put down very deep roots in the UK. In 2012, after the film series had finished, a studio tour, 'The Making of Harry Potter', was opened. In early 2016, Josh Berger, president and managing director of Warner Bros. Entertainment UK, Ireland and Spain, became chair of the British Film Institute. This cemented the relationship between the studio and the UK industry yet further. It meant that a Hollywood executive was helping oversee policy at the public body that made the strategy for the British film industry.

'It has been a really remarkable run. To have achieved that number of films in that period of time on the scale of those undertaken has been without precedent,' Mark Batey, chief executive of the UK's Film Distributors' Association, told the *Independent* at the time of the final Potter movie, *Harry Potter and the Deathly Hallows: Part 2*, in 2011.

It is a phenomenon. It has really crossed over from cinema screens into every walk of life – every bus conversation, every family breakfast table. Harry Potter is part of our lives now. Like James Bond, it is a real cultural force.[21]

One of the series' less-noted side effects was the way it has transformed the economic fortunes of Florida. The state's finances had been in a parlous condition after the sub-prime mortgage crisis and the financial crash of 2008. There were bankruptcies and home repossessions aplenty. Then, in the summer of 2010, Universal opened its Harry Potter theme park.

'There's the long version of Florida's recovery,' the *New York Times* reported. 'Here's the short one, a refrain repeated by everyone from multimillionaires like [hotel owner Harris] Rosen to security guards at Universal: Harry Potter did it.'[22] With the opening of the theme park, tourism rebounded and leisure industry jobs shot up.

The Harry Potter films had achieved a double whammy. They had turned into a movie franchise that matched the long-running James Bond series and they had also managed to compete successfully in a kids' market hitherto dominated by Disney.

'I always thought they were going to be something big but I had no idea that they were going to be that big!' Christopher Little says of the Potter books. The unsolicited manuscript which landed in his office in 1995 had spawned a brand estimated to be worth $25 billion – and counting – by 2016 (after the release of *Fantastic Beasts and Where to Find Them*). Little has had other successes with books turning into movies, notably when a diary that he found in Warsaw was eventually published as *The Pianist* and made into an Oscar-winning film by Roman Polanski, and with a thriller novel called *Man on Fire*, made into a popular film by Tony Scott with Denzel Washington in the main role. These properties may have done well enough, but none came even close to matching the magic of Potter.

CHAPTER 8

The Name Is Still Bond

Harry Potter's arrival on screen had taken some of the strain away from the franchise that had underpinned the British film industry for over four decades, namely James Bond.

It wasn't a coincidence that the Bond films hit a rough patch in the 1980s and early 1990s, in the period when the industry as a whole was in a slump. *Licence to Kill* (1989) had shot in Mexico rather than at Pinewood, for so long the home of the series. Its box-office performance was relatively disappointing (in the UK it had received a 15 certificate, the most restrictive in the series' history), there were (separate) legal disputes over rights, and even the then star of the series, Timothy Dalton, was quoted as saying that the Bond series may have run its course.

The Bond producers were dismayed that the Eady Levy (the tax on cinema tickets that yielded funding for new production) had been disbanded in the 1985 Films Act. Thirty years before, Bond producer Cubby Broccoli and Irving Allen, his business partner at Warwick Films, had been drawn to Britain in the first place at least partly by the prospect of receiving Eady support for their film *Red Beret* (1952), starring Alan Ladd. At the start of that very same year, at Goldeneye, his home on the north Jamaican coast, the 43-year-old Ian Fleming was getting to work in earnest on a long-planned spy thriller, which he wrote in 2,000-word bursts on his Imperial typewriter. 'The scent and smoke and sweat of a casino are nauseating at three in the morning,' begins the first James Bond novel, *Casino Royale*.

Fleming's early Bond novels were written long before the period under consideration in this book – but the origins of the Bond movie franchise are worth revisiting, if only because Bond continues to play such an important economic and symbolic role in the British film industry.

Broccoli and his co-producer at Eon Productions Ltd, Harry Saltzman, were both victims and beneficiaries of the *US Government vs. Paramount Pictures* anti-trust suit of 1948, which prevented the US major from owning its own cinemas. The case is reckoned to have precipitated the end of the old Hollywood studio system.

'The [US] government stepped in and broke up the system of the studios owning the cinemas. I don't think it was very good for the industry but it did lead to people forming independent companies the way we did,' Broccoli later recalled to *Screen International*. 'I think our success has encouraged people from other companies to come over and make films at Pinewood and the other studios here.'[1]

In the cases of both Bond and Harry Potter, the franchises benefited from the pooling of British and American talent. These were very British movies made with American know-how. One of the reasons the Bond novels had become so successful was that they found such an enthusiastic audience in the US. As *Life* magazine reported in an article on John F. Kennedy in the spring of 1961, Fleming's Bond novel *From Russia, with Love* was among JFK's ten favourite books.

The Bond films may have been made with United Artists' backing but, right from the outset, they became part of Britain's export drive. As journalist Alexander Cockburn has noted, 'The cycle of Bond films began just when the Labour prime minister Harold Wilson was urging the nation to cast aside the archaic vestments of the past and bathe itself in the "white heat of technology".'[2] Wilson's 'White Heat' speech was made at the Labour Party conference in the autumn of 1963. When *Dr. No* started shooting in January 1962, Harold Macmillan was prime minister. Macmillan's famous 1957 speech, 'most of our people have never had it so good', captured a new mood of self-confidence, bullish but brittle, which Bond himself seemed to embody.

Broccoli, a flamboyant ex-Hollywood agent and close friend of reclusive millionaire Howard Hughes, cut an incongruous figure when he first visited austerity-era Britain in 1948 to attend a car rally. 'Where's the King's Arms?' he asked a passer-by when he was trying to track down a pub where he had an important meeting. 'Oh, around the Queen's arse,' the passer-by responded in typically sardonic British fashion.[3] Broccoli took very quickly to British humour, even when it was sarcastic.

On his first trip to Britain, Broccoli had stayed in the Savoy. 'He came into the Grill to have breakfast. This lovely waiter came to the table and said, "What would you like, sir?" He said, "I'll have bacon and eggs and a pot of coffee,"' his daughter Barbara Broccoli remembers. The waiter sighed and said that, regrettably, this wouldn't be possible. Britain was still under rationing. A day or two later, though, the waiter arrived at Broccoli's breakfast table, saying he had a surprise. He lifted a big silver salver to reveal two boiled eggs. Broccoli asked the waiter how he got them. 'Oh, I brought them from home,' the waiter said.[4]

The film producer was so touched that he immediately became a champion of all things British. Every movie Broccoli made was filmed in Britain. He relished the lifestyle: the horse racing, the gambling clubs (where his friends included Jimmy Goldsmith, John Aspinall and Lord Lucan) and the social scene.

As Barbara pointed out, it was no coincidence that an American (Broccoli) and a Canadian (Saltzman) were the ones successfully to bring James Bond to screen. They had none of the hang-ups about class that British producers might have brought to the 007 stories. 'Had they [the Bond films] been done by people who were from Britain, maybe the class-ism in the books would have been much more a feature in the films. Probably, Sean Connery wouldn't have been cast,' she says.[5]

Bond author Fleming had made it very clear that he didn't want 'stage Englishness' with 'monocles, moustaches, bowler hats'.[6] Broccoli and Saltzman weren't likely to allow any Gilbert and Sullivan or P. G. Wodehouse-style mannerisms to creep into the films. At the same time, they were both obvious Anglophiles and made sure the films foregrounded the 'best of British', whether Aston Martin cars or Savile Row suits.

Bond himself may have been a loner but the 007 film sets were characterised from the outset by a sense of camaraderie. Broccoli himself was a family man and Bond productions were famously 'family' affairs. He liked to work with people he knew and trusted. In his autobiography, *When the Snow Melts*, Broccoli pointed out that many of the contacts he made a decade before Bond, when shooting *The Red Beret*, would stick with him for the Bond movies too:

> It was the beginning of a relationship with British technicians, stunt men, musicians and others that I would cherish for close to 40 years. Several of the people I started out with in the early '50s are still my working associates and friends. We were coming in at a time when independent production dominated the scene. John Woolf and Sam Spiegel, for instance, teamed up to make *The African Queen* with Humphrey Bogart and Katharine Hepburn. American producers and financiers were welcomed in Britain, because it kept the studios humming and technicians in work, and brought dollars into the country. Moreover, there was then, as there has always been, a tremendous reservoir of talent.[7]

Terence Young, who directed *The Red Beret*, went on to direct three Bond films. Richard Maibaum, who co-wrote the screenplay, was to write the screenplays for a dozen of the Bond movies. Other crew members on *The Red Beret* (aka *Paratrooper*) were also to join the Bond circus, among them stunt director Bob Simmons, cameraman Ted Moore and costume designer Julie Harris.

'We keep the crew together,' producer Michael G. Wilson, Broccoli's stepson, confirmed in an interview at the time of *The World Is Not Enough* (1999), the 19th film in the series. Peter Lamont, who had just won an Oscar for *Titanic*, had worked as draughtsman, set director, art director and (latterly) production designer on all but three of the films – and would stay with Bond until *Casino Royale* (2006). He served as art director under Ken Adam, the legendary production designer who gave the Bond movies of the 1960s and 1970s their distinctively sophisticated, glossy look.

Similar apprenticeships were served by other crew members who worked themselves up into prominent positions. Barbara Broccoli herself was an assistant director and associate producer before she graduated to a full producer credit on *GoldenEye*. Wilson, meanwhile, worked early in his Bond career in the legal department. 'A bunch of the crew is the same,' Wilson said. 'Sometimes it's their children and in some cases their grandchildren.'[8]

This wasn't just sentimentality and loyalty to old colleagues: it made creative and economic sense too. Technicians who had already worked on one Bond movie knew what to do on the next. They were faster and more efficient than outsiders would have been. Nevertheless, there was never the sense the Bond movies were a closed shop. During the years ahead, Eon became a prominent supporter of young people securing broader access to the UK film industry, whether through on-set internships or film educational schemes in and out of schools.

When United Artists agreed to finance the first Bond movie in 1962, they provided the £1.1 million budget on the understanding that the bulk of the money was going 'below the line'. David Picker, head of production at UA, made it clear that casting wasn't the studio's paramount concern. The look and feel of the film had to be true to the Fleming novel. On one level, then, the technicians were the stars. More of the budget was going into their work than into the salaries of the actors. (This was true of Harry Potter, too, in which the main roles were played by unknown child actors.) Broccoli and Saltzman may have fought hard to cast unknown working-class Scottish actor Sean Connery as Bond ('no, no, no' read the telegram from UA when they first made the proposal), but they weren't just choosing him because of his rugged charisma. Connery came cheaper than other potential, far better-known alternatives such as David Niven or Trevor Howard. He also appealed to a mass audience in a way they wouldn't have done. Picking up on the double-edged quality the Scottish actor brought to Bond, veteran film-maker John Boorman wrote:

> I believe that Connery touches us because he personifies the best qualities that came out of the postwar upheavals in Britain. The reform of education, the busting of the BBC's monopoly and so on allowed a lot of talent to flourish [...] he also repre-sents something timeless. His persona reaches back and touches a tradition in British life.[9]

Connery stood for a changing Britain in which class was no longer a determining factor but, at the same time, Boorman pinpointed his rugged, old-fashioned quality by suggesting characters he could play better than anyone: 'Captain Cook, Thomas Hardy, Isambard Kingdom Brunel, Tom Finney, W. G. Grace, Keir Hardie, Drake'. He was the everyman and the hero. International audiences accepted him in the same way as Hollywood stars like James Stewart or Cary Grant (once himself mooted as Bond) or Robert Ryan. His Bond was rebellious and reckless enough to appeal to audiences who'd liked irreverent Method actors like Marlon Brando, James Dean and Montgomery Clift, but he also wore suits and a tuxedo and seemed to fit seamlessly into the establishment.

On an intended franchise film, the first one is a prototype. If it doesn't work, the line will be abandoned. In Cubby Broccoli's time at the helm, all of the Bond films other than *Moonraker* (Paris-based) and *Licence to Kill* (Mexico-based) were shot at Pinewood. 'This was for budgetary reasons but we did use British crew,' Wilson notes. After Broccoli's death, *GoldenEye* (1995) was shot at Leavesden, five years before it became Harry Potter's home, and *Tomorrow Never Dies* (1997) was partially shot nearby at specially improvised studios in Frogmore, Hertfordshire. Pinewood, though, was and remains the series' main base.

Building a franchise involved taking several uncomfortable decisions. Bond was 'a blunt instrument, wielded by a government department. He is quiet, hard, ruthless, sardonic, fatalistic.'[10] In other words, he had a mean streak and didn't seem immediately ingratiating. It was a point of principle for Broccoli that they were making international films, not just British ones. Wilson noted, 'Cubby's philosophy was that a film should have a "bump" every reel. What he meant by that was that there should be a plot twist, an action sequence or some kind of surprise, every ten minutes.'

In a presentation on 'The Art of Nurturing Franchises' at the 2013 British Screen Advisory Council (BSAC) Annual Film Conference, Wilson made it clear that there was no simple formula for keeping the Bond series going.

The received wisdom, 'if it ain't broke, don't fix it', was a formula for complacency and a disaster for any film franchise. It was important to get ahead of the curve and to change before things started to taper off.

The Bond films were exercises in repetition and innovation, in reassuring audiences while also startling them and defying their expectations. The producers, whether Cubby Broccoli and Saltzman initially, or Barbara Broccoli and Michael G. Wilson from 1995 onward, would be ruthless when required. They weren't just responding to the box-office performances of the current films but taking measures that would ensure the long-term health of the franchise. For example, Barbara Broccoli and Wilson decided in 2000 to move on from the then Bond star, Pierce Brosnan, although Brosnan's four Bond films, *GoldenEye*, *Tomorrow Never Dies*, *The World Is Not Enough* and *Die Another Day*, had been highly successful. They felt that the Bond character was beginning to teeter on the edge of kitsch.

Fans had always been interested in the cars in the movies – the Aston Martins, Lotuses and Rolls-Royces. The Bond franchise had extended into merchandising lines, such as toys, games and fragrances, a decade before *Star Wars* was released. Now there were Barbie dolls too. 'Her mane of luscious brunette locks and sultry face paint capture plenty of attitude. Oh, so alluring!' runs the marketing blurb for the *Octopussy* Barbie Doll.[11] Twenty different 'brand partners' were aboard *Die Another Day* (2002).

James Bond had always been about aspiration. He drank Martini and Dom Pérignon, wore Rolex or Omega watches, drove fast cars, and was seen in exotic locations. By the end of Brosnan's stint in the role, many fans and critics felt that the high living and conspicuous consumption were getting out of hand. He was turning into more of a playboy than a secret agent.

As Wilson noted, Brosnan had become Bond at the end of the Cold War, when questions had begun to be asked about the character's relevance. Replacing him with Daniel Craig was seen as a return to the original values of the film series. 'When in doubt, go back to Fleming' was the pet mantra of the producers. Whenever they had concerns about how to move the Bond films forward, they returned to the books. Ian Fleming's novels weren't identical to one another but his characterisation of Bond was always consistent. Richard Maibaum, the most prolific scriptwriter on the early Bond films, pointed out:

> If you analyse the books, you'll see that despite certain similarities (always a monstrous villain, a super-criminal, torture scenes, card games, the female lead involved with the opposition, etc.), his storytelling technique varies from suspense to mystery, to jeopardy […] to character conflict.

The challenge was always in striking what Maibaum called 'the proper balance between the suspense, the sex and the fun'.[12]

'His new incredible women, his new incredible enemies, his new incredible adventures' read the slogan on the US poster for *From Russia with Love* (1963), the second Bond film, summing up very succinctly the attractions of the Bond franchise – sex, danger and excitement.

Bond himself needs to remain close to a cipher. You can never lumber him with too much backstory. He is an idealised figure onto whom viewers can project their own fantasies and prejudices. As Sam Mendes (director of *Skyfall* and *Spectre*) realised, 'everyone has a different version [of Bond] in their heads.'[13] Some people will grumble that the films are too funny, while others complain that they are not funny enough. The secret agent is defined by his gadgets, weapons, cars, clothes and lovers. To invoke his childhood, put him in the psychiatrist's chair or bring his family onto the screen is always risky. At the same time, viewers want to know more about him.

In the run-up to the shooting of *Casino Royale*, Broccoli and Wilson had commissioned research into what audiences wanted:

> The results showed that poker was of no interest to the public; changing the actor was risky; to reduce risk it was preferable not to play around with key elements such as gadgets, Bond girls, one-liners, Q and Moneypenny; and that audiences were not interested in Bond having a serious relationship with a woman.[14]

In the light of these results, the script they had been developing began to seem a risky and foolhardy proposition. It had 'no gadgets, no Q, no Moneypenny, no one-liners, no Bond girls, and in fact Bond fell in love and the woman died. On top of that, there was a 20-minute poker game in the middle of the story.'

The easy option would have been to abandon the script. Instead, the producers ignored the research altogether. *Casino Royale* was widely praised for re-establishing Bond as the 'hard, ruthless, sardonic' spy that Fleming had written about in the first place. It won a BAFTA and numerous other awards around the world.

'Bond is a unique cinematic hero, idiosyncratic yet utterly dependable, elegant, confident and tech-savvy,' observes FDA chief executive Mark Batey.

> He has been reinvented cleverly for each generation, so he is both of his time and reassuringly timeless. For half the lifespan of British cinema, Bond has been, and remarkably remains, the backbone. It's the cinema's longest-running franchise and hit an all-time box-office high to date with *Skyfall*, the twenty-third entry, which was the first film ever to pass £100 million in UK cinema ticket sales.[15]

Since the Bond franchise was launched in 1962, the machine has occasionally threatened to stall. Disputes over rights and casting or the financial problems of MGM, the US studio partnering Eon in the series, have led to some lengthy gaps between films. This always causes alarm within not just the film industry but other parts of the economy too. One of the best barometers of the influence of Bond is UK tourism. Bond, along with the Queen, was the face of Britain at the launch of the 2012 London Olympics, when the event began with a stunt involving them both apparently parachuting into Stratford for the opening ceremony. Bond continues to feature very prominently on the website of VisitBritain, run by the British Tourist Authority, and it is claimed that the fact that a few scenes of *Skyfall* were shot in the remote Scottish Highland region of Glencoe boosted tourism there the following year by 41.7 per cent.[16]

20. Nobody does it better: *Skyfall* was launched with a huge charity premiere event at London's Royal Albert Hall in October 2012, attended by all its stars, including Daniel Craig, in his third Bond assignment, and Naomie Harris, here making her debut as Eve Moneypenny. *Skyfall* was the first Bond film to be digitally remastered into the giant-screen IMAX format. After just ten days on UK cinema release, it became the fastest film ever to reach £50 million in box-office receipts. It won two BAFTAs and two Oscars among many international awards, and ended its cinema run with global ticket sales of $1.1 billion.

Bond was the first major franchise to be based in the UK but others were to follow. The British film industry may almost have closed down at the beginning of World War II but the Nazis inadvertently did their bit for inward investment. Britain spent so heavily on the war that the old pound versus dollar rate of just over $4 could not be maintained. In 1949, the pound was worth $2.80. In 1952, when Broccoli came to Britain to make *The Red Beret*, that had fallen to $2.50. The pound had edged up very slightly, to $2.55, by the time of the first Bond film, *Dr. No*.

The James Bond series was to have a transformative effect on Pinewood Studios. Ambitious films had been shot there before. Powell

21. Licence to thrill: the Albert R. Broccoli 007 Stage, first opened in December 1976, is a cavernous legacy of the Bond films. Built to house Ken Adam's submarine-swallowing supertanker in *The Spy Who Loved Me*, it stands as one of the largest sound stages in the world, occupying some 59,000 square feet with an interior tank. It has facilitated many spectacular sets, such as the vast chocolate-river room in Tim Burton's *Charlie and the Chocolate Factory* (2005), the Greek fishing village in Phyllida Lloyd's *Mamma Mia!* (2008) and sections of the colossal mountain in Baltasar Kormákur's *Everest* (2015).

and Pressburger had recreated a convent in the Himalayas at the studios for their lush 1947 melodrama *Black Narcissus*, and had come close to their idea of 'total cinema' in their ballet movie *The Red Shoes* (1948). David Lean had shot his Charles Dickens adaptations, *Great Expectations* (1946) and *Oliver Twist* (1948), at Pinewood. These films had been made under the 'Independent Producers' label of the Rank Organisation, which had been set up to produce big-budget, prestige films with a chance of cracking the American market. Rank, though, had retrenched in the early 1950s and had adopted a far more con-servative production policy under John Davis, its managing director and later chairman.

Some visionary technicians were working at Pinewood in the post-war years. There was make-up artist Stuart Freeborn, who collaborated with Lean on the Dickens films and whose subsequent credits included *2001: A Space Odyssey*, *Superman* and *Star Wars*. Cinematographer Douglas Slocombe shot Ealing comedy classic *Kind Hearts and Coronets* and went on 30 years later to shoot *Raiders of the Lost Ark* for Steven Spielberg at Elstree. Walter Percy 'Pop' Day was a legendary matte artist and art director who contrived some of the magical visual effects on *Black Narcissus* and *The Red Shoes*.

The reputation for technical excellence that would later help attract so many big-budget Hollywood films was already long established.

It is also possible to draw links between Bond and Carol Reed's *The Third Man* (1949), the classic British spy thriller shot at nearby studios in Shepperton. Guy Hamilton, later to direct four Bond films, had been a sound man and assistant director for Reed. He served as a double for Harry Lime (Orson Welles), running up and down stairs to simulate the sound of Lime's feet as he scurries through the sewers, looking for safety, at the end of *The Third Man*. John Glen, who went on to direct five Bond films, having served as editor and second-unit director on three others, was also part of the sound-editing team on *The Third Man*. The character of Harry Lime himself, played with tremendous charisma by Welles, has all the qualities associated with the best Bond villains. He was debonair and dapper, very articulate, and even shared the screen with a cat. (Bond's arch-nemesis, Blofeld, was frequently seen stroking a white cat in the Bond films.) It was often said that the Bond films were only as good as their villains – and Harry Lime set a template for the Bond writers and actors to emulate.

The skills for making very big movies in Britain were already in place. Rank and Alexander Korda had, at various times in the 1930s and 1940s, attempted to produce pictures that had the sweep and production values of anything being done in Hollywood. However, look at the work shot at Pinewood in the early 1960s and you'll find Norman Wisdom vehicles and *Carry On* and *Doctor* comedies. Embarrassingly, what was then the biggest Hollywood movie ever to come to Pinewood, Fox's *Cleopatra* starring Elizabeth Taylor, had started shooting in 1960 but had been abandoned… and decamped to Rome.

Fox spent a reported $7 million at Pinewood, recreating ancient Rome in full papier mâché magnificence in rural Buckinghamshire, before putting the production into mothballs, thwarted by lousy British weather and by Taylor's pneumonia, which nearly killed her. The costumes and sets didn't entirely go to waste – they were later used for the supremely vulgar *Carry On Cleo* (1964). The film, though, was recast, recrewed and shot elsewhere.

February 1962 saw *Dr. No* come to Pinewood after the Jamaican part of its shoot was completed. No one expected that Bond movies would still be shooting at the studios more than 50 years later. *Dr. No* had a big budget for its time but was hardly a blockbuster. Fox had spent far, far more on its aborted British shoot of *Cleopatra*.

Still, Bond was a supercharged departure at a time when British cinema was dominated by the *Carry On* and Norman Wisdom comedies or by social dramas like Basil Dearden's groundbreaking, gay-themed *Victim* and Bryan Forbes' *Whistle Down the Wind*, a classic yarn about a runaway convict mistaken by some Yorkshire kids for Jesus. These were all solid, modestly budgeted British pictures that would do most of their business in their domestic market. Right from the outset, however, Bond was tilting at the international market.

As the Bond films took root at Pinewood, other international projects also started to set up at the studios. Part of the spoof Bond film *Casino Royale*, whose huge cast included Orson Welles, was shot there in 1966. So was Charlie Chaplin's *A Countess from Hong Kong*, starring Marlon Brando and Sophia Loren. Billy Wilder came to Pinewood in 1969 to shoot *The Private Life of Sherlock Holmes* and Fred Zinnemann was there in 1972 to make *The Day of the Jackal*. Jack Clayton's lavish version of *The Great Gatsby* was made at Pinewood in 1973. Certain films with no British connection whatsoever, for example Norman Jewison's dystopian thriller *Rollerball*, also came to the studios. By the late 1960s, the Hollywood companies had offices in London and it was natural for them to shift much of their production to the UK. Nonetheless, the regular James Bond apart, there was nothing resembling 'franchise' film-making in the UK. That would change in the 1970s as the *Superman* films, *Star Wars* and the *Alien* series all began to be made in Britain.

Their reasons for being in the UK were very obvious. The facilities, the locations and the technicians drew them to Britain. And movie stars liked London. Many would stay in Claridge's, a relatively short commute from the studios. Bond was the bedrock.

In the period detailed in this book, Hollywood began to look ever more seriously to Britain as a potential production base. There was no sentimentality about the decision to make *Stars Wars* or Marvel superhero movies in the UK. The US studios came to the country because the facilities and the costs justified it. They could have stayed at home or gone to Eastern Europe had it been cheaper and easier to do so. They were always doing their due diligence and searching for reassurances that they were in the right, most cost-effective place. The 50 and more years that Bond movies had been made in the UK provided them with the evidence that it was possible to make the very biggest, most prestigious films in Britain. It helped, too, that the British were trying so hard to court them. The Eady Levy may have gone in 1985 but the tax reliefs that the UK government started offering them in the 1990s, and which continued to be enhanced, were a very major attraction.

CASE STUDY

CASINO ROYALE (2006)

The James Bond producers were accustomed to working backwards. The release date for the next 007 tended to be set before it had been financed, cast or shot. In April 2005, they announced that the next Bond feature, *Casino Royale*, would be released on 17 November 2006. By then, producers Barbara Broccoli and Michael G. Wilson had a director aboard, Martin Campbell, but no Bond. Pierce Brosnan, the previous 007, was stepping down.

This was a delicate moment for the long-running franchise. There had been corporate upheaval. Bond distributors MGM, which had taken over the task from United Artists, had a new financing and distribution partner in Sony Pictures. The most recent Bond movie, Lee Tamahori's *Die Another Day* (2002), had been attacked for (as critic Todd McCarthy put it) pushing 007 into 'CGI-driven, quasi-sci-fi territory that feels like a betrayal of what the franchise has always been about'.[17]

With Warner Bros. well into its stride with the Harry Potter films and the *Star Wars* prequel cycle nearing its conclusion, Bond now had plenty of competition.

'Wacky comedy extravaganza *Casino Royale* is an attempt to spoof the pants off James Bond. The $12 million film is a conglomeration of frenzied situations, "in" gags and special effects, lacking discipline and cohesion,' trade paper *Variety* wrote of the 1967 version of the film, produced by Columbia and directed by (the small army of) John Huston, Ken Hughes, Val Guest, Robert Parrish and Joseph McGrath.[18] It was agreed, even by admirers of its stars David Niven and Peter Sellers, to be a bit of a mess.

On a grey autumn morning in London in October 2005, 13 months from the mooted release date, British actor Daniel Craig sped along the Thames in a Royal Marine speedboat toward a special press event aboard HMS *President*, where he was to be announced as the new Bond. He had been cast ahead of such potential rivals as Clive Owen, Colin Farrell and Ewan McGregor because, the producers told the press, he would bring 'a contemporary edge to the role'.

Craig, best known for TV's *Our Friends in the North* and Matthew Vaughn's crime caper *Layer Cake*, was a darker, more mercurial presence than Brosnan or Roger Moore. *Casino Royale* was the first Bond novel that Fleming had written. The producers had decided to go back to basics – to remould Bond. They had brought in Paul Haggis, writer–director of Oscar-winning ensemble drama *Crash* (2005), to work on the screenplay with regular writers Neal Purvis and Robert Wade.

This was an intense, relatively pared-down approach to Bond in which performances and stunts took precedence over special effects and gadgets. The villain, Le Chiffre (played by Danish actor Mads Mikkelsen), wept tears of blood but, otherwise, realist conventions were largely followed. Its approach was exemplified in the early Madagascar-set chase scene in which Craig's Bond races on foot after a bomb maker. The relentless foot race takes them through dusty streets and undergrowth and onto a building site at frenetic pace.

Bond also showed more emotion than was commonplace from the character. He retained the usual brutality and machismo but Vesper Lynd (Eva Green) brought out an unexpected tenderness and vulnerability in him. In 2007, Eva Green won BAFTA's public-voted EE Rising Star award.

The back-to-basics approach and bold casting paid off handsomely. The film grossed $600 million worldwide at the box office and reinvigorated a franchise that had looked in danger of faltering. Its success was both a boon to the UK industry and a warning of how easily inward investment could slip away. The new tax credit system wasn't yet in place. The pound was strong against the dollar. Without sentimentality, the producers shot much of the film at the Barrandov Studios in Prague rather than back home at Pinewood.

In the summer of 2006, the 007 Stage at Pinewood burned down shortly after *Casino Royale* finished filming there. By the time it was rebuilt less than a year later, the government had put in place fiscal incentives ensuring that future Bond films like *Quantum of Solace*, *Skyfall* and *Spectre* would find it more attractive to shoot in Britain than anywhere else.

CHAPTER 9

An Uneasy Partnership — British Film and TV

The British film industry has always had an ambivalent relationship with TV. From as early as the 1920s and 1930s, the small screen was viewed as a threat.

The story of how television 'stole' cinema's audiences in the 1940s and 1950s has often been told. In Britain in 1958, exhibitors formed FIDO – the Film Industry Defence Organisation – to prevent films from being sold to TV at all. Industry bodies came together to acquire rights to keep them away from the TV companies. They effectively tried to bribe producers not to sell to the small screen. Even as their attitude slowly softened as time passed, the 'holdback' before films were allowed to be shown on television used to last for years.

In the period which this book covers, the fortunes of British cinema became more dependent than ever before on television. Many of the best British movies from 1982 (when Channel 4 was founded) to 2017 were developed and funded by TV stations. Nonetheless, for most of the last 30 years, producers continued to regard television with a mix of snobbery, suspicion and fear. They wanted their films to go into cinemas and had little desire to make them for television.

By 2017, that attitude was finally beginning to change. In a new age of Video on Demand (VoD), Netflix and Amazon, producers saw TV as their lifeline. They invariably lost money or, at best, broke even on their feature film productions. 'I do television to feed my film habit' was the phrase that they began to bandy about to describe the shift in emphasis.[1] A tax credit was now available for 'high-end TV drama' as well as for film, and there were a host of new patrons commissioning work for the small screen. The actual business of making TV drama had moved closer to that of shooting a film. The same crews and actors tended to be involved. Perhaps most surprisingly, the budget for TV drama was often higher than that for film. Television offered film producers far better 'terms of trade'. Thanks to deals negotiated on their behalf by producers' organisation PACT in the early years of the new millennium, they could hold on to rights far more easily for TV productions than they could for movies. A major patron like a Netflix or an Amazon would often fund the entire cost of production – and free the producers from the painful process of piecing together a relatively modest budget from multiple sources. The big American company would write a single cheque that covered the cost of production.

'When I arrived and started doing movies, television was dead. I wouldn't touch it,' says stockbroker turned producer Stephen Evans, whose Renaissance Films funded Kenneth Branagh's *Henry V* (1989). Evans makes his point by gesturing with his fingers. 'I was there' – he points up at the ceiling to describe his status as a movie producer. 'Television was there' – he points downward. Now, the roles are reversed. 'I am down here' – he gestures toward the floor. 'Television is up there. That is where the market is. If you can get a four-part or six-part TV series that travels round the world, it is big money. You can hold on to the rights. Also, it is less high risk. You haven't got the problem of box office.'[2]

In 2017, independent British producers were fretting that the business model for film production in the UK was 'no longer sustainable' and that to run a business in the film industry is 'impossible'. The market was flooded with titles which struggled to make any impression in an increasingly polarised marketplace, in which a handful of Hollywood titles accounted for a huge percentage of receipts.

Even when British films did well, they didn't necessarily make money for their producers. Sales agents, investors, distributors and exhibitors all tended to take out their share of the profits first. The producers relied on their producer's fee but would still be very lucky if they were to see any 'back end' profit. They had the crutch of the film tax credit, worth 25 per cent of qualifying expenditure – and, in practice, worth 15 to 20 per cent of the overall budget. Ideally, that money would have come straight to them. However, they invariably needed to use the tax credit to get their films financed. They would have to negotiate with an intermediary to 'cash flow' the tax credit. (The intermediary would advance the value of the tax credit to the producer but would take a fee for doing so. In effect, the tax credit was being used to secure a loan that helped top up the budget.)

Stewart Mackinnon, founder of Headline Pictures, would tell the cautionary tale of his project *Quartet* (2012), directed by Dustin Hoffman. This was a comedy–romance about a group of retired opera singers in a home together. It starred Maggie Smith, a major draw for older audiences. The film grossed $70 million at the global box office but none of that money trickled back to Headline. 'We've not received one penny in returns in spite of spending months with lawyers negotiating the percentage of backend and the share of corridors,' Mackinnon told *Screen International*.[3] Mackinnon and his team had spent years developing *Quartet*. It was little wonder that afterwards Headline refocused and started to work with Amazon on a TV project, the Philip K. Dick adaptation *The Man in the High Castle*.

Agents who would once have steered their actor clients away from TV now saw small-screen drama as being every bit as alluring as feature films. The biggest shift by 2016/17 was that high-end TV was by this time considered a more rewarding artistic form than feature film by many of the best writers and directors. It gave them a creative freedom they didn't have when making movies. They were able to express themselves at far greater length and to take artistic risks that wouldn't be possible in a 90-minute feature. The writers were treated with more respect. Often, they were also the 'show runners', the people who originated and oversaw the drama series.

Ironically, in the early 1980s it had been almost impossible for film producers to work in television, even when they wanted to. The union rules were so restrictive that they had to choose one form or the other. 'As an Academy Award-winning producer, I couldn't work in television at all without becoming an employee of the BBC or ITV,' David Puttnam remembers. 'It was madness.'[4]

Producer Simon Perry concurs. 'You had to decide at the time of production which union agreement you were making your film under. If you made it under the TV agreement, you couldn't show the film in cinemas.'[5]

That was why the formation of Channel 4 in 1982 was to prove so significant to the British film community. The broadcaster's founding chief executive, Jeremy Isaacs, had realised that French, German and Italian TV companies all strongly supported their local film industries, paying for and showing movies. In the UK, the situation was different: 'Exhibitors wouldn't touch anything that had been on television because they saw television as a terrible threat.'[6] This meant that British film-makers were denied any opportunity to tap TV money for their productions.

A deputation of film industry representatives visited Isaacs 18 months before Channel 4 was launched to ask the channel to support feature films — and to allow these films to be shown in cinemas before they were broadcast on TV. It helped that British cinema's most relentless lobbyist and champion, Richard Attenborough, was a board member and later chairman of Channel 4. David Puttnam also fought hard to persuade the new channel to support film-makers and encourage production.

A new 'Film on Four' label was set up under former *Z Cars* producer, David Rose. Its brief was to support 20 low-budget features a year. Film on Four had £6 million to invest annually in the project. This was all about giving opportunities to film-makers and supporting bold new work. The idea wasn't to make big commercial box-office hits. 'Directors grateful for the chance did their damnedest to do good work on a modest budget,' Isaacs recalled.

Right from the outset, the standard of films produced was extraordinarily high. On the very night the station launched, 2 November 1982, it showed Stephen Frears' feature *Walter* starring Ian McKellen as a mentally handicapped man, a lovable, very imaginative character trying to cope in a world in which he is condemned always to be an outsider. In the same week, the channel also showed Michael Apted's *P'tang, Yang, Kipperbang*, a poignant and funny coming-of-age story set in late 1940s London. David Puttnam was its producer.

The broadcast of two such memorable films by directors of the calibre of Frears and Apted underlined the new channel's commitment to film. However, the very fact that they were shown on Channel 4 so early reinforced the idea that these were TV movies. No arrangements had been made to release them in cinemas first. At this time, exhibitors were still insisting on a three-year window. 'This was a nonsense because we were paying for these films to be made and we wanted them to be seen,' Isaacs pointed out.

Channel 4's thinking at first was that the films should be shown on television in the UK but be 'for the cinema abroad'. Isaacs, though, knew that these films' directors were very eager for their work to be seen on the big screen in Britain too. He credits his colleague Justin Dukes, managing director of Channel 4, with helping talk distributors and exhibitors round to the view that if the fledgling channel had paid for its own films and wanted them seen in cinemas, this wasn't such an outrageous concept. Dukes' idea, which seemed groundbreaking at the time but only a matter of common sense from a vantage point a few years down the line, was that film and TV could help each other. Dukes told journalist Dominic Joyeux:

> the task is to persuade the television audience that cinema isn't only a diet of James Bond but that it's something that is capable of looking into issues and is enjoyable. That there is a dimension there that they go and experience. For example, it is quite impossible for television to do justice to *The Draughtsman's Contract* [one of the first films completed with the aid of Channel 4 money]. With all its detail, its subtleties, a lot of the attractions of this film are going to be lost on the small screen [...] The very first thing that we've got to do is tell the audience to take the phone off the hook, put the children to bed or tell them to keep quiet, disconnect the doorbell and watch this film. You will not get more than 40% of what it has to say if you watch it like *Benny Hill*. Even with the above precautions I don't think we'll have people getting more than 60% out of a film when it's shown on TV. So what I hope will happen, is that at the end of the film we'll be able to say that this film is on at the following cinemas. Because television is a tremendous scattergun and

I hope we can change people's concept of television and cinema. The idea is not to further damage film or cinema but in fact to develop a new chemistry of the relationships between different media.[7]

Dukes and Isaacs were floating the idea that audiences could find out about a film by watching it first on TV and then go and experience it more fully in the cinemas. They wanted films to find an audience both on TV and in cinemas. With the support of some more adventurous independent distributors and exhibitors, among them Andi Engel of Artificial Eye and Romaine Hart of Mainline Releasing, they were able to persuade the exhibitors to relax their rules. Films that cost less than £1.25 million (later increased to £2 million) were permitted to be shown in cinemas and on TV without the draconian three-year window.[8]

This meant that selected films from the second season of Film on Four, Neil Jordan's *Angel* (starring Stephen Rea as a saxophonist caught up in the 'troubles' in Northern Ireland) and Peter Greenaway's baroque and cerebral mystery drama *The Draughtsman's Contract*, were given cinema releases and then shown on TV shortly afterward.

There was growing evidence that releasing films in cinemas first boosted their popularity when they came to be broadcast on TV. Mike Radford's *Another Time, Another Place* (1983) was a Channel 4-backed film about a young woman who has an affair with an Italian prisoner of war in Scotland. It screened in the Cannes Festival's Directors' Fortnight and was given a limited cinema release. Then, a few months later, it turned up on television. 'Compared to the other Channel 4 films which had not had theatrical releases, our ratings went through the roof. We got 3.8 million,' the film's producer Simon Perry recalls.[9] It helped that the film was broadcast when the memory of its cinema release was still fresh.

Stephen Frears' breakthrough, *My Beautiful Laundrette* (1985), had been made for television. He shot it on 16 mm. It was shown at the Edinburgh Film Festival and everyone realised how special it was. The film was given a theatrical release and ended up securing its screenwriter Hanif Kureishi an Oscar nomination.

22. Bringing sharply drawn characters to life: Leicester-born Stephen Frears began directing TV dramas in the 1960s and has been much in demand for feature films since the 1980s. Throughout his career he has collaborated with some of the finest British and Irish writers, Hanif Kureishi, Alan Bennett, Christopher Hampton, Roddy Doyle, Steven Knight, Peter Morgan, Jeff Pope and Lee Hall among them. Here he is shown with Helen Mirren on the set of *The Queen* (2006).

Alamy

In the mid-1980s, British cinemagoing figures may have dropped dramatically but British television had a seemingly insatiable appetite for movies. Throughout the decade and into the 1990s, that appetite grew and grew. In 1990, there were 1,767 films screened over the year on the four terrestrial channels – BBC1, BBC2, ITV and Channel 4. By 1992, that number had gone up to 2,200. Channel 4 showed more films than anyone else. These films drew hefty viewing figures and, on the commercial channels, helped attract plenty of advertisers. If you look at the top ten 'programmes' in any given year in the 1980s and 1990s, you will almost always find a film on the list. In 1984, the year in which box-office returns slumped to an all-time low, four films were in the top ten, all with audiences over 17 million for their single screenings: *Raiders of the Lost Ark*, *Airplane*, *Kramer vs. Kramer* and *Mary Poppins*. These four alone were seen by close to 70 million people at a time when only 54 million tickets were sold in cinemas. Any sense that the British public had fallen out of love with cinema was therefore absurd. The first time *Jaws* shown on TV, it had an audience of over 23 million.[10] Given these huge audiences, it seemed perverse that the broadcasters themselves invested so little in film production.

When Channel 4 started supporting British film-makers, it was only to be expected that others would take notice. Film on Four may not have produced blockbusters but it delivered high-quality films from top directors, Stephen Frears, Peter Greenaway, Neil Jordan, Derek Jarman, Mike Leigh, Ken Loach and Mike Newell among them. Their films were respectfully reviewed by critics and found decent audiences. TV executive Antony Root, who worked for Euston Films and then went on to head up the television arm at Working Title, recalls:

> Suddenly you had the opportunity for people who were producing, writing and directing films for television to go and make feature films. It became incredibly fashionable. Those of us who worked in television used to complain a lot because the thing people aspired to was to make a Film on Four rather than making television series, miniseries or TV movie.[11]

The BBC eventually began to respond. Former film critic turned producer Mark Shivas became head of BBC Drama in 1988. One of his first actions was to change what was called the 'Plays Department' into the 'Films Department'. As Shivas told the *Independent*, the BBC still felt a little queasy at the very idea of becoming involved in something as shady as the movie business. Shivas remembered:

> When I took the job of Head of Drama in 1988, I encountered the general feeling that the BBC shouldn't be involved in films – you know, 'Films aren't mentioned in the Charter', 'the film industry is full of thieves and sharks and louts', and 'why should we have anything to do with them, we're in television'. But it seemed that this policy was losing us a lot of very good writers and directors to the other place [Channel 4], because it's obviously frustrating to put a lot of time and effort into something that will only be shown once or twice [...] And

the fact that there's nothing about film in the Charter can be used in another way – it means there's nothing preventing us from taking the BBC into the film industry, which is something British film-makers have been trying to do for twenty years.[12]

'The BBC's historic relation to film was tentative and equivocal,' agrees producer David M. Thompson, who ran BBC Films for over a decade, until 2007. 'They [the BBC] were often quite resentful of film and for very understandable reasons.'[13]

There were reasons for this 'equivocal' attitude. If a film backed by the BBC was a success, the corporation would rarely be credited. It would take a considerable time for the holdback period to end and for that film to be aired on the BBC – and when it was finally shown, the original buzz around it would almost certainly have subsided. Money was tight anyway and many BBC controllers felt it made more sense to invest in television drama which they could control themselves. The arrival of Sky complicated matters further. The satellite operator was able to show some of the films that BBC Films had backed long before they appeared on terrestrial TV.

Executives like Thompson, Mark Shivas and George Faber were determined that the BBC should embrace cinema as well as single TV drama. The counterargument they made was that, over time, investing in film was 'very economical' for the BBC. The movies it backed could be shown many times. Films like *Billy Elliot* and *Mrs Brown* reached huge audiences not only the first time the BBC showed them but when they were repeated as well. It didn't help, though, that the BBC wasn't keen on partnerships. It wasn't in a position to finance feature films on its own and therefore had to work with outsiders – and this caused great wariness.

The official launch of BBC Films came in June 1990. One of the first films it supported was Anthony Minghella's *Truly, Madly, Deeply* (1990), which was screened at the London Film Festival. The story of a bereaved woman (Juliet Stevenson) whose deceased musician lover (Alan Rickman) comes back to her from the dead, this very poignant romantic comedy–drama was made for the BBC's Screen Two strand but was highly enough regarded to be given a cinema release. The project launched Minghella as a film-maker. He would go on to make such epics as *The English Patient* and *Cold Mountain* and to chair the BFI.

Having ignored British film-makers (or only supported them when they were making dramas for the small screen), the BBC and Channel 4 were soon to become key players in the industry. There were reasons for scaling up. It was hard to raise money for single TV dramas. Budgets were bigger for movies and the best directors, writers and producers aspired to work in cinema.

For film-makers looking for public support, the broadcasters were becoming crucial patrons. There was either the BFI (or later the Film Council) or the two broadcasters' film arms. There was nowhere else to go. They had relatively modest amounts of money but the talent became dependent on them. Big-name US producers like Scott Rudin and Harvey Weinstein quickly realised that BBC Films was nurturing film-makers whose work might have a global appeal. 'We would be the engine rooms of these films. In numerous cases, we would develop them and get directors attached,' Thompson recalls.[14]

The BBC Films name was regarded as a stamp of quality. In certain circumstances, that was the problem. When US distributors released projects developed by the BBC, they would sometimes ask for the BBC Films credit to be removed. They worried that audiences would see the logo and would then expect the movie to be dull and worthy, in a Masterpiece Theatre sort of way, but not commercial or enjoyable.

The irony now was that instead of being too cautious about the film business, many felt that the BBC and Channel 4 became too reckless. In the early years, BBC Films wasn't inundated with projects or 'spec' scripts. During the early 1990s, the industry wasn't booming. This meant that Thompson and his fellow executives had to develop features in-house. They set up offices in central London, something which their colleagues back at Television Centre in White City resented. It didn't help, either, that BBC Films executives were jetting off to festivals and working with movie stars. Thompson remembers:

> I always described my time at the BBC as fighting with one sword in front of me and one sword behind my back because you had to protect yourself all the time. It [BBC Films] was

constantly under threat. If I had a pound for every time someone told me BBC Films was about to be shut down, I would have been a rich person.

In the case of Channel 4, the company eventually set up its film arm, FilmFour, as a separate business, complete with production, sales and distribution arms and with its own gleaming offices in Charlotte Street in central London. Under its chief executive Paul Webster (ex-Palace), it began to tilt at the world market in much the same way that PolyGram and Goldcrest had a done a few years before. As Webster told the press, the original mandate for FilmFour in the Jeremy Isaacs era had been 'to stimulate filmmaking in this country, and to support films that deserved to be made. Economic considerations came second.'[15]

Under Webster, the economic considerations were foregrounded. As so often happens in British film, attempting to be more commercially minded backfired and ended up having the reverse effect to that which was intended. Buoyed by the successes of *Four Weddings and a Funeral* (1994) and *Trainspotting* (1996), FilmFour struck a deal with Warner Bros. in 2000/1. The idea was that they would co-produce films together and that these films would then receive distribution through the Warner Bros. global machine. Back in Britain, FilmFour had its own distribution arm, through which it released not just its own films but a few American pick-ups too, among them such commercial fare as American high-school romantic teen comedy *She's All That* and Woody Allen's *Small Time Crooks*. 'I can't sustain distribution on our own productions, especially the art-house ones,' Webster told the *Daily Telegraph*. '*She's All That* made money for us. Nothing wrong with that.'[16] There was indeed 'nothing wrong with that', but the problem was that FilmFour's own productions didn't follow suit.

Access to international distribution had always been the holy grail for British film-makers. Briefly, after the alliance with Warner Bros. was first struck, it appeared that FilmFour had achieved it. As it turned out, this wasn't the case at all. The films that the British company and the American major made together turned out to be uncomfortable hybrids. There was the Sebastian Faulks adaptation *Charlotte Gray*, a British-made, largely French-set wartime drama directed by an Australian, Gillian Armstrong, and starring Cate Blanchett. It was one of those movies in which all the French characters spoke in English but with heavy Gallic accents. Then came Danny DeVito comedy *Death to Smoochy*. In his interview with the *Telegraph*, Webster justified the partnership with an American major as follows:

> One's nervous of being swallowed up. At the same time, you can't fly your kite on your own any more. If you have international ambitions, which we do, you have to talk to these people. We're a little company learning to live with a giant global conglomerate.

Neither *Charlotte Gray* nor *Death to Smoochy* worked at the box office; the Warner Bros. deal was summarily ended and FilmFour was forced into a major period of retrenchment. The stand-alone company closed in 2002, only four years after it was set up. There were reported losses of £3 million in 2000 and £5.4 million in 2001 – more than the Channel 4 board would accept. This was like the PolyGram story but on a smaller scale. Webster told the press that it had been more expensive to close the film arm down than it would have been to keep it open. In the event, Film4, as it was rebranded, was folded back into Channel 4 under the highly respected executive Tessa Ross. A few years later, it had one of its biggest ever successes with *Slumdog Millionaire*. Ross oversaw a mini golden era, which saw Film4 backing such films as *Four Lions* (2010) and multiple Oscar winner *Twelve Years a Slave* (2013).

The upheavals at FilmFour in the early 2000s underlined the difficulties British broadcasters still faced when it came to working out their relationship with the British film industry. Satellite broadcaster Sky continued to infuriate producers by refusing to invest in British production at all and by buying in almost all its movies in big packages from the studios. Individual ITV companies occasionally invested in film (for example, Granada briefly had a film arm in the late 1990s), but the BBC and Channel 4 were the two crucial players who were fully committed to supporting the British industry. Neither was in a position to finance films entirely. They developed projects and then brought on other backers.

There was a 'damned if you do and damned if you don't' aspect to a lot of the broadcasters' financing decisions. For example, BBC Films was criticised in certain quarters for its involvement with Sam Mendes' American-set *Revolutionary Road* (2008). This was a movie which reunited the stars of one of the biggest box-office hits of all time, *Titanic*. However, even with Leonardo DiCaprio and Kate Winslet leading the cast, its box-office performance was relatively modest and the familiar complaints were made about BBC Films gadding about with Hollywood stars when it should have been working with home-grown talent. *Revolutionary Road* was clearly a movie which could have been made without the involvement of the BBC. The same applied to the Mel Gibson political conspiracy thriller *Edge of Darkness* (2010), developed from a BBC TV miniseries from the mid-1980s.

From the BBC point of view, at least they were getting titles which they could show on prime time on one of their main channels and with which they could reach a hefty audience. That wasn't always the case with the more 'artistic' British titles they backed. For example, Andrea Arnold's bold and sexually explicit *Red Road* (2006), set on a Glaswegian housing estate and dealing with bereavement and venge-ance, won plaudits when it screened in competition in Cannes, but was 18-rated – and so could only be shown on TV very late at night, when it would reach a tiny fraction of the licence-fee payers whose money enabled it to be made. It wasn't 'schedule-friendly'.

The argument that Thompson made to the BBC top brass was that such films made up in prestige what they lacked in mainstream viewing figures. The BBC could bask in their critical and festival success and accept the plaudits for discovering new talent. 'That's why we survived and thrived, because people did buy into that,' Thompson recalls.

As long as we were successful at doing that, building new talent, winning awards, going to festivals and the [BBC] flag could be seen flying around the world, people did buy into that. Of course, in a perfect world, you get films that are both brilliantly innovative and very commercial and popular.[17]

Before catch-up TV, when films could be made available on the BBC iPlayer, the more commercial BBC Films titles would go onto BBC1 and the more challenging fare onto BBC2. There were far more films on the latter than on the former. 'That reflects where the talent is and how it works,' says Thompson.

Senior executives at the broadcasters were also frustrated by the long wait to be allowed to show the films that they backed. Film production was still regarded by these executives as a 'non-core' activity, something they dabbled in on the margins. They little realised the crucial role the BBC and Channel 4 were now playing in British film on both the creative and business sides as investors, distributors and supporters of new talent.

What hadn't been considered was just how important so-called 'high-end TV dramas' were going to become to the British industry. In the internet era, there was a growing internationalisation of the business. Everyone knew that TV dramas from big-name directors like Leigh, Loach, Frears and Alan Clark had reached huge audiences in Britain in the 1980s, at a time when there were only three or four channels for viewers to choose from. During an ITV strike, 16 million people watched Mike's Leigh's TV play *Abigail's Party* on BBC2 – an astonishing figure. These dramas, though, didn't have much of a profile outside the UK.

The growth of the internet saw the beginnings of what became known as box set TV and binge viewing. The 'millennial generation', those born between 1980 and 2000, quickly grew accustomed to watching film and TV when and where they wanted, on their laptops, desktops and smartphones as well as on their home computers.

It was reported that one of the online giants, US streaming company Netflix, had a $6 billion acquisition budget for 2016 alone. The company's business plan involved acquiring and commissioning vast quantities of TV dramas and films. Wherever you were in the world – as long as it wasn't China, Syria or North Korea, and as long as you had a decent internet connection – you could log into Netflix and devour box sets and movies.

Netflix and Amazon, the major players in the burgeoning VoD market, and the longer-established cable and satellite companies like

HBO and Starz, weren't thinking locally. All their decisions were on a global basis, even if they did support local production everywhere from Latin America to Iceland in order to strengthen their foothold in new markets. There was a voracious appetite for content everywhere, whether miniseries or films.

This was where the UK had a surprising new role to play. The UK film tax credit was already luring the Hollywood studios to Britain. In 2013, the tax credit was extended by the then Chancellor George Osborne to 'high-end TV drama', that's to say small-screen productions whose budgets were not less than £1 million per hour.

By 2016/17, it appeared that almost everything was being made in Britain. The *Star Wars* films, the Harry Potter sequels, the Marvel superhero movies and the Bond films were all shooting at British studios, as were TV dramas, from HBO's *Game of Thrones* (whose main base was in Belfast, at the Titanic Studios), Starz's *Outlander* (which filmed in Cumbernauld in Scotland) and *Da Vinci's Demons* (at the Bay Studios at a converted factory in Swansea, Wales).

While established studios like Pinewood, Shepperton, Elstree and Leavesden were booked for big international features, one noticeable recent trend has been the use of alternative, expanded and non-traditional studio spaces. This has guaranteed that film-making is taking place all over Britain, not just in the traditional heartland of the south-east but around the country. Britain finds itself in the midst of a prolonged production boom. Its film industry has seldom, if ever, been busier. With the upsurge in production, the visual effects and post-production houses are also flourishing. The boom has been driven not by indigenous production but by international film and TV, most of it originating in Hollywood.

'The truth is that what we do is […] export. Even though we call it inward investment, what we are actually doing is exporting goods and services,' explained Iain Smith, chair of the British Film Commission, in the summer of 2017. 'There is a serious money stream coming in, letting British crews and facilities work on content that they would never be able to do within the British context […] we've benefited to the tune of billions.'

In Hollywood itself, all the studio sound stages had filled up with game shows and reality TV programmes. The US studios found themselves having to look further afield to make movies. It didn't help that California lacked its own incentive programme to match the UK tax credit or the fiscal incentives offered by so many other countries and even by several US states. Smith observed:

> In Britain, we are in a very good position because the hook of the tax relief brings them [the US films and TV dramas] in, but the skills [of the British technicians] are what make them want to come back because they get reliability.[18]

After the Brexit referendum in the summer of 2016, during which the UK decided to leave the European Union, the British currency fell against the dollar and the euro. That made the UK yet more appealing to US film and TV producers. By late 2017, *Screen International* was reporting that UK film was worth $5.6 billion (£4.3 billion) to the economy and is the UK's fastest-growing sector. The industry employed 66,000 people, more than 70 per cent of whom worked in film and video production.

Netflix and Amazon may have been stealing away some of the cinema audience but, in theory, the VoD 'platforms' (whether accessed on TVs, tablets or smartphones) are providing a new and potentially kinder environment in which films can be seen. No longer are movies judged exclusively on the basis of their opening weekend. Now, in theory, they can 'sit' on the internet platform and wait for their audiences to discover them. In practice, it doesn't happen quite like that. Films that aren't showcased on the home pages of the VoD providers struggle to be noticed. With so many new titles vying for attention, older films quickly slip from view. This isn't a new utopia – but it demonstrates that, just as in the 1980s and early 1990s, when the four British terrestrial TV channels showed over 2,000 movies a year between them, there is still a voracious appetite for filmed entertainment.

Some argue that it was reductive even to think of the UK film industry in local terms. 'The modern paradigm is internationalist. Content has to be sold and delivered to an international audience.

That is hopeful for creators because they [the patrons] need diversity in their storytelling,' says Iain Smith.

Intensely British stories, especially heritage dramas like *The Crown* and *Downton Abbey*, are now reaching global audiences. However, independent British movies are struggling more than ever to make an impression in the international marketplace. 'If they are really good, like *The King's Speech*, they can get away with it, but [producers] have to be much more aware of the cultural appetite of the larger audience,' Smith noted.

Independent British producers remain in an invidious position. The general wisdom is that they should avoid 'overhead' costs and stay as small as possible. This means, though, that they are singularly ill-equipped to deal with their own successes. There is still the tendency to wager everything on one or two movies rather than to build businesses with long-term prospects.

Some producers try to 'play both sides'. They work as hired guns on the big projects being funded by the US studios or the new 'disruptors', as Netflix and Amazon have been called. Andrew Eaton, a British independent producer who used to tell the trade press hair-raising stories about using his own money to give cash flow to productions when backing from elsewhere was slow in arriving, produced *The Crown* for Netflix. Smith produced *Mad Max: Fury Road* (distributed by Warner Bros.). At the same time, these producers would also pursue their smaller passion projects.

'It's an imperfect way of doing it. I look at more idealistic producers and I wonder how they do it,' Smith, one of the UK's most experienced producers, reflects on the challenges facing producers as they try to keep their businesses afloat while making films for the love of it. 'We are never going to be hugely wealthy. If you want to see producers driving Bentleys, look to TV.'

A common lament is that the DVD market has collapsed. Partly as a result, it is far harder to pre-sell feature films (to help put together their budgets by licensing them to foreign distributors in advance of their completion). Budgets for independent features are therefore being forced downward. However, the boom in high-end TV drama and the ever-increasing number of big blockbuster movies shooting in the UK means that competition for crews is fiercer than ever – and that means that wages for the best technicians are going up.

After he left BBC Films in 2007, David Thompson set up his own company, Origin Pictures, which enjoyed success with such films as *Woman in Gold* starring Helen Mirren, *The Sense of an Ending* starring Jim Broadbent and Charlotte Rampling and poignant family drama *What We Did on Our Holiday* with David Tennant and Rosamund Pike. 'High-end television is so good and so well funded that you often wonder what the point is of a small independent film,' Thompson notes.[19]

By a strange reversal of the old norms, the 'point' of independent film-making is now often to provide the talent that could go on and flourish in high-end TV. The epic Netflix series *The Crown* is partly directed by Stephen Daldry, who had made *Billy Elliot* for BBC Films. In 2012, renowned playwright Tom Stoppard, who had scripted such films as *Enigma* and *Shakespeare in Love*, adapted *Parade's End* for HBO. There are far more 'players' in the industry than when Film on Four and BBC Films were first being launched. There may be more potential patrons too but, even with Netflix, HBO and Amazon on the prowl for new projects, it remains as tough as ever to get either films or TV commissioned.

'Notwithstanding people's desire to work in television drama, there are only so many shows that are going to be made at any given time,' notes television executive Antony Root. 'It is more difficult than it seems. You've got to look at how many new dramas are produced in any given year and then work out who is producing them.'[20]

Do the analysis, Root suggests, and you discover that there is still a very limited number of 'suppliers' providing TV drama. The idea that this is a new world in which independent film producers can flourish is only partly true.

Thompson tries to put the pessimism in the independent film-making community in late 2017 in context:

Ever since I can remember, people have always said this is the most challenging time. What is encouraging is that there are a lot more good British films [being made] than there were ten or 15 years ago. There are more hits. The quality is higher. People don't have that sinking feeling when they are going to see a British film that they're going to see grey skies, red buses, people wearing funny uniforms.

The 'dreariness, depression and miserability' that some used to associate with British films has dissipated as more and more decent British movies are made.[21]

CASE STUDY

SLUMDOG MILLIONAIRE (2008)

'There are no second acts in American lives,' F. Scott Fitzgerald famously wrote in *The Last Tycoon* (1941), his posthumously published, unfinished novel based on MGM wunderkind Irving Thalberg. That truism doesn't apply to the British film industry. Survey any given period and you will see a continual oscillation in the fortunes of directors, producers and the companies they work for.

When FilmFour, the self-contained mini studio that Paul Webster had run for broadcaster Channel 4, closed in 2002, the assumption among most industry observers was that the Channel's film activities would now slow down considerably. Instead, Film4, as it was rebranded, was about to enter a golden age under executive Tessa Ross. A decade of eye-catching success would culminate with Steve McQueen's Oscar-winning *Twelve Years a Slave*, which made an astonishing $187.7 million at the box office in spite of being about the most grim subject matter imaginable.

Ross, a former BBC executive and script editor, had a knack for nurturing talent from unlikely sources. Film4 didn't have the means to fully finance films or even often to be the leading partner on them but its success was in identifying projects and putting together the creative teams to make them.

Film4 had optioned Indian author Vikas Swarup's debut novel, *Q&A*, at manuscript stage. This is the story of a young Indian waiter from a very humble background who wins a fortune on a TV quiz show but is then accused of cheating by those who resent his good luck. At the time, Film4 didn't have a producer or indeed anybody else attached to the project but, as Tessa Ross later told *Screen International*, 'It had a fantastic landscape, a clever plot and a way of telling the story of a boy's life in the present that I liked.'[22]

Film4 assigned Simon Beaufoy (best known for *The Full Monty*) to write the screenplay. In the name of research, Beaufoy made several fact-finding trips to India.

Film4 eventually partnered with Celador, the British company which had originated TV hit *Who Wants to Be a Millionaire*. Celador had a films arm run by young producer Christian Colson. The involvement of Celador enabled the producers to get the permission they needed to refer to *Who Wants to Be a Millionaire* in their movie. *Trainspotting* director Danny Boyle came on board quickly after reading Beaufoy's screenplay.

This was a very left-field idea — an Indian-set drama partly shot in Hindi and with three sets of actors playing the main characters at different times in their lives. The 18-year-old London-based Dev Patel and actress Freida Pinto were already emerging talents but the kids were unknowns who had been discovered in the Mumbai slums by the casting team.

Boyle shot the film in the same irrepressible, wildly energetic way as he had *Trainspotting* just over a decade before. He was working with Anthony Dod Mantle, a British cinematographer with a flair for improvisation who had made his name in Denmark on low-budget Dogme movies like *Festen* and *Mifune's Last Song*. Beaufoy's screenplay had the comedy, pathos, vivid characterisation and epic sweep of a Charles Dickens novel.

Slumdog Millionaire, the project which Tessa Ross and her team had developed from almost nothing, went on to become a huge crowd-pleaser. When it was first unveiled, it won the audience award at the Toronto Film Festival. That gave it the initial momentum that would eventually lead it to amass close to $400 million at the box office globally, a huge return on a budget of $15 million. It went on to win Oscars too. The film was set in India but conceived in Britain, underwritten by the UK film tax credit and coaxed into existence by a British broadcaster whose annual budget for film was a paltry £10 million. This was one occasion on which the British industry did punch above its weight.

CHAPTER 10

A Taxing Business

During the summer of 2016, a middle-class north London wife and mother began posting a series of sharply observed, very poignant blogs about the way her life had suddenly fallen apart. *A Prison Bag*, as her blog was called, expressed what it was like to be leading an affluent, relatively cosseted existence one day – and then to be visiting your husband in prison the next. The husband, Robert Bevan, was a well-known film financier and producer whose credits included an early film from Keira Knightley (Gillies MacKinnon's *Pure*), a Ralph Fiennes and Penelope Cruz movie (*Chromophobia*) and features which had screened at Sundance and Cannes. He was one of the principals of the immensely prolific company Little Wing, which had used tax breaks to make dozens of lowish-budget British, US and even Latin American movies. Now, he was in prison, serving a sentence of nine years.

Bevan's wife, Josie, was a script reader and freelance script editor who had retrained as a nutritionist. Now, to stave off her despair and loneliness, she was writing very frankly about both her experiences as a prison wife and what she saw and learned of prison life from her visits to her husband. Her blog was well written and often heart-rending to read. It helped her achieve a very minor celebrity. But when she was profiled in Sunday newspapers or wrote a column or appeared on the radio, the comments from the public were often very harsh. They saw her husband as a swindler.

Along with his business partners, Bevan had been found guilty in Birmingham Crown Court of running a fraudulent film investment scheme used to claim £100 million of tax repayments. Little Wing's high-net-worth investors (many of them footballers and celebrities) had pumped money into the company's schemes, thinking they were both supporting British film production and securing themselves tax advantages. The prosecution had accused the company of inflating budgets, generating artificial losses and then using offshore companies to hide the money, which they were keeping for themselves. Nobody likes a tax cheat.

'It can feel as if you are married to a dead person who materialises in brief calls and visits. You are changing and so are they,' Josie Bevan wrote in a newspaper article.[1] Often, her misery and loneliness were overwhelming. 'I dramatically declare to my friend that I would cut body parts off to get Rob home again. Which ones? he asks. I imagine myself as an amputee and reconsider,' she confided in her blog in November 2017.[2]

Her plight wouldn't immediately seem to contain any particular lessons for the British film industry. She was married to someone who had been convicted of white-collar fraud. However, that alleged fraud came about precisely because the UK government had been determined to attract investment into British film-making and had set up tax breaks for that purpose. In 2018, at the point at which this study ends, the film and TV tax credits are the bulwark of the industry. It's largely because they are in place that Disney, Warner Bros. and others are making huge-budget movies and TV dramas in Britain. There were, though, a lot of teething problems before those tax credits were established. Earlier attempts at providing tax relief to the film industry had started off British cinema's own answer to Klondike fever. There were movies to be made and money to be had. The tax-relief legislation was a work in progress, full of loopholes, and plenty of mountebanks and chancers wanted to take advantage. Throughout the 1990s and early in the new millennium, HM Revenue and Customs (HMRC), the politicians and film financiers were engaged in continual skirmishing as the legislation was tweaked and financing schemes that had previously been legal were outlawed. Sometimes, the changes in film tax rules caused outrage and resulted in movies having to be abandoned.

This was the case when, in the second week of February 2004, the letters began arriving in bagfuls at the office of the Paymaster General,

Dawn Primarolo. Their tone was desperate and accusatory. Thanks to an announcement about 'limited liability partnerships' made on 10 February, production on over a dozen British films had stopped. Their financing had collapsed because of a change to the law, and now projects which producers had spent years putting together stood to be abandoned. As Adam Dawtrey wrote in *Variety*, 'The British film industry felt last week like a shanty town after a hurricane had hit it.'[3]

One of Hollywood's most highly paid actors, Johnny Depp, star of *The Libertine* (one of the films at risk), tried to telephone the Treasury. He didn't get through. The trade press dubbed the day of the law change (10 February) 'Black Tuesday'. Furious missives were sent off to the Film Council, the lead agency for UK film, asking why it hadn't intervened or forewarned the producers that film financing practices considered acceptable on 9 February had been outlawed on the tenth.

'In one fell swoop, your decision took away 30% of our production finance,' the producers of a romantic comedy, *The Truth about Love*, due to shoot in Bristol, complained to the Paymaster General. They pointed out that their production finance was being provided

23. During Tony Blair's premiership, Dawn Primarolo was Paymaster General from 1999 until 2007. For her political service she was appointed a Dame in the Queen's Birthday Honours of 2014.

Jeff Overs/Getty Images

by Grosvenor Park's 'First Choice' scheme, 'one of the most highly regarded non-studio sources of film finance in the UK'. The name of their financier certainly sounded respectable enough.

Grosvenor Park, like fellow financier Ingenious Media, had been using 'generally accepted accounting principles' (GAAP) to write off production costs as tax losses. The Treasury decided that this was no longer permissible. 'If the situation is not resolved speedily, your decision will instantly have put hundreds of British people working on this film out of work,' the politicians were warned. Restaurants, bars, taxi firms 'and the like' would all suffer.[4]

Other producers struck a politer but equally forlorn note. 'I'm not sure if it is possible to convey the extreme sense of despair I had at this news,' Sarah Curtis, about to make a film called *On a Clear Day*, also with Grosvenor Park funding, wrote to the Paymaster General in an email.[5] She had worked 'flat out' for over a year to put the film together, during which time she had had no other paid employment. This was a relatively modestly budgeted project but she was now personally liable for £30,000 'pay or play' deals on actors and had no way of paying her legal bills. She predicted bankruptcy for herself.

Plenty of others wrote in to 'protest in the strongest possible terms' or to say they were 'appalled' about the unthinking, knee-jerk way the Inland Revenue had effectively closed down 'a large sector of UK film production overnight'. People's livelihoods were 'in jeopardy'. The government was accused of sending a 'very negative' message about shooting films in Britain to the international film community. Those whom the government decision was going to hit hardest were the poor, beleaguered independent British producers. The US studios would simply walk away and make their films somewhere else.

The coverage suggested that the government, on a whim or out of some random malice toward British cinema, had closed down the schemes. Of course, it was more complicated than that. For years, the British film industry had been trying to attract investment from the City. In the early 1980s, such investment had been forthcoming. As historian John Hill points out, in 1979 the Inland Revenue ruled that films could be treated as 'plant' and were therefore eligible for 100 per cent capital allowances in the first year.[6] This had the desired effect, bringing city money into such movies as *Chariots of Fire* and *Local Hero*. However, there was also 'substantial tax avoidance' and the rules were tightened up.

In 1984, Chancellor of the Exchequer Nigel Lawson announced he was abolishing the capital allowances. Investment in film fell sharply, declining from £270.1 million in 1986 to £49.6 million in 1989. The Tory government didn't seem unduly concerned. 'I know that people have been anxious about the tax changes that have been made, but I believe that there is evidence of a high level of activity,' the films minister, Norman Lamont, told Parliament in late 1984, citing the production activity of Goldcrest, Thorn EMI and Virgin as well as that of Channel 4 as evidence that there was plenty of work going on. The following year, 1985, was to be British Film Year (see Chapter 11) and Lamont blithely claimed that there were so many new opportunities for film-makers thanks to the rise of video and cable that public support was barely needed. Of course, this wasn't the case. As investment dried up, the industry lobbied intensively for tax breaks to be reintroduced.

In 1996, Sir Peter Middleton's Advisory Committee on Film Finance was set up to work out what was stopping private investment into the industry and to consider introducing a 100 per cent write-off.[7] There had already been a concession with Section 42 of the Finance (No. 2) Act 1992, which allowed expenditure to be deducted over a minimum of three years on a British film of any size. This was expected to give producers setting up sale and leaseback deals 'an immediate cash sum of between four and eight per cent of a film's budget', which was 'of considerable value for productions of £10 million or more' but 'often not worth the time, trouble and expense of setting up the deal for lower budget films'.[8] It was very welcome but not a big enough incentive on its own to have a major impact. Much more promising from the local industry's point of view was Section 48 of the Finance (No. 2) Act 1997, which allowed for immediate tax savings but only applied to films budgeted under £15 million.

It all seems very dry when written about in memos from bankers and financiers, but sections 42 and 48 were about to usher in a new gold-rush era in British film financing. Hundreds of millions of pounds were to pour into the industry, supporting films of very variable quality, many of which wouldn't be shown in British cinemas; there was to be the rise of a new breed in British film-making, the so-called 'middleman'; wealthy footballers, celebrities, industrialists and even politicians were to pump their money into the film financing schemes – and a decade or more later, some of those behind the schemes were going to end up in prison.

This was the era of 'sale and leaseback' film financing. The banks would buy the rights to completed British films and lease them back to their producers over a number of years. When the accelerated tax relief of a 100 per cent write-off in the first year was introduced by the Labour government in 1997, the market opened up for high-net-worth individuals looking to invest in film structures. These investors could defer tax payments until the films they backed had been released and made a profit. However, they could claim tax relief on 'the whole of their pledged investment, including the deferred payment'.[9]

Under some of the film schemes offered on the market, there was a guaranteed return for the investor of between 13 and 15 per cent and the producer could access finance at a better rate than he or she would have done if dealing with a bank. It was as if the British film industry had suddenly stumbled on its very own answer to alchemy. This was a financial tool that worked regardless of a film's box-office performance – or, indeed, of whether the film was actually seen in cinemas or not. The trade press began to fill with stories mentioning 'sideways loss relief', basically film investment schemes generating trading losses which high-net-worth individuals were able to offset against their earned income. The sideways loss schemes were separate from the statutory tax reliefs.

'Everybody knows how to do it. The producers all know how it's done. There's no skill or cleverness in it. It's absolutely standardised,' one film financier told the trade press. When asked what was likely to happen if Section 48 was scrapped, the executive admitted frankly: 'The terrible thing is that when it's taken away, the activity will go away again.'[10] In other words, this production boom was built on extremely shaky foundations.

'Theoretically,' Alexander Walker noted in *Icons in the Fire*, 'it would now be possible for a producer to make a film, never have it released, yet enter a profit for himself and his investors on the strength of the write-off value and the sale and leaseback deal.'[11]

Blair's Labour government also offered tax breaks for research and development in pharmaceuticals and aerospace engineering. Film, though, was one of the first sectors it supported. Section 48 was intended to boost local British production. It did so, but one of its unforeseen consequences was to transform the UK almost overnight into one of the most attractive co-production partners in global film.

As a generalisation, the British were no longer very good at co-production. In the latter part of the British Screen era, from 1991 to 2000, almost 60 per cent of the 144 films supported by the organisation were co-productions (85 out of 144) and there were still a number of producers (Jeremy Thomas, Rebecca O'Brien, Christopher Sheppard, Andy Paterson, Julie Baines, Keith Griffiths and a few others) who successfully looked to Europe and elsewhere for support. However, the British had left Eurimages (the Council of Europe's co-production fund) and would only ever turn up in small numbers at the various co-production markets held every year at film festivals around the world. Their European counterparts were well accustomed to financing their movies by piecing budgets together from many different foreign partners, broadcasters, film funds and the like. This was a skill, though, that the new generation of British producers either had never possessed or had somehow lost along the way. The idea of becoming minority partners on French or German features on the understanding that the French and Germans would then become minority partners on their films in return simply didn't appeal. The language difference was an added hindrance. The British made films in English, not in other languages. They looked to the US for support, not to Europe. Nonetheless, the Europeans (and the Canadians too) were now looking to them. It became possible for British producers to make substantial amounts of money on films on which they had no creative input whatsoever. On 'financial only' co-productions, the British producers simply needed to sign papers confirming that the films they were supporting were British-qualifying and could therefore access the UK's tax breaks. In particular, UK/Canadian co-productions were very intensely scrutinised. It was recognised that some producers were using the UK/Canadian co-production treaty to access the 100 per cent UK tax write-offs on movies in which as little as 20 per cent had been spent in Britain.

This was a cat-and-mouse game with the sense that the industry, at least at first, was one step ahead of the government and HMRC as it attempted to exploit the loopholes in the Section 48 legislation. It was a measure intended for film but TV soap operas, kids' shows and even weather forecasts took advantage of it... at least until the government belatedly stopped them from doing so. Former British Screen boss Simon Perry told trade magazine *Moving Pictures*:

> There were huge screams from the television industry but nobody cared because they didn't need that money anyway. It was never intended for them. What that meant was that for all the investors who appeared, using the system for film and TV, they only had film. There's now a massive amount more money than there are projects which can use the money.[12]

At times, the sparring between the film financiers and the Revenue took on a comic aspect. Rules changed so that film partnerships hoping to claim tax reliefs had to demonstrate that they were carrying out a trade. They needed to prove that they were devoting at least ten hours a week to their film business interests. This led the financiers to masquerade as producers, pretending that they were reading scripts and attending production meetings.

Companies like Visionview, Grosvenor Park, Ingenious, Baker Street and the Future Film Group raised hundreds of millions of dollars from private investors to pump into movie production. Accountants, tax experts and lawyers were all queuing up to support an industry which in normal times (and after past experiences) they would not have gone near.

The trade press couldn't help but notice that the Cannes market in the late 1990s and early years of the new millennium was suddenly becoming 'flooded with low-budget films financed by British tax incentives', most of them with very dubious commercial prospects.[13] This was turning into what one sceptic called 'a churn and earn business. The more you churn, the more you earn [...] in the churn and earn game, you don't send anybody away. The only questions are: is the film going to get made and is it British-qualifying?'[14]

British film-makers themselves were startled at how easy it had suddenly become to get their films green-lit. Every spring, there was a frenzied rush to complete financing amid suspicions that the movies had been pushed ahead prematurely to meet the deadline for the end of the tax year. Such matters as script development, casting or ensuring that the new pictures would receive UK distribution were secondary. The main concern was to get the movies finished as quickly as possible. 'Usually financiers would want to ask a lot more questions about a project,' one film-maker whose film was backed with tax-incentive money told trade paper *Moving Pictures*. 'It was a surprise that they were prepared to give us so much money without having more certainty about what was going to happen at the other end.'[15]

The new films' subject matter didn't inspire much confidence either: they were a traditional mixture of comedies and genre thrillers, most starring TV actors or once-significant Hollywood names whose careers were now in terminal decline. In other words, they were films with a strong whiff of 'quota quickie' about them. (In the 1930s, in response to quota legislation insisting that a certain percentage of films shown in British cinemas were made by British producers, there had been another artificial boom. Films were made quickly and cheaply simply to fulfil the legislation. They were programmed to be shown at the least popular times so as to free up the lucrative evening screenings slots for the Hollywood productions. It used to be joked that nobody at all saw them apart from the cinema cleaners doing their morning shifts.)

Suspicion about the cavalier way Section 48 relief was being treated was exacerbated by the case of Evolution, a Chester-based production company which claimed 100 per cent tax write-offs on total budgets of its films although (as *Screen Finance* pointed out) 'it only invests about

30 per cent (of those budgets) up front with deferrables payable out of any sales revenue'.[16]

'A new company, Evolution Films, has set alarm bells ringing across the British film industry by using tax breaks to pour millions of pounds directly into production,' *Variety* reported as Evolution began cranking up in earnest in 2001.[17] The company claimed it had raised £23 million ($33 million) from private investors to produce seven British films and one short. It was raising another $85 million to shoot 20 more films in the next 12 months, among them the imaginatively titled *Revenge of the Swedish Bikini Team*.

Evolution's initial projects included *Al's Lads*, a thriller epic clearly made on very modest means. This co-starred Richard Roundtree (of *Shaft* fame) and was set in Al Capone-era 1920s Prohibition America but shot, to save money, on the mean streets of Liverpool instead. Another one was *Mrs Caldicot's Cabbage War*, starring Pauline Collins, about a little old lady leading a revolt at an old people's home, and *Arthur's Dyke* starring Pauline Quirke (a well-known TV actress), about a mum who leaves her family 'to walk the length of the Welsh border'. Everything about Evolution's projects seemed just a little dubious. These were films with improbably big budgets and very modest casts. Their directors weren't well known. The films were represented at markets by small independent sales agents. Distributors certainly weren't clamouring to acquire the rights.

Another company turning out films in industrial quantities was Little Wing Films. Their proposition, which proved highly attractive to footballers, pop stars, bankers and any other high-net-worth individuals, was that for every £100,000 invested, higher-rate tax payers could reclaim £130,000 in tax repayments from HMRC. Little Wing was later to be accused of inflating expenses and budgets. Fifteen years later, in the summer of 2016, its principals were to receive stiff jail sentences. Keith Hayley, Robert Bevan and Charles Savill were each sentenced to nine years' imprisonment with conditional license available after four and a half years. One other defendant, Norman Leighton, was sentenced to a two-year suspended sentence. However, for a brief period at the start of the century, this was one of the British film industry's most prolific production companies.

One of its most notorious features, *Crust*, was about a seven-foot-tall boxing crustacean. The storyline concerned a pub owner who bought a giant shrimp that had been washed up on shore and taught the mollusc to box. The film, which was screened in the Cannes market by its sales agent, Park Entertainment, later became the subject of a celebrated law suit. Banker and private equity investor Guy Hands (whose Terra Firma group was later to buy Odeon) and his wife Julia were among 75 investors who had invested in a package of Little Wing projects on the advice of accountants Baker Tilly – with the giant pugilist crab at the heart of the investment. They were all expecting an easy return on their investment. In the event, when HMRC came after the scheme, Hands was forced to pay back £15 million in disallowed tax relief and £2.3 million in interest.

'The reason I invested in the films was to obtain the benefits of the tax reliefs which would at least ensure I got my principal investment back,' Hands told the High Court after he launched legal action against Baker Tilly in 2008.[18] He had been told he would obtain tax relief on the money invested in the film – and also on deferred payments for it. (In the parlance of the time, this was 'double dipping'.) If he had been informed that there was any chance he would lose 60 per cent of his investment, Hands insisted he would never have invested. Hands and the other investors reached a settlement with Baker Tilly after confidential negotiations.[19]

Crust didn't secure professional distribution in the UK. (That the film later achieved cult status in Japan appears to have been accidental and certainly wasn't envisaged in the producers' business plan.) Nor did many of the other Little Wing movies make it into British cinemas.

Screen Finance had estimated that 40 per cent of films that went into production in the UK in 1999 had not secured a distributor by 1 May 2001. This was not as grim a statistic as it first seems. (Three years earlier, the figure was closer to 60 per cent.) Still, it underlined the exhibitors' and distributors' continuing suspicions about the commercial prospects of modestly budgeted British independent films. The distributors were wary about handling such fare because of the exhibitors' terms. The less successful a film, the higher the proportion of the box-office receipts that the cinemas held on to. 'With less successful films, we keep more of the take because of the severe fixed costs which we now face, particularly with multiplexes,' Odeon's managing director Richard Segal explained.[20]

There was evidence of a chasm between the film-makers themselves and the new generation of financiers who were backing their work.

'To be blunt about it, we have built financing structures and we need raw material to go through those structures and our raw material happens to be film,' Tim Levy, boss of Future Film Group, one of the more prestigious of the new breed of film financiers, told the trade press in 2002.[21] Future Film has been involved in more than 200 films, raising over £750 million in the process. His company had just launched three new funds: Fusion, targeted at studio-level films; Microfusion, targeted at films budgeted between £5 million and £15 million; and Mezzanine, aimed at films between £1 million and £15 million. 'They're highly complex financing tools and the problem is that the industry is full of people who don't understand them,' Levy lamented.

By the turn of the millennium, there was a huge amount of tax-driven film production activity in the UK. Everybody was in on the game. Small British companies and US studios alike were taking advantage of the legislation. 'The studios played fast and loose with sale and leaseback, claiming tax credits on their productions and then selling them [back] to themselves and claiming [against tax] on the purchase price,' recalls one senior UK Film Council executive.[22]

There was no sign that the new wave of financiers had any particular affection for film or even any interest in it. Former British Screen chief executive Simon Perry worked for a year as 'head of co-production' at Ingenious Media. This was the company founded by Patrick McKenna, the executive who had made his name as accountant to *Phantom of the Opera*, *Cats* and *Evita* composer Andrew Lloyd Webber. He had gone on to become CEO of Lloyd Webber's Really Useful Group and had founded Ingenious in 1998.

'They [Ingenious] were in the money business. They were in the business of persuading high-net-worth individuals, mostly footballers, some rock stars and one or two other people, to sign up to their schemes,' Perry recalls. The 'beauty and horror' of the schemes was that the box-office performance of the films was immaterial. The schemes generated 'free money' for the investors and their intermediaries while providing the films with around 12 to 13 per cent of their budgets. Ingenious itself charged as its fee 8 per cent of the entire transaction. 'It was just something that the accountants had managed to make fly with the Revenue,' Perry said of the schemes.

> I always thought that this just cannot last because the wastage is so enormous, the cost of it to the country, the money not going on the screen is so vast. The money not going to the Revenue was out of all proportion to what was actually going in to enhance the film.[23]

The Treasury's concern was that the so-called 'middlemen' (intermediaries like Ingenious and Future Film) looking for raw material for their financing structures were reaping benefits that were intended for the producers. 'This is a cycle which will continue until Doomsday,' Mike Kelly, head of finance at the Film Council, told *Moving Pictures*.

> Whenever a government tries to make a particular move to sustain a particular industry, there will be a huge entrepreneurial group that tries to exploit that in the quickest, easiest and most effective way. It's up to the government and the Department of Culture, Media and Sport to police the tax relief so that it is not abused.[24]

Paymaster General Dawn Primarolo wasn't in the slightest apologetic that the government had outlawed some of the schemes used by the 'middlemen'. The Labour government took exception to the 'aggressive tax planning' that had been going on around the film industry since 1997. This was a case of 'wealthy individuals joining tax schemes that were allegedly funding the development of a film when actually it [the investment] was a way of buying somebody else's losses to reduce their tax'.[25] The government had tried to close the loopholes by introducing anti-avoidance measures. Every time it did so, the middlemen found a new way of exploiting the system.

The GAAP schemes, dependent on 'sideways loss relief', were just the latest in what the Treasury viewed as wheezes for avoiding tax. As noted, such schemes worked by generating trading losses which high-net-worth individuals were able to offset against their earned income. Sceptics felt that as much creativity went into designing the schemes as into the films that they were ostensibly there to support. The partnerships always had a veneer of respectability. They were put together with the cooperation of leading banks, 'magic circle' lawyers and top accountancy firms.

Representatives from the UK Film Council were regular visitors to Parliament. They did their best to reassure the government that tax breaks for the film industry should be kept at all costs. 'They went to the Prime Minister, they went to the Chancellor. They said it would be the end of the film industry [if the tax breaks were cut],' recalls one senior Treasury official.[26]

Lord Attenborough and Lord Puttnam were continually making the same point. Leading film finance companies would also seek meetings in Parliament. The lobbying was relentless and generally effective. Government ministers listened but their patience was beginning to run out. They felt that the tax breaks had become (as Primarolo calls them) 'tax reduction vehicles for wealthy individuals'. The actual films that were being made were incidental. This was a case of the tail wagging the dog. Treasury officials advised the government that the Exchequer was losing huge amounts of revenue because of the schemes.

Many within the government felt that the tax schemes were immoral and that the wealthy individuals benefiting from them should have been paying their taxes like everybody else. The legislation certainly hadn't been designed to help rich people defer their tax bills or buy somebody else's losses. There was also sympathy within government for the film-makers themselves. These film-makers weren't tax experts and were simply looking to get their movies financed. If the money was offered to them, they could hardly be blamed for taking it. However, any sympathy toward the film-makers was countered by the anger and even revulsion toward the financiers with whom they were working.

Film Council deputy chair (and later chair) Stewart Till would visit Paymaster General Primarolo, by then a close ally. Their meetings were akin to those between an errant pupil and a head teacher. Again and again, she would make the point that the government was 'putting loads of money' into the industry but that only a percentage of it was reaching the film-makers themselves. The rest was going elsewhere, into the pockets of the financial advisers and their wealthy clients.

'I saw them a lot. I liked them, they were good friends,' Primarolo recalls of the film lobbyists who visited her so frequently. Nonetheless, she made it very clear to them that if the abuses weren't stopped, the tax benefits would become untenable. 'I would go, you have to help me because I can't go to the Chancellor and say, "Look, I know they [British film-makers] aren't getting very much but let's stick with it."'[27]

This was taxpayers' money, after all, and the government also had to find money for the Health Service and education. It would have been disastrous from a PR point of view if it had begun to appear that the government was subsidising fat-cat financiers rather than cash-strapped British producers.

Primarolo made it very clear to the lobbyists that if the tax relief couldn't be fixed, it wouldn't be kept: 'You, the industry, have the obligation to help us, government, to get this tax credit right, because if we can't get it right, we can't keep it!' The tax relief had to benefit the film-makers rather than the tax planners and the high-net-worth individuals whose money they were looking to squirrel away out of the grasp of the Inland Revenue. Even so, when the GAAP schemes were outlawed on 'Black Tuesday' the industry was shocked.

From the Treasury's point of view, the 'Black Tuesday' announcement couldn't have been introduced in any other way. The public hated tax avoidance. The National Audit Office wasn't keen either on aggressive film tax schemes that seemed to result in hundreds of millions of pounds leaking away from the public coffers. Anti-avoidance measures were always introduced immediately, without prior warning, because the object was to stem future losses. 'Illegitimate' tax avoidance schemes were often hidden alongside legitimate schemes. The only way to deal with them was to close them all down at once.

By February 2004, it didn't look as if there was a solution. In the eyes of the Inland Revenue, the old system didn't work. There wasn't a satisfactory replacement.

Historically, the British film industry had had its share of South Sea Bubble moments, when money had poured into production and then, after a string of failures or scandals, the financing had disappeared. The case of Max Schach, whose Capitol Film Group had persuaded insurance companies and banks to invest heavily (and disastrously) in the film industry in the 1930s, stood as an earlier example of a period in which a generation of 'middlemen' had attempted to fleece the British film business.

Seasoned industry observers had long known that tax breaks and soft-money schemes in the film business came and went. They were dependent on the whims of government. If one country or jurisdiction gave its film-makers a significant advantage, others would cry foul and introduce their own schemes which, eventually, would cancel each other out. Britain was a member of the EU and there were strict 'state aid' rules to ensure that no EU member states had unfair advantages over their rivals.

In the aftermath of 'Black Tuesday' there was a very real possibility that the Blair government would tell the film industry that it had had its chance and blown it. The government had repeated again and again its desire to help the film industry, but wasn't prepared to sanction tax avoidance schemes any longer.

In late 2004, it emerged that the next James Bond film, *Casino Royale*, was set to shoot mainly at Barrandov Studios in Prague. The Czechs didn't offer tax breaks but their rates were significantly cheaper than those of the major British studios. In 2005, Pinewood Shepperton plc issued a profits warning as the rate of production activity in the UK fell sharply. This was the backcloth as the Labour Party pondered just what to do about cinema. The thinking in government was that the film industry had squandered its opportunity. The Treasury wanted to abolish the tax incentives.

'Our losses were so great and we couldn't really find our way through it,' Primarolo says of this period.

We had spent a huge amount of time. I was reporting regularly to Gordon [Brown, the Chancellor], telling him how well it was going. If we had £400 million at that time to spend, we

had Sure Start, we were trying to raise money to invest more
to get the Health Service to the European average. Let's not
forget that this is not government money, it is taxpayer money.
We didn't think we could find a way. We tried and it was like,
OK, this is the end.[28]

The politicians didn't like being portrayed as the villains. After all, they
had pumped hundreds of millions into the film industry, with lottery
money as well as tax breaks. They had negotiated co-production treaties on behalf of the industry and had listened to its sometimes shrill
cries for assistance. Now, they were taking an 'absolute hit publicity-
wise' and the long-term goal of building a sustainable British film
industry seemed as far away as ever.

David Puttnam recalls making a last-ditch attempt to persuade
government to reform rather than scrap the system.

I went to see Dawn Primarolo. I made a whole plea to her that
the idea was right and the industry was worth supporting, but
that it had to be re-looked at. At the end of the meeting, she said,
'I hear you, I'll have to talk to Gordon [Brown] about this but
I'll see what I can do.' Gordon, bless him, agreed to revamp the
system and try again. Dawn has an unsung heroic role. When
I walked in the room, she was alas under instruction that she
would kill this. When I walked out, she agreed she would go and
talk to Gordon about finding a way of giving it a second life.[29]

A great deal of resuscitation work would be required before the UK
film tax system in its revamped form was to flicker into life.

In the short term, in the immediate aftermath of 'Black Tuesday',
the Treasury did what it could to minimise the damage to films already
in production and which had had their financing taken out from under
them. Transitional relief measures were put in place. The Johnny Depp
feature, *The Libertine*, was able to replace its lost tax-based support
from Grosvenor Park's First Choice scheme with funding from the
Isle of Man. As Grosvenor Park's managing director had made clear,
getting Johnny Depp to work on an independent British film with a

first-time UK director had been an achievement in itself. If the film had been allowed to collapse altogether, it would have been a public relations disaster.

'We got to a good position by trial and error, but it was such hard work,' Primarolo remembers of the attempts to put a new film tax relief system in place.[30]

Gordon Brown's special advisor Stewart (now Lord) Wood was a key figure in ensuring the film tax credit was put in place. 'We absolutely held our breath and they [the government] came up with a 20 per cent credit on low-budget British films and 16 per cent [for bigger budget films],' remembers Stewart Till.

At one stage, it was going to be 20 per cent for British films and 12 per cent for inward investment. I went to Dawn [Primarolo] and said, 'It is better you do nothing than 12 per cent. It won't be enough. Twelve per cent won't cut it with the Hollywood studios and you'll look silly because you will announce it and no one will come.' She said, 'It's pretty set in stone.' I said, 'Obviously I can't force it,' but she did listen and the next day she announced it would be 16 per cent – and subsequently it went up to 20 per cent. It was a huge turning point, obviously, for the British film industry.[31]

Under the new UK Film Tax Relief system, which was finally introduced and granted EU state aid approval in 2007, the risk to the Exchequer was minimal. This was a measure specifically designed to benefit production companies. Smaller players might have had to work with intermediaries in order to get their tax relief cash-flowed (they needed the money up front to complete their budgets), but the relief was very different from the old schemes.

Sale and leaseback was an invention of the shipping and aircraft industries that had been 'borrowed' for film-making. It had an in-built inefficiency when applied to film and was open to sharp practices by opportunistic financiers. It couldn't be used without intermediaries to oil the wheels. By contrast, the 2007 tax relief was custom-made for film.

244 | STAIRWAYS TO HEAVEN

'All I wanted at the time was to have something that worked for the film industry and give them a base to build on and that didn't give me any more headaches and problems,' Primarolo remembers.[32] What she and others didn't realise was that the new tax relief was going to underpin arguably the biggest boom in production and inward investment in British cinema history. The film industry was to play a crucial part in the UK's economic growth as a whole. By 2016, the spend on film production in the UK had reached £1.6 billion, a record-high figure.

As an ironic and poignant footnote, at the time film-related inward investment was breaking records, many of those high-net-worth individuals involved in the film tax partnerships from a decade before were being shamed in the media and some were facing bankruptcy. They had been forced to pay back money which they didn't always have any more as HMRC won a series of high-profile victories against the originators of the schemes and their investors. Public sympathy was in very scant supply. *The Times* quoted a source from HMRC as saying that it had 600 film schemes under investigation and that 'such schemes are a £5 billion risk for us at least'. 'Scams for scumbags' was how one HMRC source characterised the schemes.[33] Solicitors Pannone LLP wrote in 2012:

> Sports stars, celebrities and leading City figures who ploughed money into the controversial Film Partnership schemes, in a move to defer tax payments, are facing unexpected and devastating multi-million pound tax bills of up to ten times their original investment as the schemes begin to unravel.[34]

One of the goals of the *Bigger Picture* report in 1998 was to lure City money and investment into the British film industry. As those behind the schemes were given ferocious grillings and accused of being 'utterly immoral' in televised hearings of the Public Affairs Committee under its ferocious chair, Labour MP Margaret Hodge, it was little wonder that the investors were thoroughly spooked. They no longer wanted to go anywhere near the film industry. By now, though, they were hardly needed anyway.

At the time of writing, in early 2018, on films that qualify as culturally British at any budget level, any film production company can claim a payable cash rebate of up to 25 per cent of UK qualifying expenditure through the tax relief. That relief is now also available to high-end TV, video games and animation, along with similar reliefs which apply to other parts of the creative industries. It has helped the UK become the destination of choice for Hollywood blockbusters and the most ambitious international television dramas alike. The Coalition government of 2010 may have dismantled the UK Film Council but it continued every other aspect of the Blair Government's policy toward the industry. The Tory Chancellor, George Osborne, pushed for a higher rate of film tax relief and made it clear that he wanted as many superhero and sci-fi epics to shoot in British studios as possible. The visual effects and post-production industries have grown at an extraordinary rate. New studio spaces opened up all over the country, tax revenue shot up and training and employment opportunities rose. The US studios set up British offshoots or opened visitor attractions and embedded themselves more firmly in the UK than ever before.

There were still anomalies. As film-makers were quick to point out, under the rules governing the tax credit, British-made films with British actors that were shot abroad didn't qualify for relief, but big US studio films with American actors could qualify as British. If the British industry benefited from Hollywood investment, Hollywood was benefiting too, and to a huge extent. The Motion Picture Association of America (MPAA) was a quiet presence behind the scenes, lobbying for incentives to shoot in Britain. Harry Potter played its part too. Insiders talk of the 'Leavesden effect'. This was the studio complex where Warner Bros. had housed and shot the Potter films. If there was ever a need to convince a government minister of the benefits that film was bringing to Britain, all that needed to be done was to arrange a trip to the studio. Even the most myopic politician couldn't help but see the vast number of craftspeople, actors and technicians working away on movies that would make hundreds of millions of pounds at the box office and put Britain in the shop window in the process.

'It [the Potter experience] brings to life in a visual way what we were trying to achieve in policy terms. It was absolutely crucial,' suggests Stephen Bristow, a partner in the film and television unit at the accountancy firm Saffery Champness, another key, behind-the-scenes figure who had formerly worked for the UK Film Council. 'Warner Bros. was a phenomenal tool in our armoury, in terms of convincing the government what a great incentive [it was].'[35]

The tax relief didn't solve on its own the problems that still bedevilled independent British producers. They still couldn't hold on to rights to their films and they still couldn't build businesses. They continued to live a hand-to-mouth existence. Nonetheless, the relief very quickly became a pivotal part of their film-financing plans.

For the industry as a whole, these were boom years and the film tax relief was behind the new-found prosperity. Oxford Economics estimated that without it the UK film sector would have been over 70 per cent smaller.[36] 'Certainly, in terms of inward investment, we just wouldn't be on the map,' says Bristow.

As Primarolo says now, 'We didn't know it would be as good as this. How could we?'[37]

CASE STUDY

ONE DAY IN SEPTEMBER (1999 – DOCUMENTARY)

Documentaries in the UK used to be regarded as something best left to television.

Pioneering Scottish film-maker John Grierson (1898–1972) may have been acknowledged as the founding father of the form and Humphrey Jennings (director of *Fires Were Started*) as one of British cinema's visionaries but, by the mid-1980s, very few feature documentaries were being seen in British cinemas.

Over the period this book covers, that situation changed completely. By 2017/18, 80 or more documentaries were being given (limited-scale) cinema releases each year and the 'doc' had become a fundamental part of British film culture.

If there was a single movie that ushered in the new era in which British documentary found its place on the big screen, it was Kevin Macdonald's Oscar-winning *One Day in September* (1999). This was the story of the slaying of 11 Israeli athletes at the 1972 Munich Olympics by Black September terrorists. It was exhaustively researched, just as might have been expected. Macdonald tracked down and interviewed Jamal Al-Gashey, the one surviving Black September terrorist from the Munich mission. He interviewed the widow of one of the murdered athletes. He accessed rare archive footage. Again, that wasn't so unusual.

What was different about *One Day in September* was the attempt to make the film cinematic and to distinguish it from TV documentaries. Macdonald recruited Hollywood star Michael Douglas to provide the narration; he edited the film as if it was a thriller and he used rock music from Led Zeppelin and Deep Purple to give his documentary a sense of drama and scale.

One Day in September had originally been suggested as a project to Macdonald by producer John Battsek, who had previously made fiction films. Battsek had been heavily influenced by two US sports documentaries that had been successes in British cinemas – *When We Were Kings*, about the 'Rumble in the Jungle' fight between Muhammad Ali and George Foreman, and Steve James' *Hoop Dreams*, a lengthy and very poignant film telling the story of two African American youngsters trying to make the grade as basketball players. There was drama, pathos and a sense of scale about both these films. They seemed best suited to cinema.

Battsek managed to recruit Arthur Cohn, a veteran Swiss producer whose credits included Vittorio De Sica's Oscar-winning *The Garden of the Finzi-Continis*, to produce the film alongside him. When they met in London, Cohn asked: 'Will there be lots of archive? It's essential to have lots of archive because if you don't, you won't win the Oscar.' Battsek had thought Cohn was joking – but *One Day in September* did feature plentiful archive. It was given a full-blown awards campaign and won the Oscar.

Macdonald would go on to make several other documentaries that played as well in cinemas as fictional films, among them mountaineering epic *Touching the Void* and music film *Marley*.

In the wake of *One Day in September*, more and more documentaries became mainstream cinema successes in the UK, among them such titles as *Searching for Sugarcane*, *Senna*, *Amy* and *The Imposter*. Independent companies such as Dartmouth and Dogwoof sprung up that specialised in distributing documentaries. Production values for documentaries rose and BAFTA, which had ignored documentary in its film awards, began to acknowledge the form alongside every other type of film-making; some cinemas set up dedicated screens to show documentaries. By 2018, documentaries were an accepted and flourishing part of the British film distribution and exhibition landscape.

CHAPTER 11

Flying the Flag — Marketing Britain on Screen

We need to poke people into remembering that cinema is there [...] we wouldn't know what washing powder to buy if we weren't told.
                                        —Actress Jean Marsh at the beginning
                                                    of British Film Year, 1985

It may have seemed at first like a forlorn attempt at fanning flames out of ashes, but 'British Film Year' in 1985 was a bold and overdue initiative. Audiences had plummeted the year before to record lows. This was the very moment that the Thatcher government was passing its free-market-oriented Films Bill, getting rid of the Eady Levy and dismantling the National Film Finance Corporation.

The idea had first been hatched by Fiona Halton, director of producers' trade body the Association of Independent Producers (AIP) in late 1983 but, at first, little attention was paid to it.

Fiona Halton had written a letter to Kenneth Baker MP, then the Minister for Information Technology. She explained the plans to run competitions nationwide, to set up studio tours and to publish a 'British Film Compendium' as part of the Film Year and asked for government endorsement and support.

To the cynics, this belated attempt at promoting and marketing British cinema was nothing more than a symbolic gesture. They would later argue that the real reason that film-going figures began to increase again after 1985 was nothing to do with British Film Year. It was simply that Hollywood was again providing movies that British audiences wanted to see – *Rambo: First Blood Part II*, *Back to the Future*, *Beverly Hills Cop* – and luxurious venues in which to see them. This was the year that, starting with AMC's The Point in Milton Keynes, the out-of-town multiplexes began to be built in earnest.

At first, AMC had been shunned by the established players in the industry. The UK's most powerful exhibitor, Odeon, had responded to the arrival of AMC by declaring at an annual film conference in Torquay that it would do all it could to drive the American exhibitor 'into the sea'. Thankfully, other, more forward-thinking figures in exhibition and distribution accepted that the American company was helping to re-energise the business. They saw that a British Film Year could help them too.

'Our cinemas are dirty, discourteously handled, with appalling projection,' Richard Attenborough told the *New York Times*. 'They were built in the main street where people came on trains or bicycles or walked. Now people want a car park and they don't want to queue out in the cold and get soaking wet.'[1]

The big chains, which owned the high-street cinemas, now vowed to change. Rank, EMI and Cannon all agreed to invest considerable sums in refurbishing their venues and bringing them closer to the shiny standards of the new multiplexes.

The notion of 'British' cinema was itself under threat. Research had revealed that film-making and film-going were both overwhelmingly concentrated in the south-east. According to 1985 figures published by Mintel, London accounted for 17.9 per cent of cinemas in the UK, 25.1 per cent of admissions and 31.9 per cent of box-office takings, with just 12.4 per cent of the total population.[2] These were startling numbers. Almost a third of the receipts were coming from a single city, albeit the capital. There were parts of the country in which the cinemagoing habit had seemingly been all but lost.

This was the situation as British Film Year was launched. Its logo was a piece of celluloid in the shape of a British flag. The first 'roadshow' was held in Leicester Square, London, with Dame Anna Neagle and Charlton Heston in attendance, but the Film Year's focus was to be far more on the regions than on the capital.

The government, perhaps conscious that its free-market policies toward the film industry hadn't been at all warmly welcomed by the producers, eventually agreed to invest £250,000 in British Film Year and gave the scheme its 'wholehearted' approval. From the government's point of view, supporting British Film Year was akin to a tacit apology for its decision to remove the Eady Levy.

The total budget for the Year was just over £1 million. Exhibitors and distributors, among them EMI, Rank, Cannon, Virgin and Goldcrest, also chipped in but the organisers had far less than the £2.9 million they originally hoped for – and less than the £1.25 million that the organisers claimed to the press they had raised.

'For the first time in memory, all sections of the industry have been invited to join forces and to re-sell cinema to the British public,' was how *Screen International* characterised British Film Year, which began in earnest in April 1985 (and ran to April 1986).[3] Many were still reeling in alarm at the prediction by Jack Valenti, head of the Motion Picture Association of America (MPAA), that British audience figures would continue to plummet. As mentioned, having tumbled to the nadir of 54 million in 1984, Valenti predicted admissions would carry on falling and could drop to 45 million or below by 1986.

In time-honoured fashion, many within the industry responded by burying their heads in the sand. Those who potentially had most to gain had reacted to British Film Year with what *Screen International* described as 'cynicism and sheer apathy' when the event was formally announced in Cannes in May 1984.[4]

'There was a lot of scepticism,' Halton remembers. She was in her twenties, a woman who had studied publishing and had only recently entered the industry. As she points out, that scepticism was understandable. 'The scepticism was because there hadn't been anything like it before. You are trying to raise the money and sell the concept at the same time as everybody is quite sceptical that it will actually work at all.'[5]

There was a whiff of sexism in the way some of the industry veterans treated her. 'But being a woman helped. If you had done this as an older person who was a man and who was on the inside of the industry, you would have [been] perceived as a threat,' Halton suggests. She was young, female and an outsider. She didn't see hurdles that may have put off others.

An exasperated David Puttnam, who was vice chair of British Film Year in charge of 'national events', described the initial response as 'niggardly, fragmented and uncohesive'. 'Instead of saying, "Here's an opportunity, let's make it work," they wanted it to go away,' Puttnam stated.[6]

Puttnam and Richard Attenborough had lobbied hard for British Film Year. Inevitably, some within the industry resented their high profile in the media and would sneer about them behind their backs. Heads of the distribution companies would meet for their usual long and liquid-fuelled lunches in Soho and some would scoff at what they perceived as the 'self-aggrandising' ways of British cinema's two most energetic champions. Distributors and exhibitors expressed little interest in putting up any of their own money for British Film Year. To Puttnam, their attitude reeked of defeatism and petty-mindedness.

Even so, the Film Year quickly picked up momentum. Regional committees were set up all over the country. Education officers, local councillors, members of local chambers of commerce, business leaders and print and radio journalists all rallied to the cause, alongside regional arts associations and film-makers. British Film Days and mini festivals were organised around the country and there was a concerted attempt to remind the British public that they still had a film industry to be proud of. The 'FROGS' (Film Regional Organising Groups) were unleashed.

There were roadshows all across the country. Some of these events had a vaguely surreal hue. Big-name movie stars would turn up in regional city centres. For example, Omar Sharif appeared one rainy afternoon in Lincoln. As the *New York Times* reported, half an hour before he arrived, 400 fans were waiting for him, shouting, 'We want Omar!'[7]

Jean Marsh, who was on screen in 1985 as the witch in Disney's *Return to Oz* and was best known for co-creating and starring in TV's *Upstairs, Downstairs*, appeared in costume at a roadshow event in Portsmouth. Kids were delighted to have the witch, and many of the girls joined in enthusiastically in a 'Dorothy lookalike' competition.

The organisers quickly discovered that stars were happy to travel back to their home towns to tub-thump on behalf of British Film Year. One hundred and fifty of them took part. It was estimated that the roadshows attracted on average between 10,000 and 15,000 people at each venue.

Cinema managers who had hitherto been known for their Scrooge-like behaviour toward their customers went on an unlikely charm offensive. During British Film Year, they would meet and greet film-goers before and after screenings in the foyers of their cinemas. They would also go out into their towns to meet the public.

The British Film Year roadshow travelled all over the country. Stop-offs included Brighton, Nottingham, Hull, Bradford, Liverpool, Southampton, Peterborough, Cambridge, Glasgow, Portsmouth, Birmingham, Manchester, Swansea and Norwich. At every venue there would be a celebrity in tow.

Stunt artists, make-up designers, costumiers and assorted other technicians would turn up too to let the public in on some of their trade secrets. Omar Sharif, Charlton Heston, John Mills, Alan Bates and Anna Neagle were among the stars who placed their handprints in wet cement in Leicester Square. (The handprints didn't survive a

24. Casting call: Sir John Mills and Dame Anna Neagle leave their handprints before a phalanx of photographers in Leicester Square in May 1985, during British Film Year.

Photo by Bob Workman, courtesy of Fiona Halton

2012 redevelopment of the square but Film Distributors' Association has preserved them for potential future display.)

The costumes from such films as *Greystoke* and *A Passage to India* were put on public display. A special exhibition, 'Stars of the British Screen: Photographs from the 1930s to the 1980s', opened in Preston, travelled around the country and eventually reached the National Portrait Gallery in London. Five stamps were issued with faces of stars (Charlie Chaplin, Peter Sellers, Vivien Leigh, David Niven and director Alfred Hitchcock) on them. There were Rambo lookalike competitions. British Film Year piqued the curiosity of the international media and was covered in the *New York Times* and the German press. There were also dozens of articles in British national and regional newspapers.

A special book, *A Night at the Pictures: Ten Decades of British Film*, by respected critics Gilbert Adair and Nick Roddick, was published in conjunction with British Film Year. Thanks to David Puttnam, *Chariots of Fire* and *Blade Runner* composer Vangelis was persuaded to write a special theme for the year. Harrods mounted commemorative window displays.

For Halton, the significance of British Film Year lay in the way it brought different sides of the industry together in pursuit of a joint goal, namely increased admissions: 'There was no central body promoting film. What [British Film Year] did was that it became the first body to pull these different people and organisations together.'[8] An inward-looking, London-centred industry began, tentatively at first, to look outward. There was a concerted attempt to engage with the public, rather than to treat cinema spectators as a necessary evil.

Accountancy firm Deloitte was commissioned to produce a report on the impact of British Film Year. By the end of 1985, audiences were rising very swiftly. 'There is gathering support for the view that British Film Year must receive some of the credit for rising cinema attendances. We would endorse that view,' Deloitte's researchers wrote. They concluded that the year-long initiative had offered 'focus and publicity to what was becoming an inherently more attractive proposition'.[9]

Another key factor mentioned again and again in contemporary accounts was the terrible weather in the summer of 1985. Gales and rainstorms were commonplace as the roadshow rolled into town. The crowds braved the elements to greet the stars... and then headed into the cinemas for refuge. At the start of British Film Year, the goal had been a 4 per cent rise in admissions. The figure actually achieved was closer to 40 per cent.

Even before British Film Year was up and running, industry bodies had belatedly begun to realise that they didn't need just to market and promote films. They had to remind an apathetic public that cinema-going itself was still the best way to experience a film. This had led, in 1984, at the same time as British Film Year was being prepared, to the creation of AIM, the All Industry Marketing for Cinema group. It brought together distributors, exhibitors and screen advertisers, who all had a shared interest in broadening the film-going public. The original members were the Cinema Exhibitors' Association and Film Distributors' Association. They were later joined by the Cinema Advertising Association and the British Academy of Film and Television Arts (BAFTA).

The chair of AIM from 1984 to 2000 was John Mahony, chief executive of National Screen Service, the organisation that distributed trailers, posters and publicity materials on behalf of the industry. As Mahony recalls, distributors and exhibitors in this period still had a ferocious antipathy toward each other. 'The thought of them being together was rather like oil and holy water.' Nonetheless, times were 'desperate'. The two warring factions were forced to get together. He was considered to be 'neutral' and unlikely to favour distributors over exhibitors or vice versa. Both groups were his clients, after all.[10]

Mahony had taken his role at AIM on the suggestion of Tom Nicholas, the UK managing director of Columbia Pictures. Nicholas had just overseen the highly successful British release of hit American supernatural comedy *Ghostbusters* (1984). This was a movie that had been marketed with energy and ingenuity. It had spawned a hit song ('Who you gonna call? Ghostbusters!'). It had attracted kids and adults alike, fans of horror and of comedy, and was credited (as *Forbes* magazine later put it) with 'breaking down the once strictly church-and-state divide between television and film actors'. Many of its cast members were from American TV's *Saturday Night Live*.

Nicholas saw the personable Mahony as someone who could bring distributors and exhibitors together without there being a trail of broken glass and smashed furniture left in the room. Mahony told Nicholas that he didn't know anything about marketing. 'Don't worry about that. We've got enough of them,' the Columbia boss reassured him.

'So I took the job on, which was very daunting,' Mahony recalls. 'When I went into the room at Royalty House [in Dean Street, Soho], I was facing the managing directors of all my customers.' Years later, Mahony could still remember precisely what he said to the exhibitors and distributors at that first AIM meeting: 'There is nothing like the prospect of imminent death to concentrate the mind.' The remark may have been tongue-in-cheek but the sentiment was real enough. In the mid-1980s, as the UK's two major companies, Rank and EMI, dithered and lost interest in film, there was a very real danger of the industry dying on its feet.

As its very name suggests, British Film Year was a short-term measure. However, AIM was intended to continue indefinitely. One of the new group's insights was that the industry didn't just need young cinemagoers to watch *Ghostbusters* and *Beverly Hills Cop*. For the longer-term health of the industry, it would be crucial to broaden the range of titles they might consider watching.

25. First class: a series of study guides, indicating how film may be deployed to illuminate aspects of the primary or secondary school curriculum, as appropriate, was disseminated to teachers as an initiative of British Film Year (1985). The set included a guide to *A Passage to India*, a John Brabourne/ Richard Goodwin production based on an E. M. Forster novel set in the 1920s. It was the final film, a characteristically large-scale undertaking, directed by David Lean, who had been knighted in 1984 and died aged 83 in 1991.

British Film Year/TESE

With this in mind, another new organisation, Film Education, was created, to encourage the use of film in teaching. By the late 1990s, with financial support from AIM and individual film distributors, film study guides were being mailed to 14,000 secondary school teachers and 20,000 primary school teachers. As they faced cutbacks to their budgets, the schools were desperate for learning materials and therefore welcomed the well-written study guides with all the more enthusiasm. 'Film Education wasn't a totally altruistic exercise, although we felt we were helping children and helping education,' Mahony says. 'Of course, we were looking to develop future cinemagoers, which I think we did fairly successfully.'

In the meantime, AIM was striking some clever new alliances. In the 1990s, it was to bring on board both TSB and Barclays banks as generic partners. There were various wheezes to the joint benefit of the cinema industry and the banks. For example, when a new customer opened an account at Barclays, that customer would receive £2 toward the price of admission at any participating cinema. This effectively meant at the time that they could go and see a movie for half price or less. The net result was that almost every new customer took advantage of the offer – and with some, the habit stuck. 'Great night out, brilliant way in' was one slogan used to advertise the scheme. 'Barclays: all the best features' was another. Barclays also came up with their own trailers, advertising the bank in the style of actual movie genres.

'We said [to the banks], "We can offer you targeted publicity,"' says Mahony. 'For example, we would top and tail the trailer reel with an advertisement. That was the thing they liked most of all.'

At the same time, cinemas were advertised in the banks' own publicity materials. The puns may have been feeble and the trailers irritating, but they did their job. At first, none of the money that TSB or Barclays invested through AIM went back directly to the distributors and exhibitors; it was all used for the generic marketing of British cinema. 'The view that I took right from the beginning was that AIM was not in business to publicise films but to promote cinemagoing – and cinema as the best place to see a film,' Mahony explains.

26. Saying yes to cinema: the UK cinema industry's generic marketing committee pioneered sector-wide promotions, to raise the profile of cinema as a night out, complementing individual film campaigns. Partnerships with TSB and then Barclays Bank each lasted two years, while their successor, Orange Wednesdays, ran for 11 years and boosted midweek cinema visits. This in turn was followed in 2015 by Meerkat Movies, sponsored by price comparison website Compare the Market.

TSB Bank/FDA archive

Inevitably, exhibitors were resistant to certain aspects of the schemes. It pained them to offer cut-price tickets to blockbusters or to allow cinemagoers to pay anything less than the full whack at weekends. Mahony's response was that the only way to avoid 'a punch-up at the box office' was to ensure the schemes ran for 'any film, at any time and at any cinema'. After all, no one was certain in advance which movies would turn into blockbusters.

It wasn't just the UK exhibitors who were wary about losing potential revenue in the short term, even if the schemes helped grow and attract audiences in the longer one. The US studios didn't like to see their wares showing at anything less than full price, but they were talked around by some of their own senior executives in the UK.

Mini-festivals were staged, for example Cinema '87 and Cinema '89 in Brighton. Mahony remembers movie-star husband and wife Don Johnson and Melanie Griffith turning up at one of the events with their baby child in tow (presumably their daughter Dakota, who would star in *Fifty Shades of Grey* a quarter of a century later). While Johnson and

Griffith went on stage, the wife of Fred Turner, the managing director of Rank Film Distributors, looked after their baby. His Royal Highness Prince Edward was another high-profile visitor. He was introduced to maverick British director Ken Russell and the cast of Russell's latest film, D. H. Lawrence adaptation *The Rainbow*. There is no record of what they discussed together.

The year 1995/6 marked the centenary of commercial filmgoing. It was just over 100 years since, in December 1895, the Lumière brothers had first charged customers to watch a selection of their short films at the Grand Café in Paris, a presentation first shown in London's Leicester Square in March 1896. The centenary was used as another promotional tool – as a way of reminding audiences that cinema wasn't just about the latest blockbusters in their local cinemas but an artistic form with a long and fascinating history.

On Sunday 2 June 1996, AIM launched the first 'National Cinema Day', an initiative through which the public could see any film in any of the country's 750 or so cinemas for just one pound. It was estimated that 2.5 per cent of Britain's population took advantage of the offer. 'The strange thing was that, even then, there was a rather old-fashioned attitude in some quarters,' Mahony remembers.

> One or two distributors were heard to grumble that too many people had gone to see their films, a novel complaint. It was felt they had got in too cheaply although, of course, there is no guarantee they would have seen a film at all without the all-industry promotion.

Complementing National Cinema Day was Film Education's first-ever National Schools Film Week, through which 81,000 children were lured to cinemas to see 45 different films at over 400 free screenings. There were workshops for the kids on scriptwriting, animation and direction. Film-makers, stars, publicists, producers and journalists all supported the scheme.[11]

There were common-sense initiatives such as special screening events for regional journalists who, at this stage, found it hard to see the films they were writing about (as trade previews all tended to be held in London). In April 1988, AIM helped stage 'Film Days at Wycombe 6', a series of screenings and network events held over three days for the Guild of Regional Film Writers. The journalists were shown such movies as *Good Morning Vietnam, Planes, Trains and Automobiles* and *Wall Street* well in advance of their UK releases.

Some of this activity may have appeared small-scale, even parochial. It's a long way from Hollywood and West End premieres to regional screening days in High Wycombe. That, though, was precisely the point: AIM was trying to remind the public and the industry that cinema was for everyone, not just for the metropolitan elite. The reason that UK admissions had hit such astronomical levels 50 years before (1,635 million tickets in 1946 alone) was the accessibility of cinema. Everyone wanted to go (very few people owned television sets). Everyone could afford to go. By the late 1980s and early 1990s, there were many other competing leisure activities and evidence of a divide between London and the rest of the country. Nonetheless, AIM was helping to repair the bond between the industry and its audiences. It was also taking other practical measures, for example launching a touch-tone service for cinema information with British Telecom (these were pre-internet days, after all) and devising the UK's first anti-piracy commercials.

As part of Film Education (set up by teacher Ian Wall in 1984), leading critics were dispatched to the provinces to try to drum up interest among schoolkids, many of whom hadn't ever visited a cinema. Mahony, who became chair of Film Education as well as of AIM, has vivid stories of heading up to Nottingham with the former jockey turned *Guardian* film critic Derek Malcolm, to make a presentation to an audience of six- and seven-year-olds: 'They would stream in and be absolutely awestruck.'

As part of a 'Five Senses' programme in cinemas, kids would be shown excerpts of Disney movies without the sound. The sound would then gradually be phased in and the kids would begin to realise the craft that went into film-making. The presentation would end with 'taste', which was basically an excuse to give the kids lots of ice cream. At the same time, students in the sixth form would be invited to write reviews of films like Spike Lee's *Malcolm X*. Derek Malcolm would then assess their work. These sessions would be held in the morning.

The cinema operators were very supportive. They, too, realised this was a chance to reach their future customers at a key formative point in their lives.

One of the effects of the multiplex boom was that cinemagoing in Britain shifted slightly. No longer were profits overwhelmingly concentrated in a handful of successful cinemas in the south-east. The new multi-screen cinemas tended to be found on the outskirts of towns or between towns in places where they could be easily reached by car. At the same time as British Film Year was tub-thumping on behalf of British cinema, it helped that there were decent films (American and home-grown) being made and that the venues themselves were at last being upgraded or replaced by the big, shiny new multiplexes. After all, the worst of the old city-centre 'fleapits' were an ordeal to enter. They were dark and gloomy, reeked of nicotine and had lavatories which were in a shocking state of squalor and disrepair. By contrast, the AMC and other new multiplexes that opened in its wake – among them the eight-screen Cannon in Salford Quays and similar venues in High Wycombe (CIC's Wycombe 6), Slough and Warrington – seemed airy and palatial. They were transforming the UK's cinema landscape and consequently the ways in which distributors were able to book – and market – films around the country.

However entrenched some of the old exhibitors were in their views, and however resistant to modernisation, the parade was moving on. They had to move with it.

As AIM, Film Education and British Film Year were championing British cinema at a grassroots level, the distributors themselves were beginning to take a far more active and inventive approach toward the marketing of their films. Mahony noticed the emergence of a 'young and more professional' type of distributor whose way into the industry was 'more than simply starting as a boy in the office' and working his or her way up. Companies like Palace Pictures (see Chapter 2) were bringing 'a breath of fresh air to film marketing'.[12] That new-found savvy was felt at every level of the industry. Given the structural problems that still faced the business, the ingenuity was very badly needed.

One British executive hired by a US studio tells a revealing story about visiting California to meet his new bosses shortly after being appointed to his job in the early 1990s. On his way to a meeting, he was accosted by one of the most senior figures in the company. He was pushed up against the wall and the American hissed into his face some home truths about the British market.

> Here's my problem with the UK. Your rentals are shit, the terms are shit. Your advertising costs are the highest in the world. There's no more expensive place other than Japan [...] and you have the most vicious press in the world.[13]

On a big studio movie, the rough rule of thumb was that you wouldn't start making profits on a theatrical release until you reached £8 or £9 million at the box office.

In the 1980s and 1990s, US studio films still tended to be marketed in the UK in a very formulaic way. British execs working for the US majors remember the 'great excitement' they used to feel when the 'pouch' arrived in London from Burbank. This was the film marketing team's equivalent of a ready meal. It would have a U-matic tape with all the TV advertising spots on it, 35 mm transparencies, production notes and posters. Little space was left for the US major's British offshoot to come up with any ideas of its own. 'It was like, "Here is your pack of stuff. Go ahead and do with it what you can,"' recalls one senior exec working for an American major in London in the late 1980s and early 1990s. It was still possible to 'open' certain movies — Steven Seagal action thrillers for example — without any extra work. They had an in-built audience. Finding an audience on video was like 'shooting fish in a barrel [...] everything worked. It propped up every studio and every independent for a long time.'[14] Even when films flopped at the cinema box office, the home video market provided them with a very soft landing. Fewer films were being released in the UK. British audiences weren't worried that the films they were seeing had been shown in US cinemas several months earlier.

There was no tracking of the audience. The distributors weren't compiling exhaustive data-driven charts in advance of release (as they do today) telling them about cinemagoers' 'unaided awareness' or 'prompted awareness' of new titles or their 'definite interest' in going to see them.

In the mid-1990s some 300 films were released in UK cinemas each year, around a third of the quantity released in 2017. Audiences were predominantly 15- to 34-year-olds, drawn very largely to mainstream US-produced films. In 1994, *Four Weddings and a Funeral* was the only British film in the year's top ten; the others included *Mrs Doubtfire*, *The Lion King*, *The Flintstones* and *The Mask*.

Other executives who worked for the major distributors feel a twinge of nostalgia for a time in which viewers weren't being 'bombarded' with content and could make their choices about what to see in cinemas in a more leisurely way. For companies handling star-driven US projects in the British market, there was a reassuring feeling that they could 'buy' their audience. If they spent the money on TV and print advertising, they'd reach their audience. In an era before satellite television, let alone digital distractions, TV advertising for films could reach tens of millions of people. The same applied to print advertising. In 1997, Britain's most widely read tabloid, the *Sun*, had a circulation of 3,877,997 while the *Daily Telegraph*'s circulation was 1,129,777 and the *Guardian* was at 428,010.[15] Kezia Williams, Head of Theatrical Distribution at Entertainment One (eOne), and a former marketing executive at Warner Bros. and Universal, and media account director for Sony Pictures, says:

> There would be a very significant TV buy. Most distributors would be starting at least three weeks out, leading up to the release of the film. There would be a very substantial campaign committed to support the film post-release as well. I just think that the amount of money on media was a lot bigger.[16]

In a changing marketplace, even the biggest distributors now realised that their films needed to stand out. The independents had never had the luxury of being able to 'buy' their audiences. They were faced with the lowest rental terms that any distributors faced in Europe.

A new generation no longer followed the mechanical strategies of the old guard. Instead, they came up with their own distinct campaigns.

Together with academic and critic Mark Kermode, Warner Bros. exec Ian George oversaw the British rerelease of William Friedkin's 1973 horror classic *The Exorcist* in the late 1990s. It was test-released first (at Warner Bros.' insistence) in 31 cinemas in Scotland in June 1998 on one of the hottest weekends of the year, during the beginning of the 1998 football World Cup, whose first match was Scotland vs. Brazil. In theory, it stood little chance. In practice, it turned into a huge hit. George had advertised the film very aggressively and had drummed up plenty of publicity too.

Putting *The Exorcist* back in cinemas wasn't exactly revolutionary. Nonetheless, this was an example of a studio film being given a bespoke release in the UK and benefiting from it. There was no pouch from Burbank with 'how to' instructions for the British on releasing the film. They had to come up with their own ideas.

The Exorcist made £151,000 on its opening weekend in Scotland and £7.37 million by the time it had been released across the rest of the country (to tie in with Halloween later in the year). *Starsky and Hutch* star David Soul was hired to record voice-over spots. Friedkin and *Exorcist* author William Peter Blatty came over to the UK to do publicity. *The Exorcist*, 25 years old, ended up becoming one of Warner Bros.' biggest-grossing films of the year (1998) in the UK, second only to *Lethal Weapon 4*, and then was finally released, extremely profitably, on video. The BBFC had previously denied it a video certificate.

The UK distribution market remained very lopsided. Box office was still dominated by the majors. After the closure of PolyGram, no new UK companies had emerged that could compete on equal terms with the US studios – or withstand the losses when a run of films underperformed. What had changed was that some of the most enterprising UK executives were now working for the studios.

The old 'pouch' system had gone. No longer was it a case of the studios' UK offshoots waiting for a special delivery of all the materials they would use in their own marketing campaigns. Nonetheless, the UK campaigns were often very close to those in the US. 'Nine times out of ten, the US campaign would be appropriate,' says George.[17]

There were signs that the 'gonzo' tactics used by some of the more enterprising video companies in the 1980s were being embraced by the majors too. This wasn't that surprising given that executives from Palace and PolyGram had taken up some of the most senior positions in the industry. For example, Daniel Battsek had been one of the most tenacious and innovative executives at Palace, renowned for his 'aggressive poster policies' (as Angus Finney notes) and creative approach to marketing.[18] 'If it was written that this was the way you did things by the book, we tore it up and did the opposite,' Battsek recalls of the Palace years. 'Our campaigns were very driven by publicity because that was the one thing we could afford. We couldn't buy TV ads like our competitors so we had to build awareness through editorial.'[19]

Battsek did his share of fly-posting. He and his team 'tented over Leicester Square' for the premiere of Julien Temple's *Absolute Beginners* (1986). They were equally inventive with other releases:

> I do remember that we decided the best way to publicise [gangster thriller] *The Hit* was to do a deal with the crookedest people we could find. We had the event for that in a bar above a Kentucky Fried Chicken in a very low-rent part of town. It was one of those things like not advertising a concert at a private venue by Prince. Everybody wanted to go and no one knew where it was!

This was the reverse of the usual West End premiere. The bar ended up 'rammed with people fighting to get drinks'. The guest list was eclectic and included 'some interesting types of a somewhat gangsterish disposition'. It was debatable whether the rest of the guests were enjoying themselves but Battsek's tactics were certainly making an impression.

Flash forward to the early 1990s and Battsek had been tasked by Jeffrey Katzenberg and Bill Mechanic at Disney with forming the studio's stand-alone distribution company, Buena Vista International, in London. He may have had the might of the 'Mouse House' behind him but BVI was set up originally in a buccaneering spirit reminiscent of Palace. 'Bill's attitude was that he didn't want Buena Vista to be just another international studio, peopled by someone from Warner Bros. here, somebody from Universal here, somebody from Sony here.'

The original team that Battsek put together all came from independent film companies or from outside the business. Battsek regarded himself as 'a left-field appointment' who had been chosen because of his connections with the British independent sector. The company started with a tiny staff of only Battsek, an assistant, a rented office and a kettle. At this stage, Disney wasn't releasing huge numbers of films. There were not yet Marvel superhero films or Pixar animated features under the Disney umbrella. Disney's animation studios were at an all-time low, albeit on the verge of a mighty renaissance. Nonetheless, BVI quickly grew.

One title which Battsek later nurtured at BVI, developed, fully financed and helped to turn into a huge international hit was Nigel Cole's *Calendar Girls* (2003), a whimsical and poignant comedy about some middle-aged, middle-class Yorkshire matrons who pose naked for a calendar in order to raise funds for cancer research. 'Rather than just take Buena Vista into the British film-making community and put a huge net out there, my feeling was that we needed to focus on a genre and work within that,' Battsek said.

He believed that British comedy had the best chance of travelling internationally. There were misfires. For example, *High Heels and Low Lifes* (2001), directed by comedian Mel Smith (who had also helmed Working Title's *Bean*) didn't work at the box office. This was an action comedy starring Minnie Driver about a nurse and her friend trying to blackmail some hardened criminals after eavesdropping on their heist. However, it was modestly budgeted. With a studio behind it and DVD as a safety net, its failure wasn't catastrophic. Meanwhile, *Calendar Girls*, in the year of its release, was the most profitable film on the Disney slate. Worldwide, *Calendar Girls* grossed almost $100 million at the box office – ten times its reported budget – and went on to sell very strongly on DVD too. It also helped to spawn a new genre of films aimed at older audiences – and often featuring older stars like Helen Mirren, Maggie Smith and Judi Dench in the leading roles. But just because it was targeting the 'grey pound' didn't mean BVI marketed it any less aggressively. 'I adapted my gonzo Palace stunts for an older demographic,' Battsek recalls.

27. Dropping everything for a good cause: Helen Mirren and Julie Walters, here promoting the upcoming release in Cannes, led the terrific ensemble cast of *Calendar Girls*. Co-scriptwriter Tim Firth has subsequently adapted the joyous work into a stage play and a musical, co-written with Gary Barlow.

Steve Finn, Getty Images

Calendar Girls wasn't selected for Cannes but that didn't stop BVI from taking it to the festival and giving it a screening in the market. The cast were all in attendance and so were the real-life matrons who had appeared nude in the calendar. A special tea party was arranged for them, complete with cucumber sandwiches. They were photographed on the beach as if they were Brigitte Bardot-like starlets.

Battsek and his team realised that the film, unlike most other releases, would work as well or better during weekdays than at weekends. Exhibitors noticed that it was attracting significant (older-skewing) audiences at times when cinemas tended to be at their quietest. They were prepared to give it a long run.

'It's an audience that grew up going to the cinema,' Battsek says of the older demographic.

They're not the sort of people who are watching movies on their iPhones and so why not make movies for them? They know what they like and can afford to go out. They enjoy going to the cinema and have never really grown out of the habit. The only thing they've grown out of the habit of is finding movies that actually speak to them.

As managing director of Warner Bros. UK, Nigel Sharrocks oversaw the release of the first three Harry Potter films, *The Philosopher's Stone* (2001), *The Chamber of Secrets* (2002) and *The Prisoner of Azkaban* (2004). Sharrocks, a highly successful advertising executive before he came into the film business, was tasked with making Potter the biggest success possible in the UK. The overall marketing campaign was overseen by Sue Kroll, president of marketing at Warner Bros. Pictures International.

'Firstly, because of the size of the film and the investment from the studio, even though it was made in Britain, to all intents and purposes, it felt like a studio picture with a worldwide release pattern,' Sharrocks recalls of *The Philosopher's Stone*.[20] This wasn't a case of slowly building an audience or using gonzo marketing tactics. The 'Harry Potter' brand and books were already known globally – the first four books had been published by the time the first film opened. Warner Bros.' task was to launch the first film as 'wide as we could and on as many screens as we could possibly get it on'. The pressure was on to make the opening 'huge'. The film series was going to be sold to the public partly on the basis of its own success. There were one or two days of previews for *The Philosopher's Stone* before the official release.

Sharrocks talks of waiting late at night for the 'EDI numbers' (the UK box-office gross receipts as reported by Entertainment Data, Inc.) to come in screen by screen. 'You've got a good idea of what those screens normally take for big movies and so you can project pretty quickly how big it is going to be.' The ambition was to make the film the biggest box-office success in UK history. Warner Bros. spent heavily hoping to achieve this. In the event, *The Philosopher's Stone* grossed $84.5 million in Britain, considerably less than the $114 million achieved by James Cameron's *Titanic* (1997) but still a huge number, especially given its relatively high proportion of child-price tickets. 'We just ran out of steam at the back end. Had we done another day of previews, we probably would have done it.'[21]

Harry Potter and the Philosopher's Stone was a phenomenon. Cinema screens playing it were packed. The joke among the execs was that the only way they could have increased the box office further would have been to build bigger car parks at the cinemas. The scale of the Potter series was underlined when, in 2001, Coca-Cola signed a £103 million multi-year deal to be the global marketing partner of the Potter series. Other huge brands, Lego and Mattel among them, also struck Potter deals.

Releasing Potter films wasn't just an exercise in 'blitzkrieg' tactics. Some guile was needed too. One of the bolder initiatives was to launch the third Harry Potter film, *The Prisoner of Azkaban*, on a Bank Holiday Monday – 31 May 2004, in spring half-term week – rather than waiting for the following Friday, 4 June (films traditionally opened on Fridays by this time, and that was the date when the film went out in the US). The result was one of the most successful weeks in UK box-office history.

Other US companies were equally enterprising in the way they marketed their films in the UK. As managing director of 20th Century Fox from 2006 to 2010, Ian George was handling some of the biggest franchises around, among them *X-Men* and the *Ice Age* animated features. He also oversaw the release of several smaller gems which came to the studio from its deal with UK production company (and lottery franchisee) DNA, or through its 'speciality' arm, Fox Searchlight. These included *Little Miss Sunshine*, *The Last King of Scotland*, *Notes on a Scandal* and *The History Boys*.

In theory, *The History Boys* was a tough sell. Adapted from an Alan Bennett play, it was about a group of very bright young students at a grammar school and their relationship with their larger-than-life, very camp history teacher, Hector (played by Richard Griffiths). George wasn't excited by the initial campaign that Fox devised. He suggested instead that *The History Boys* should be marketed as if its young leads were members of a boy band. He wanted the kids 'to look cool, a bit rebellious' and not like pimply schoolboys. The original stage production at London's National Theatre had been overseen by the same creative team (writer Bennett and director Nicholas Hytner) who had now made the movie, but George was determined to reach beyond the theatre lovers who had made the play such a success. The tactics helped the film to gross over $6.5 million at the UK box office.

'I do think there is definitely an audience still for quality British stories and for quirky British stories, but I think where we really struggle is when we try to ape America,' George suggests. 'They're fantastic at doing that; let them do that.'[22]

In the pre-digital era, there had been a sense of 'cause and effect' about film marketing. If a distributor spent 'X' amount of money, the box office would be 'Y'. That was changing. In the digital age, many costs were coming down. Thanks to Facebook and social media, the distributors were able to target their potential audiences far more precisely than ever before. No longer did they have to spend massive amounts on TV advertising or print campaigns. They may have been able to reach an audience of 20 million in the 1980s by advertising a film on TV in the breaks in an episode of a popular soap like *Coronation Street* but there was a huge amount of 'wastage' in the process. Their real interest was in only a small percentage of that audience. In the digital era, they could reach exactly the consumers they wanted without any wastage whatsoever.

The very notion of spending big amounts on outdoor advertising, on bus shelters, on buses themselves or on billboards, has also begun to seem old-fashioned. What is the point of paying for billboards when many potential customers are so busy looking down at their smartphones that they won't look up at the posters anyway? The same applies to newspapers and teen magazines. In the early 2000s, such publications had huge readerships and print ads would be seen by hundreds of thousands of people. A decade later, newspaper and magazine circulation have shrunk and the teenagers are communicating via Snapchat, Instagram and whatever other photo-sharing apps are today most popular. Now, the talk is of 'earned media', that's to say the coverage of films that distributors can generate through reviews, social media 'likes', reposts, endorsements from popular 'YouTubers' and shares.

For all its benefits, the technological changes have confronted film distributors with daunting new challenges. 'The explosion of content has made the job almost impossible,' George observes. 'With most films that we release now, every weekend, if you had spent double on that film, the result would have been the same and if you had spent half, the result would have been the same.'

It is a paradox. The audience is easier and less expensive than ever before to reach, but also more fragmented. As Kezia Williams puts it: 'You just can't reach large swathes of people within one medium.'[23]

Reaching them is anyway only part of the challenge. Consumers are becoming increasingly savvy and far more selective. They can find information about films long before their releases. If a new movie is damned on social media, they know about it instantly.

Another shift is that the US studios are far more controlling of how the films are marketed internationally than they were in the 'pouch' era. Foreign box office has become massively more important to their balance sheets than in the 1990s.

'The first time international box office revenues for studio movies surpassed domestic [US/Canada] was in 1997,' box-office analyst Stephen Follows noted.

> It was mostly due to the strong global performance of just three films: *Titanic* (70% of the global take came internationally), *Men in Black* (57%) and *The Lost World: Jurassic Park* (63%). But it wasn't until 2003 when international revenues came to over-shadow the domestic market for good.[24]

As Hollywood's focus on international markets increased, so did its concern about how its wares were presented abroad. Nigel Sharrocks says:

> You've only got one shot at these things. The balance of risk and reward in changing something that might have worked in the US and maybe doing something slightly different in the UK was probably a risk not worth taking.[25]

The emphasis now was on 'global consistency' and making sure that films were marketed in the same way pretty much everywhere. If they were already successful in the US, there would be little appetite to develop new customised campaigns elsewhere.

Decision-making processes have changed. No longer are campaigns for films being put together well in advance. Now, everything tends to be done at the last minute. Decisions are postponed for as long as possible. Distributors can then respond instantly to tracking or what is being said on Twitter or Instagram or by the critics. If the response to a film on social media is negative, they can do some damage limitation and 'try to change the conversation'. Newspaper circulation may be falling but the influence of leading film critics is rising. That is because their reviews are aggregated on websites like Rotten Tomatoes, which audiences turn to in huge numbers – and if a film is deemed to be not fresh on the 'Tomatometer', audiences are more likely to turn their noses up at it.

'Tracking and research don't lie,' the distributors were told. At the same time, they all still talk of the importance of 'gut instinct'. They don't just mould marketing campaigns on the basis of the huge amount of focus group data available to them. 'That's not your job. You're not paid just to do research and then act on research,' says George. 'Your job is to use experience, guile, intuition, as well as common sense, to work out the most appropriate marketing tools you have.'[26]

Besides, tracking isn't always fail-safe anyway. It's akin to political opinion polls. In the US, pollsters were wrong about the 2016 presidential election when Donald Trump was elected. In Europe, many polls about the likely result of the Brexit referendum were likewise very wayward. There are examples of films that hadn't been noticed by the public, or that had scored badly in focus-group screenings, but then performed much better than expected when they were finally released. And the tracking may work on big studio blockbusters, but it isn't much use with smaller, independent films for which audience awareness has to be built gradually.

Piracy remains an issue. One of the ironies is that the distributors are sometimes making the pirates' jobs easier. They upload trailers on YouTube, whetting the appetites of the fans, but then a pirated copy of the actual movie might be posted alongside the trailer and all those fans can watch the film illegally. The distributors have succeeded in creating interest in the movie but not necessarily in getting the fans into the cinemas.

The knowledge that distributors have about their customers is more sophisticated and comprehensive than it has ever been before. Not only can they narrow it down to age, class and demographics, but they know now precisely which others films the cinemagoers have seen and liked.

Distributors may be able to target these consumers more precisely than ever before but that, itself, is a problem. They are getting the message about any given film out to those in the 'core' audience who may already want to see it. What they aren't always managing to do is reach the 'persuadable' further audience who might be prepared to take a gamble on a movie if the buzz and marketing catch their imagination. Marketing veteran Paul Lewis suggests:

> If you're dealing with a franchise movie with a huge budget, and you can buy a massive amount of television and digital [advertising], then it's fine, but when you're dealing in a middle ground of movies where you've got to make your money work harder, you can make it [the campaign] run very efficiently online, but you end up becoming so targeted that there's a risk you haven't become the event that people feel they need to go and see.[27]

What is apparent is the resourcefulness of British distributors. In a hi-tech world, they still often achieve the best results from using traditional grassroots marketing techniques to build an audience. For example, eOne went to extraordinary lengths to ensure that Ken Loach's Palme d'Or winner, *I, Daniel Blake* (2016), reached as big a British audience as possible. This is a film about a 59-year-old joiner in Newcastle who has a heart attack and has to stop working. He is confronted with a Kafkaesque and unsympathetic welfare system. Made in Loach's familiar social realism style, *I, Daniel Blake* was a polemical film in which the director was trying to highlight how he felt 'the most vulnerable people in society are being humiliated, impoverished and put through terrible hardship in a very cruel way [...] that's happening throughout Europe'.[28] A popcorn movie this wasn't.

'It [the film] felt so relevant in the wake of Brexit and a heightened interest in debate and politics in the UK,' says eOne's Kezia Williams, who oversaw the release.[29] Williams and her team were determined to make sure that the campaign for the film didn't seem 'London-centric' and that it appealed to a wider demographic than 'the natural *Guardian*-reading audience who loved Ken Loach'.

> We didn't even want it to feel like people in London had cre-
> ated this marketing campaign. We wanted genuinely to give
> it [the campaign] organic roots in the north [of England] and
> in Scotland – in places where we hoped the film would really
> resonate.

With this in mind, eOne hired regional marketing executives all over Britain to work on the film. They also worked very closely with trade unions and the Labour Party itself. Facebook had alerted them to the fact that the trailer wasn't just being picked up on by film lovers but also by political activists. The distributors were told (in the language of the day) that their 'algorithms were becoming very strong in a way that is unusual for a piece of film content'.

The distributors held screenings for all the different political parties at their autumn conferences, and MPs talked about the film in Parliament, drawing attention in particular to its harrowing and heart-breaking scenes of a young mother failed by the welfare state, unable to feed her family and obliged to use food banks. 'Sick and disabled people are also more likely to be hit by social security sanctions and forced to use food banks, as the film *I, Daniel Blake* so poignantly showed,' Debbie Abrahams, Labour MP for Oldham East and Saddleworth, commented during a debate in the House of Commons on government welfare policy.[30]

The campaign wasn't just about maximising box office. Equally important for Loach and the distributors was the possibility of changing government policy. In early November 2016, Labour Party leader Jeremy Corbyn stood up at Prime Minister's Questions and encouraged the Prime Minister, Theresa May, to go and see the film in the hope that it might persuade her to change what he called the 'institutionalised barbarity' of the welfare system.[31]

I, Daniel Blake took over $4 million at the UK box office, an impressive amount for a low-budget, polemical drama without stars. Distributors eOne had defied conventional wisdom and had shown that politics could be a draw in cinemas.

British distributors will sometimes spend years developing campaigns for films. This was certainly the case with Steven Spielberg's *The BFG*, which eOne also released in 2016. Spielberg had worked very closely with UK marketing executives right from the start of his career. One executive, Gerry Lewis, had been working for Cinema International Corporation, the joint UK distribution venture between Paramount and Universal, when he was sent various made-for-TV movies to see if there was any scope for releasing them theatrically. In the words of his son, Paul Lewis (also a marketing executive), most were 'rubbish'. One, though, caught his eye, a film called *Duel* (1971), which was Spielberg's debut. It was released on a double bill with a low-budget British horror film, *Asylum*, and the respectful reviews it received from certain leading British critics helped to ignite the young director's career. Spielberg admired Lewis' work on his behalf and continued to work with him throughout his career; both Gerry and Paul Lewis were to work directly for DreamWorks SKG, the studio created by Spielberg with Jeffrey Katzenberg and David Geffen in the 1990s. Even after leaving DreamWorks, Gerry Lewis continued to serve as Spielberg's overseas marketing consultant.

In Williams' words, eOne made 'a very big play' to be allowed to create a 'bespoke' campaign for *The BFG* in the UK. They wanted to play up the British elements. The British distributor also emphasised the Roald Dahl connection (2016 marked the centenary of Dahl's birth) and the TV ads made sure that the corgis were in the foreground (the Queen features prominently in the story). Entertainment One worked for two years preparing the release of *The BFG*. Their preparations paid off. The film grossed $40 million at the UK box office, a very strong figure for a film that underperformed in other markets (for example, grossing only $55 million in the US).

The problems facing UK distribution today remain acute. There are still too many films – 122 suppliers providing 900 releases in 2016 – chasing too few film-goers. The market remains heavily polarised. Trading terms are still onerous and not helped by the 'Virtual Print Fee', which obliges distributors to pay for most of the costs of the installation of digital equipment in cinemas.

Everyone knows the problems. Nonetheless, the contrast with 1984/5 is startling. In the three decades since British Film Year, the distribution sector has become very much more resourceful and dynamic than in the years when Rank and EMI were going through the motions. From the majors to the independents, there is huge energy and chutzpah in everything from dating releases to digital marketing. That gloomy sense in the mid-1980s that the industry was in its death throes has long since been vanquished.

CASE STUDY
PADDINGTON (2014)

In the toxic political atmosphere of pre-Brexit Britain, it perhaps wasn't all that surprising that a little bear from Peru should be seen as a beacon of tolerance and decency. Paddington, the marmalade-loving bear in question, arrived on screen in Paul King's 2014 feature just as debates in Britain about immigration were becoming very heated indeed.

'This is propaganda for the little un's, apparently designed to ensure they never vote Ukip. Paddington, who has always been London's best loved illegal immigrant, here stands for every other immigrant,' the *Spectator* magazine wrote of the film, referring to the Eurosceptic, right-wing and proudly intolerant UK Independence Party.[32] Somehow, the little bear, created by author Michael Bond in 1958, became caught up in arguments about Britishness. In his blue duffel coat and red hat, he was regarded by many as a very British figure indeed, even if he had arrived at Paddington Station without proper papers. The Brown family took him in and treated him as one of their own but there were nasty neighbours who wanted him sent straight back to deepest, darkest Peru.

Harry Potter producer David Heyman announced his plans to make a big-screen version of *Paddington* in 2007. He had optioned the book and was developing the project with Warner Bros., his partners on the Potter franchise, but Warner Bros. got cold paws. The film finally made seven years later was produced and distributed by StudioCanal, the French company which had offices all around Europe.

'It was a great opportunity to work with someone like David Heyman and to be involved in a project that was anchored in Europe but could travel everywhere,' Ron Halpern, StudioCanal's executive vice president of international production and acquisitions, told film trade publication *Deadline*.

> It doesn't make sense for us to make a film about a bunch of kids running around a U.S. city. We don't add any value there. But with the film set in London, and given the history of films like *Mary Poppins*, *Harry Potter* and [*The Chronicles of*] *Narnia*, we knew that audiences around the world get British children.[33]

In other words, the Britishness was one of the main selling points. Paddington stood for an idealised vision of the UK: a country where (at least on screen) decency and tolerance still ruled. This was part of its attraction to British audiences. It was offering a reassuring and old-fashioned picture of a consensus that, in real life, had long since fractured. *Paddington* was a European-made movie with a budget of $55 million but StudioCanal marketed it with an energy that few US studio releases could match. Paddington statues popped up all over London. There were tie-ins (marmalade in department stores, advertising with VisitLondon, a special campaign with Hamleys gigantic toy store on Regent Street) and huge amounts of social media activity. Even bakers got in on the act. Warburton's rebranded its loaves as 'War-bear-tons' and offered cut-price tickets to kids who bought the bread, presumably in the hope that they'd follow Paddington's example and eat marmalade sandwiches too.

Paddington survived a minor controversy just prior to release when it was given a PG certificate (Parental Guidance) by the British Board of Film Classification (BBFC) rather than a U and the media mischievously suggested it was for sex references and bad language! It went on to become one of the highest-grossing non-Hollywood films ever, spawned an impressive 2017 sequel, and established a new British movie franchise in the process.

CHAPTER 12

Stepping Up

In the summer of 2017, when Britain's Office for National Statistics (ONS) issued its quarterly report, one piece of data stood out. Growth in the UK economy as a whole was sluggish at 0.3 per cent from April to June. However, the largest contributors to growth and services were retail and film production and distribution. Over these three months, 'motion picture activities' grew by 8.2 per cent and 'contributed 0.07 percentage points to GDP growth'.[1]

This was a very stark contrast to 1984, when cinemas were closing, capital allowances for films were phased out and it was announced that the Eady Levy was to be abolished. Back then, the question was whether the British film industry would survive at all, not whether it could stimulate employment and growth. The idea that, three decades later, film would be one of the fastest-growing sectors in the economy would have seemed unthinkable. Nonetheless, thanks to the UK's much-vaunted film studios, its technicians and its generous tax credit, which had also been extended to high-end TV drama, production activity and inward investment were at record levels.

In the late summer of 2017, the BFI launched its Future Film Skills plan for growing the industry further. Its prediction was that 30,000 new jobs would be available in the industry over the next five years. 'Once you factor in the effects of Brexit, it is clear that even more home-grown skills will be needed,' the report predicted as it outlined a new programme to increase the size and diversity of the workforce in film and TV.[2] Business, it appeared, was booming.

'What we are looking at is a fantastically, wonderfully buoyant sector,' the BFI's chief executive Amanda Nevill told the trade press in a briefing in summer 2017.

> We all know about aerospace, we all know about pharmaceu-ticals and we all know about finance, but somehow, because film, television, special effects and animation are so pleasur-able perhaps, we often forget that they are a huge and growing economic driver.[3]

This was boosterish rhetoric but the statistics appeared to bear out Nevill's remarks. Fifty-six features had begun production in the first three months of 2017 alone – and that figure didn't include the increasing numbers of TV dramas. The growth of British film and TV was (Nevill said) 'a good news story' at a time of depressing headlines elsewhere. 'The great thing about the UK is that what we seem to have mastered is that growth is about the fusion of the technical and the storytelling skills.'

Of course, the idea that British cinema had been almost moribund in the mid-1980s and has miraculously revived over the following three decades is somewhat simplistic. As this book has attempted to show, the film 'business' has grown. The efforts of companies from Goldcrest and Palace in the 1980s to PolyGram in the 1990s have galvanised the sector. From the Downing Street summit of 1990 onward, there has been consistent government support of the industry. Lottery money and tax credits have underwritten production. The decade of the Film Council, from 2000 to 2010, helped professionalise the industry. The broadcasters played a crucial role in supporting new film-making talent.

The distribution and exhibition sectors were transformed. In 1995, for example, Stephen Wiener had founded Cine-UK, opening its first 'Cineworld' multiplex in a relatively small yet underserved town, Stevenage, the following year. The son of a New York truck driver, Wiener loved the movies. As a child he used to sneak into his local cinema and later got a job in the exhibition business at Warner Bros. When the studio transferred him to lead its cinema operations in the

UK in 1991, it was the first time he had been abroad. Warners intended to help reinvigorate UK cinema with new multiplexes, then move on to other underperforming markets around the world. Wiener identified an opportunity in the UK and, with his wife, wrote a business plan for their own cinema company. They'd expected to build a small circuit with a handful of sites and sell it on to a larger operator. In the event, their management team and investors stayed the course and Cineworld expanded rapidly. In October 2004, now with some 35 cinemas, the company was acquired by Blackstone Group, a US-based private equity firm. Two months later it announced the acquisition of UGC Cinemas (formerly the Virgin circuit), which were rebranded as Cineworld. By December 2012, when Cineworld took over the Picturehouse chain of city-centre cinemas, it was the UK's largest cinema operator and Steve Wiener had retired and returned to America.

The UK now has more than 750 cinemas with over 4,000 'digital' screens. Three-quarters of these screens are in purpose-built multiplexes. The first digital cinema projector in the UK – succeeding 35 mm celluloid reels – was trialled at the Odeon, Leicester Square for the release of Disney/Pixar's digitally animated *Toy Story 2* (February 2000). It was a Texas Instruments Digital Light Processing system with a server and a projector housing three optical chips, each containing an array of tiny computer-controlled mirrors which would turn beams of light into high-resolution images on the screen. With digital presentation, there were no reels that might snap or scratch; every showing could be as pristine as the first.

As we saw in Chapter 6, the Film Council launched its Digital Screen Network in 2005. It was a lottery-backed initiative to convert over 200 cinema screens UK-wide to digital, to encourage more specialised, independent films to be shown. Nevertheless, all of the US studios encouraged the UK-first intervention. Today, the UK cinema estate is fully digital, with just a handful of 35 mm projectors remaining in situ for archive screenings. This has been much more than just a change in format – digital systems have enabled 'event cinema' (operas, plays and other entertainments) to develop, while screen programmes around the UK can be remote-controlled from their circuits' head offices.

Three-quarters of the population goes to the cinema at least once a year. The industry, by common consensus, has become more outward-facing. The Harry Potter and Bond movies, Marvel's superhero and Disney's *Star Wars* films have ensured that Britain has become the home of the blockbuster.

However, whether British film 'culture' is richer now than in the 1980s remains open to debate. British film history is always open to radically different interpretations.

'The tax credit has turned out to be more important than any of us realised,' FDA president David Puttnam reflected in the summer of 2017 on the single measure most responsible for the boom in activity. 'The correct thing is to say we've become a film-making nation as opposed to a film-creating nation. You could argue that we're so busy making that we have no time for creating.' Puttnam suggests that the UK has become 'a successful film-making factory, very successful, probably more successful than any of us would have imagined 20 or 30 years ago'.[4]

To extend the metaphor, the question now is how that factory copes when there is a downturn. As Puttnam acknowledges, the industry has been very dependent on a handful of individuals. Remove J. K. Rowling (the Harry Potter creator) and David Heyman (the Potter producer), and take away Barbara Broccoli and Michael G. Wilson (who oversee the Bond franchise), and the business might quickly begin to stutter. 'That's worrying. Where are the next generation coming from?' Puttnam asks. 'The problem is that we are not producing enough talent.'

It has been instructive to listen to independent producers discussing the state of the industry. They are far less upbeat than Nevill about the possibilities for film-making in Britain.

'It [independent production] is almost impossible at the moment because the value of the international market has fallen so much,' producer Andy Paterson told *Screen International*.[5] His point was clear. Big American companies might be coming to the UK in record numbers to shoot film and TV dramas but indigenous British film-makers are struggling to get their movies financed, let alone seen. They can no longer rely on foreign pre-sales to complete their budgets. 'A model we've used for 20 years really doesn't work any more,' Paterson said.

In the late spring of 2017, UK producers' body PACT had issued a report, *The State of the UK Independent Film Sector*. It makes for downbeat reading. The report reveals that 78 per cent of the British producers canvassed by PACT's researchers have had to defer some or all of their fees since 2007.[6] Given that these producers were often completely dependent on fees for making any money from their movies whatsoever (and often had to give up rights to profits to other financiers in order to get the films made), this meant that they were still living a completely hand-to-mouth existence.

Look back to the 1980s when British production was seemingly in the doldrums and you will see a decade in which 'talent' was emerging just as quickly as it was in 2017. Supported by the BFI Production Board, Terence Davies was making his first films, the 'Trilogy', and then, in 1988, his Golden Leopard winner, *Distant Voices, Still Lives*, about growing up in a working-class Liverpool family.

The 1980s and early 1990s are described by critic Michael Brooke as 'a golden era' for the BFI Production Board, a time when directors like Davies, Sally Potter, Margaret Tait, Derek Jarman, Peter Wollen and Laura Mulvey, and Peter Greenaway were making films with its support.[7] As academic and producer Colin MacCabe, who ran the Production Board from 1985 until 1989, recalled, the set-up was akin to that of a mini studio. 'I had cutting rooms, I had technical staff, I had people selling, I had people distributing. It was a time of incredible enthusiasm [...] Our job was to make films that would please long [into the future] as well as a few at the time,'[8] MacCabe remembers of a period in which Working Title was making Derek Jarman movies like *Caravaggio* with the BFI rather than romantic comedies.

Precisely because the British industry seemed so sclerotic and hidebound, it was possible for a new generation of film-makers, producers and distributors to make a mark. This was the era in which Palace emerged (see Chapter 2) and maverick independent companies like Virgin and Hemdale backed major movies. Jeremy Thomas was winning Oscars with *The Last Emperor*. Andi Engel was expanding Artificial Eye, the most adventurous of the British art-house distribution companies. In the early 1980s, Engel had borrowed money to open the Lumière cinema in St Martin's Lane, a venue in the tourist heartland, the West End, at which there would be queues around the block for the latest Krzysztof Kieślowski or Peter Greenaway movies. (Artificial Eye's other venues, the Chelsea Cinema on the King's Road and the Renoir in Russell Square also did very brisk business.) Romaine Hart's distribution company, Mainline Pictures, had its own cinemas, too, among them the Screen on the Hill and the Screen on the Green (both in north London), which programmed independent and foreign-language fare. The Gate Cinema in Notting Hill did likewise.

It's easy to fall prey to false nostalgia but in London, at least, the 1980s were an exciting period for independent distribution. The market wasn't yet as dominated by the US majors as it was to become. Channel 4 and the BBC were regularly programming foreign-language and independent movies. Early in its existence, Channel 4 held seasons of films by François Truffaut, Jean-Luc Godard and Rainer Werner Fassbinder, among others. This helped stimulate the curiosity of audiences who would then go to see the work of these directors in cinemas.

It helped that US independent distributors had rediscovered their appetite for British films. The joke among producers was that whereas these companies had looked for 'Swinging London' films in the late 1960s, now they wanted 'burning London' films – movies which reflected the tensions and undercurrent of violence in Thatcher's Britain.

There was even the utopian dream of an alternative industry that wasn't dependent on Hollywood. The AIP briefly became the voice of a new generation of film-makers who aspired to make movies reflecting life in British society and who weren't simply concerned with box-office receipts.

Throughout the last 30 years, outstanding British films have continued to be made, but the work of directors like Clio Barnard, William Oldroyd, Terence Davies, Lynne Ramsay and Andrea Arnold still feels marginal. Their films achieve relatively modest box office and are invariably eclipsed by the huge British-made but Hollywood-produced blockbusters being shot at Pinewood and Leavesden. Their producers struggle to build businesses.

The paradox is so obvious that it hardly needs observing. In 2016, expenditure on making films in the UK reached the highest level since records began in 1994, at £1.6 billion – and yet many producers were in just as invidious a position as they had been in 1984.

Meanwhile, the extreme volatility of the film distribution business remains clear to see, as the market share of any distributor rises and falls from year to year according to the films on its release slate. In 1983 and again in 1994, the Monopolies and Mergers Commission (MMC) examined the film sector, producing thorough, well-informed reports. In 1994 it made two recommendations that sought to increase competition in the supply of films to cinemas, keeping pace with the changes in the sector which by now had numerous substantial circuits (including UCI, Showcase and Warner cinemas), not simply the 'duopoly' of Odeon and ABC/MGM. The MMC's measures restricted the minimum period of exhibition for a first-run film to two weeks, and brought about an end to 'alignment', the booking practice whereby certain circuits had favoured relationships with certain distributors. In the multiplex era, such practices were completely outmoded.

Independent British distributors face particular travails. In an increasingly polarised market, in which a handful of US studio titles accounted for a huge proportion of overall profits, these distributors are fighting over what, relatively speaking, are breadcrumbs. In 2015, 853 films were released in British cinemas but the top ten on their own generated close to 40 per cent of all ticket sales. The share of box office is dropping for films outside the top 40. Industry analysts comScore revealed that, in the last ten years, while the number of UK cinema visits has remained broadly level, the quantity of films released has more than doubled.[9]

Nonetheless, the arguments that the industry has been transformed for the better are overwhelming. Admissions to British cinemas slipped to 54 million in 1984. Thirty years later, admissions had stabilised at around the 170 million mark (see Appendix). Increases in ticket prices haven't diluted the numbers of cinemagoers. Even if the independent sector is still struggling, the business as a whole is markedly more buoyant and dynamic than it was in the 1980s.

The film industry has won a fundamental argument with the politicians. Both the Thatcher and the Blair governments had accepted the economic case the industry had made on its own behalf. The debate about public intervention in the film industry is no longer couched in cultural terms. The politicians have been won over by talk of inward investment and exports. Movies generate tax revenues and employment; they put the nation's goods in the shop window. They are a fundamental part of the creative industries – and government sees those industries as crucial.

'It was a terribly depressing time to come out of film school into this film industry that was on the floor,' remembers distributor–exhibitor Philip Knatchbull of the mid-1980s, the period in which this study starts.[10] Those entering the film business were looking to pop promos and commercials as the most likely way of getting into production. Film itself was 'impossibly difficult'. The industry seemed stuck in a time warp. Innovation was frowned on. Before the MMC report of 1994, barring was still practised by exhibitors. Knatchbull discovered as much when he tried to open a small cinema in Richmond on the disused site of a former Gaumont and found himself targeted both by Odeon, which had a covenant to stop rival operators from using its sites, including old Gaumonts, as cinemas, and by independent distributors, who wouldn't let his venue have films.

These, though, were the perfect conditions for rebirth. The story of Knatchbull's faltering attempts to run a little cinema in Richmond seems in hindsight like a parable about the British industry as a whole. No one wanted the cinema to succeed and no one believed that it would. The local council raised objections. The landlord refused to accept that Knatchbull wanted to run a cinema. He was told that everyone else had looked at the site – the majors and the independents alike – and had decided that it wasn't viable. Knatchbull was fresh out of film school, with no experience. No one else wanted to run the Richmond Filmhouse cinema but they weren't going to let Knatchbull do it either. Knatchbull's complaints to the Office of Fair

Trading resulted in the MMC's full-blown inquiry into restrictive practices in film supply.

The saviour, as was so often the case in this period of British cinema, was the tireless Dickie Attenborough, who lived in Richmond. He made a tub-thumping speech to the inquiry, saying that the industry desperately needed young entrepreneurs like Knatchbull. The landlord's QC tried to argue that cinema was dead as a medium. In the end, the landlord reluctantly agreed to give Knatchbull a lease. 'That was when my troubles really began,' he jokes. Odeon didn't want him there and denied him permission to use the site. 'They just blanked me completely and said no.' He therefore called the indomitable Attenborough into action.

Attenborough contacted Odeon and made a passionate case as to why Knatchbull should be allowed to run the cinema, covenant or no covenant. As ever, he was so persuasive that the big exhibition chain relented, albeit only on the condition that Knatchbull paid them compensation. 'I started looking [at the site] in 1984 but I didn't open until '89.'[11]

When he did finally open the site, no one would give him any films. He couldn't get any of the mainstream titles that were going into the local Odeon but nor was he able to book the independent titles. 'We showed crap, basically, or really old rep,' he recalls. Knatchbull persevered, though, and the cinema flourished, at least for a time.

Thirty years on, the film-making infrastructure in the UK is far more robust and extensive than ever seemed possible in the 1980s, as Knatchbull was first trying to open his little cinema in Richmond at a time when audience numbers had shrunk to their lowest ever. A huge transformation has taken place since then.

'Compared to what it was, it is like a day on the beach. There are so many financing opportunities for films today and so many films being made,' Knatchbull suggests. 'The industry has absolutely changed out of all recognition. I think the culture is taking longer to change. The ability to finance, book and distribute films – it is a proper business now.'

Up to a dozen new films are being released into the UK market each week (as opposed to the three or four features 30 years ago). The problem now is one of oversupply.

28. Transformative: digital projection systems, which have replaced 35 mm celluloid equipment, have redefined what the cinema can be for contemporary audiences. As well as movies, digital venues have greater flexibility to offer 'event cinema' presentations. Since the digital roll-out, accelerated by the huge (3D) success of James Cameron's *Avatar* (2009), the sheer number of weekly releases available to cinemas has soared.

Getty Images

The industry remains in flux, just as it always has been. Digitisation ('the fourth industrial revolution', as it has been dubbed) has caused as much disruption as the conversion to sound or the arrival of television as a mass medium. The talk now is of data analytics and of social media as a marketing tool. Some exhibitors have begun to refer to their venues as 'entertainment hubs' where, as Sony Digital Cinema premium content executive John Bullen put it in an interview with *Screen International*, 'you can go and have myriad cultural experiences on screen'.[12]

'Cinema will be an antiquated term in a few years' time,' Bullen predicted, suggesting that what used to be called the cinema would now be defined as a communal space where audiences could enjoy all sorts of 'digital content', whether it's gaming, live theatre, sports or music.

Opinion is sharply divided as to whether the UK film industry is on the brink of a new golden age – or about to re-enter the dark ages. Ben Luxford, BFI's head of UK audiences, spoke to *Sight & Sound* about the disappearance of foreign-language films from British cinemas. He tried to put the dip in context – 'Foreign language has only ever been at best knocking on two per cent of the market for the year' – but suggested that foreign-language and 'independent' cinema are suffering because the old distribution models are fracturing. 'The opportunity to take risks in the first [theatrical] window is less and less because of the lack of a meaningful back end on these films,' he said. Broadcasters aren't buying foreign-language fare, the DVD market is in decline and VoD isn't making up the shortfall in revenue.[13]

At the same time, others see a new world of plenty. In the 1980s, independent distributors could release films on cinema and VHS and maybe sell them to free TV. Today, there are 'multiple' platforms on which they can reach their audience and many more ways of 'monetising content'. They can license work not just to VoD giants like Netflix and Amazon, but to a host of smaller players too. They can sell airline rights. Even if their film underperforms in its home market, they can still make it work internationally, on TV or on the home entertainment platforms.

'Is film dead?' That was the question some pundits were asking in the autumn of 2017. This was even the theme of the Zurich Summit for Film, Technology and Business during the Zurich Film Festival that year. A slow summer for box office in the US, the collapse of the foreign sales market, the disruptive influence of Netflix, excessive ticket prices, 'franchise' fatigue and the ageing profile of the audience have all been cited as symptoms of the industry's perhaps terminal decline. Just as in the UK in 1984, when this study starts, there are plenty of Cassandra-types forecasting the worst. The delegates in Zurich may have been talking about the US industry but the point now is that everything is interrelated. Many of the Hollywood films that have underperformed have been shot in British studios or had their VFX done by British companies.

One of the biggest problems in the independent sector, prominent American producer and sales agent Greg Shapiro told the delegates, is the parlous state of UK distribution. Whereas in the past, one of the high-profile US productions with which he was associated (films like *The Hurt Locker* or *Child 44*) would look to attract well over 10 per cent of its overall budget by pre-selling to a British distributor, Britain can no longer be factored in as a reliable source of funding. Big independent distributors in the UK always appear to be skirting close to severe financial problems. It costs them fortunes to launch their films into the market and if one or two of those films doesn't perform they will find themselves saddled with debts they couldn't repay.

The UK film financiers are also in a state of perturbation. They are relying heavily on the government's Enterprise Investment Scheme (EIS) to incentivise investors to support British film production. However, the government is continually tinkering with the regulations surrounding EIS. The financiers fear that their investors will either be frightened away or prevented from benefiting from the EIS relief as part of the so-called 'Patience Capital Review'. They fired off letters to the Chancellor of the Exchequer, warning that EIS underpinned independent film-making in the UK. Without it, production levels would plummet. Veteran film financier and producer Paul Brett (whose credits included Oscar winner *The King's Speech*) warned the government that

> international soft financing structures in Europe, Canada, Australia and New Zealand, with their strong tax credits (some yielding over 40 per cent of qualifying spend), are realities which the British Film and TV industry must compete and work with. Removing EIS as a financing tool from British film and television will have an utterly destructive effect on these industries. We find it incomprehensible that this prospect should even be considered. It may well be the expert's view (or HMRC's approach) that the EIS rules need to be reviewed but the emasculation of EIS is completely irrational and economically unsound.

Brett predicted 'havoc and destruction' in the film and TV sectors if the government pressed ahead with proposed changes.[14]

Some of the same financiers had written similar letters after so-called 'Black Tuesday' more than a decade before, when the GAAP schemes had been outlawed (see Chapter 10). In the event, the furore over the loss of EIS turned out to be misplaced. The Treasury listened to the film industry and accepted their arguments. However, all the anxiety that was unleashed points to the cyclical nature of the British film business. Each generation seems to hold variations of the same debates, even as the film business evolves.

The Brexit referendum result has been another source of extreme uncertainty. The EU's MEDIA Programme, of which the UK is a part, has provided both generous support for single projects 'with international potential for cinema, television or digital platforms' and substantial 'slate funding' (funding for a number of different projects rather than just for an individual film). Some of the UK's best-known and most adventurous companies are beneficiaries of the slate funding, among them Sixteen Films (*I, Daniel Blake*), Number 9 Films (*Carol, Their Finest*), Baby Cow (*Philomena*) and See-Saw (*The King's Speech*). European Union MEDIA money has also been seeping into TV drama, animation and documentary projects, underwriting training programmes, subsidising UK-based markets and co-financing forums, supporting the distribution and sales of UK films internationally and boosting independent exhibition through a pan-European cinema network, Europa Cinemas, which has many British members. The referendum result of June 2016 raises the very real threat that this support would be removed.

Another vexing subject relating to Europe is the proposal for a connected Digital Single Market (DSM). 'Europeans will soon be able to fully use their online subscriptions to films, sports events, e-books, video games or music services when travelling within the EU,' a press release blithely said of the agreement reached by the European Commission on 'portability' in early 2017. That is one issue. Another is the idea that as soon as a film is available digitally in one European country, it will be available everywhere else too. Some European politicians are pushing for this, seemingly oblivious to the way that films are financed and released. These politicians fail to acknowledge the principle of 'territoriality', the way that films are licensed and shown in countries one by one.

'Within Brussels, they think this is a wonderfully populist and popular announcement to make,' David Garrett, founder and CEO of international sales company Mister Smith, told film trade website *Deadline* in late 2016.

> But this is Trumpism or Brexitism at its worst – selling the idea of freely-available content across Europe without anyone understanding the repercussions of making it available is putting everything in the hands of large corporations that can control content across the board. It's frankly insane.

'Film distributors invest millions of pounds, dollars and euros in effectively adapting a film for their territory,' Garrett continued.

> They translate it, market it, and create vast amounts of advertising for titles, and they deserve to reap the rewards of promoting a title in their territory if they can. If these regulations come into place, we can't finance these independent titles and it would completely destroy our business.[15]

Yet another concern is EU state aid regulations. Measures like the film tax credit and even EIS have to be approved by the European Union. Post-Brexit, the British in theory would no longer have to seek EU state aid approval and could shift the value of film tax credit up yet further if they so desired. Doing so, though, would be to risk a mini trade war or 'arms race'. Many other countries in Europe and beyond offer fiscal incentives to film-makers. If the British increased the value of their incentives, it would be inevitable that other European states would either complain or bring their own incentives into line.

As former Arts Council chairman Peter Bazalgette noted in his September 2017 Creative Industries Report, 'Other countries have sought to emulate the UK's success and have developed their own Creative Industries strategies.' These other countries were clearly 'targeting the same Foreign Direct Investment, overseas talent and export markets as UK businesses'.[16] The competition was severe. Bazalgette also noted that the creative industries, including film, are still overwhelmingly based in London and the south-east and still full of white middle-class types. 'If you were a kid from a deprived background and your parents were ambitious for you, the last thing they'd want you to do is go into the creative industries,' Bazalgette commented at the launch of his report.

> They'd regard it as worse, probably, than drug dealing or prostitution. Why would that be? Because it doesn't look like a proper career path. We in this room know it's a proper career path, but I don't believe we've properly communicated it.[17]

Today, then, there is arguably even more turbulence within the industry than there had been in 1984, when the Thatcher government was busily cutting public support at every level of the industry. There is still anguished talk about the plight of independent British producers and distributors and the threat to cinema from other leisure forms.

Alan Parker reflects on the landscape in the summer of 2017:

> In the UK, we have always punched above our weight, and with the BFI as a passive, almost mute, leader, maybe a cottage industry is all we will ever have or deserve – sitting alongside a rich, service industry that employs our skilled technicians.[18]

He pointed out, though, that these were halcyon days for British television, with British production companies really thriving and, amazingly, cashing in around the world. Parker even acknowledged the hope that new technologies and ways of consuming film result in the 'death knell of the US studios' hegemony'.

It helps, too, that the British industry now has a mirror in which to see its own reflection. That is perhaps an overly poetic way of referring to the Research and Statistics Unit (RSU) set up in the early Film Council years. One of the reasons politicians are now able to crow about the strength of British cinema is that they have data at their fingertips which tells them everything from how many movies are being shot in the UK to how many tickets are being sold at the box office.

The unit was launched in early 2001 under former Nielsen EDI managing director Steve Perrin. Its origins lay in the 1998 *Bigger Picture* film policy review when committee members realised to their dismay that they were facing a complete shortage of 'accurate, up to date and comprehensive information on the performance of the industry'.[19]

As veteran analyst Sean Perkins, who worked at the RSU between 2001 and 2017, recalls: 'It [the RSU] was all about being able to understand data better from across the industry because although data existed within individual elements of the film value chain, it was fairly compartmentalised within those individual silos.'[20]

'The lack of authoritative, widely available statistics for UK film, video and television, is both a symptom and a cause of the troubles affecting the industry,' the BFI itself acknowledged in the *BFI Film and Television Handbook 1993*.[21] Perkins points to the confusion that existed before the unit was set up: 'It was difficult to measure the direction of travel of the industry because of this lack of narrative.'[22]

The information garnered was vital not just for public bodies like the Film Council (who wanted to measure the effect of their own policies) and to the politicians and civil servants at the DCMS or HMRC deciding how investment into the sector should be handled. It was also of equal importance for the private sector.

'The UK film industry is characterised by the relatively large number of small businesses. Those businesses lack the infrastructural capabilities or analytical sense to make the most of market data,' Perkins observes, drawing a sharp distinction between the UK and the US studios, which invest huge amounts in data gathering and analysis.

Blind spots remain. At the time of writing, the unit is still struggling to map VoD and SVoD (streaming or subscription video on demand) statistics and is in discussions with Netflix and Amazon about how it could access (as Perkins puts it) 'a certain amount of data which we could use to give a full picture of the film value chain'. Some raise eyebrows at the relentlessly upbeat 'spin' placed on the unit's data gathering from the BFI in their periodic press releases. As the lead organisation for film in the UK, the BFI will invariably attempt to tell as positive a story as possible about the state of the industry.

'As providers of official statistics, we are very clear that there is a separation between our statistical output, which is objective and independent, and a press release,' says Perkins. 'We aim to ensure that the stats are fully understood… then it's up to the press team to produce a release.'

Thanks to the thoroughgoing work of the unit, it is now possible to tell the story of the progress of British film in an accurate and transparent fashion. 'It is fair to say that the information collected, collated and analysed by RSU has formed the bedrock on which many reports on the UK film industry over the last ten years have really progressed,' says Perkins.

Another sign of the industry taking itself more seriously is the transformation of its annual film awards event, the BAFTAs. This used to be held in the spring, after the Oscars and when the public was tired of the annual awards hoopla. British cinema and television were in the spotlight together with sometimes disconcerting results. Amanda Berry, who started working for BAFTA in 1998 and became chief executive two years later, remembered:

> What had happened was that the Film and TV awards used to be together. It was one ceremony. You'd have wonderful scenarios where you would have [movie star] John Travolta sitting in the audience next to [cast members from British TV soap] *EastEnders*.[23]

The British soap opera actors would know exactly who Travolta was but the Hollywood star didn't have the foggiest clue about Dirty Den, Angie or any of the other British TV household names sitting next to him.

Berry separated the film awards from the TV ones and moved the ceremony to a mid-February date. Now, instead of following the Oscars, it acts as a bellwether for them. It is broadcast in a prime-time slot by the BBC and both its prestige and its relevance to the industry have increased enormously.

294 | STAIRWAYS TO HEAVEN

Even with the steady stream of BFI press releases highlighting different areas of progress and British films winning BAFTA awards, it is still clear the dream of the 'sustainable' British film industry hasn't been realised and perhaps never will be.

There is plenty to be anxious about. In late 2017, two reports commissioned by the BFI several years before were unearthed by researcher Stephen Follows following a Freedom of Information request. The reports, undertaken by chartered accountant Northern Alliance, revealed, among other disturbing insights, that independent British production companies 'typically' had 'weak, illiquid balance sheets, often reporting retained losses at their last balance sheet date, though many appear to do so because the owners take out as much cash from their companies as soon as possible'.[24]

Leading distributor Zygi Kamasa, the chief executive of Lionsgate UK and Europe, was quoted in the *Guardian* as saying that the success of British films was being threatened by 'a loss of funding caused by Brexit' and that successes like *Slumdog Millionaire* would be increasingly hard to make.[25] Kamasa had agreed to chair a BFI commission looking at the health of independent British film. Its proposals, due in 2018, are keenly awaited by a sector facing brutally competitive market conditions.

The December 2017 announcement that the Walt Disney Company was to acquire 21st Century Fox for $52 billion, and that two of Hollywood's biggest studios were effectively planning to merge, reveals the scale of the competition that British independent producers and distributors face from giant US corporations.

Nonetheless, some very significant steps have been taken up the stairway to heaven (to borrow the American title of *A Matter of Life and Death*, one of Britain's most celebrated films of the 1940s). Even the most pessimistic observer has to acknowledge that this is a story now well very well worth telling. The British film industry in 2018, as it shakily confronts Brexit and unprecedented technological change, is in a far healthier state than in 1984, when it really did seem to be on the critical list. In 2017, spending on film production and high-end television in the UK increased by 11 per cent on the 2016 numbers (themselves a record) to reach almost £3 billion. The haul comprised

£1.69 billion on feature films, a 23 per cent increase on 2016, and £684 million on high-end television, the high st level ever and an increase of 27 per cent on 2016. These are staggering figures given the parlous situation of the industry only a few years before. When it comes to defining 'Brand Britain' and boosting the balance of trade, the film industry is having a far more galvanising effect than anyone 30 years before would either have anticipated or believed remotely possible.

APPENDIX

THE HIGHEST-GROSSING BRITISH FILMS OF ALL TIME IN UK CINEMAS

(as at 5 January 2018; box-office data courtesy of comScore)

STUDIO RELEASES

	FILM	UK DISTRIBUTOR	YEAR OF FIRST UK CINEMA RELEASE	UK CINEMA BOX-OFFICE RECEIPTS (£m)
1	Star Wars: The Force Awakens	Disney	2015	123.0
2	Skyfall	Sony	2012	102.9
3	Spectre	Sony	2015	95.2
4	Star Wars: The Last Jedi	Disney	2017	73.2 *
5	Harry Potter and the Deathly Hallows: Part 2	Warner Bros.	2011	73.1
6	Beauty and the Beast	Disney	2017	72.4
7	Mamma Mia! The Movie	Universal	2008	67.9
8	Rogue One: A Star Wars Story	Disney	2016	66.0
9	Harry Potter and the Philosopher's Stone	Warner Bros.	2001	63.8
10	Dunkirk	Warner Bros.	2017	56.7
11	The Dark Knight Rises	Warner Bros.	2012	56.3
12	Casino Royale	Sony	2006	55.5

* Still on UK cinema release as at 5 January 2018

INDEPENDENT RELEASES

	FILM	UK DISTRIBUTOR	YEAR OF FIRST UK CINEMA RELEASE	UK CINEMA BOX-OFFICE RECEIPTS (£m)
1	The Inbetweeners Movie	Entertainment	2011	45.0
2	The King's Speech	Momentum	2011	45.0
3	Paddington 2	StudioCanal	2017	39.4 *
4	Paddington	StudioCanal	2014	37.9
5	The Inbetweeners 2	Entertainment	2014	33.4
6	Slumdog Millionaire	Pathé	2009	31.6
7	Chicken Run	Pathé	2000	29.5
8	Four Weddings and a Funeral	Rank/PolyGram	1994	27.8
9	The Woman in Black	Momentum	2012	21.3
10	Legend	StudioCanal	2015	18.4
11	The Imitation Game	StudioCanal	2014	16.4
12	Tinker Tailor Soldier Spy	StudioCanal	2011	14.2

* Still on UK cinema release as at 5 January 2018

MILESTONES IN UK CINEMAGOING

YEAR	CINEMA VISITS (MILLIONS)
1980	101.0
1985	72.0
1990	97.3
1995	114.6
2000	142.5
2005	164.6
2010	169.2
2015	171.9
2017	170.6

NOTES

PREFACE

1 'George Osborne: *Star Wars* release a "huge day" for British film industry', *Herald* (Glasgow), 16 December 2015, http://www.heraldscotland.com/news/14149634.George_Osborne__Star_Wars_release_a__huge_day__for_British_film_industry/.

2 Hansard, HC vol. 618, col. 934 (15 December 2016), 'British Film Industry', https://hansard.parliament.uk/Commons/2016-12-15/debates/723587BC-C8D0-43E7-B8D3-7AF6981BF506/BritishFilmIndustry.

3 Ibid.

4 Hansard, HC vol. 276, col 353 (24 April 1996), https://publications.parliament.uk/pa/cm199596/cmhansrd/vo960424/debtext/60424-02.htm.

5 Sandy Lieberson, interview with the author, *Moving Pictures*, May 2000.

6 Geoffrey Macnab, *J. Arthur Rank and the British Film Industry* (London: Routledge, 1993), p. 56.

INTRODUCTION

1 Margaret Thatcher, *The Path to Power* (London: HarperCollins, 1995), p. 14.

2 Alexander Walker, *Icons in the Fire: The Decline and Fall of Almost Everybody in the British Film Industry 1984–2000* (London: Orion, 2005), p. 113.

3 Wilf Stevenson, interviewed by author at the House of Lords, February 2017.

4 *The UK Feature Film Sector: Background Research Part 2* (10 April 1991).

5 Thatcher, *Path to Power*, p. 14.

6   Charles Moore, *Margaret Thatcher: The Authorized Biography, Volume One: Not For Turning* (London: Allen Lane, 2013), p. 23.

7   'Campbell, John Arthur – the man who brought the cinema to Grantham', *Grantham Matters*, 18 May 2013, http://www.granthammatters. co.uk/campbell-john-arthur/.

8   John Campbell, *Margaret Thatcher: Volume One: The Grocer's Daughter* (London: Jonathan Cape, 2000), p. 27.

9   Walker, *Icons in the Fire*, p. 119.

10 Jeremy Thomas, interviewed by author, Hanway Street, London, February 2017.

11 David Puttnam, interviewed by author, Pimlico, March 2017.

12 Stevenson, interview.

13 Puttnam, quoted in Walker, *Icons in the Fire*, p. 113.

14 Stevenson, interview.

15 Jonathan Kandell, 'Lew Wasserman, 89, is dead: last of Hollywood's moguls', *New York Times*, 4 June 2002, http://www.nytimes.com/2002/06/04/ business/lew-wasserman-89-is-dead-last-of-hollywood-s-moguls.html.

16 Connie Bruck, *When Hollywood Had a King: The Reign of Lew Wasserman, Who Leveraged Talent into Power and Influence* (New York: Random House, 2003).

17 Lord Lamont of Lerwick, 'Death of a member: Baroness Thatcher – tributes', TheyWorkForYou, 10 April 2013, https://www.theywork- foryou.com/lords/?id=2013-04-10a.1165.0.

18 Puttnam, interview.

19 Thomas, interview.

20 Simon Perry, interviewed by author, London, March 2017.

21 Stevenson, interview.

22 Robinson is quoted in Walker, *Icons in the Fire*, p. 119.

23 Stevenson, interview.

24 Dominic Lawson, 'Saying the unsayable about the Germans' (inter- view with Nicholas Ridley), *Spectator*, 14 July 1990, p. 8.

25 Stevenson, interview.

CHAPTER 1: BACK TO THE 1980S

1   Terry Ilott, interviewed by author, London, March 2017.

2   David Puttnam, interviewed by author, Pimlico, March 2017.

3   Stan Fishman, interviewed by author, telephone, March 2017.

4   Tina McFarling, interviewed by author, July 2017.

5   Fishman, interview.

6   Nicholas Parsons, interviewed by author, telephone, April 2017.
7   Alan Parker, '*Our Cissy* and *Footsteps*', http://alanparker.com/earlywork/our-cissy-and-footsteps/.
8   Peter Miskell, 'The Film industry in twentieth century Britain: consumption patterns, government regulation, and firm strategy', in Richard Coopey and Peter Lyth (eds), *Business in Britain in the Twentieth Century* (Oxford: Oxford University Press, 2009), p. 322.
9   Hansard, HC vol. 64, cols 523–30 (19 July 1984), http://hansard.millbanksystems.com/commons/1984/jul/19/film-industry-policy.
10 Puttnam, interview.
11 Quoted in Geoffrey Macnab, 'The big picture: tribute to British screen', *Moving Pictures*, October 2000, pp. 40–1.
12 Kenneth Baker, *The Turbulent Years: My Life in Politics* (London: Faber, 1993), p. 90.
13 Puttnam, interview.
14 Baker, *The Turbulent Years*, p. 90.
15 Steve Knibbs, interviewed by author for *Screen International*, October 2017.
16 Ilott, interview.
17 Michael G. Wilson, quoted at BSAC Film Conference 2013, 'Exploring the blurring boundaries between film and other forms of content', 14 March 2013.
18 Baker, *The Turbulent Years*, p. 90.
19 Hansard, HC vol. 64, cols 523–30 (19 July 1984).
20 Hansard, HC vol. 60, cols 1406–12 (25 May 1984).
21 Hansard, HC vol. 64, cols 523–30 (19 July 1984).
22 Ibid.
23 Hansard, HC vol. 68, cols 29–110 (19 November 1984), http://hansard.millbanksystems.com/commons/1984/nov/19/films-bill.
24 Simon Perry, interviewed by author, London, March 2017.
25 Hansard, HC vol. 64, cols 523–30 (19 July 1984).
26 *The Sunday Times*, 10 January 1988.
27 Geoffrey Macnab, 'Alan Parker: "Bugsy Malone" financier Rank was a "disgrace"', Screen Daily, 5 December 2016, https://www.screendaily.com/alan-parker-bugsy-malone-financier-rank-was-a-disgrace-/5111899.article.
28 Macnab, 'The big picture', p. 42.
29 Ibid.
30 'Simon Relph on Bill Douglas', *400 Blows*, 18 October 2005, http://www.400blows.co.uk/inter_relph.shtml.
31 Macnab, 'The big picture', p. 42.

32 *Screen International,* 31 January 1987.
33 Ibid.
34 Ibid.
35 Ibid.
36 David Puttnam, interviewed in 'Cinema – the last picture', *This Week,* Thames Television, 5 July 1990, www.youtube.com/watch?v=bc9y4DtGIGI.
37 *Screen International,* 31 January 1987.
38 Ibid.
39 *Screen International,* 5 February 1986.
40 Michael Winner, interviewed in 'Cinema – the last picture'.
41 *Guardian,* 31 March 1993.
42 *Guardian,* 20 February 1993, 15 August 1992.
43 Relph is quoted in Macnab, 'The big picture', p. 45.
44 Alexander Walker, *Icons in the Fire: The Decline and Fall of Almost Everybody in the British Film Industry 1984-2000* (London: Orion, 2005), p. 120.
45 Ibid, pp. 190–3.
46 Raymond Durgnat, 'The ploughman's (just) desserts', *American Film,* November 1985, http://www.raymonddurgnat.com/publications_full_article_ploughmans_just_desserts.htm.
47 Hansard, HC vol. 240, col. 255 (22 March 1994).
48 Labour Party, *Arts and Media, Our Cultural Future* (London: Labour Party, 1991).
49 Letter from Percy Livingstone, president of the SFD, to Mr Stephen Pride at the DTI, 1 February 1991 (held in FDA archives).
50 Private memo reporting on Labour arts event at the National Film Theatre, 1 September 1991, chaired by Gordon Brown MP, Shadow Trade Minister, and Mark Fisher MP, Shadow Film Minister (FDA archives).
51 Letter from FDA president Percy Livingstone to Mr Gordon Brown MP, 1 October 1991 (FDA archives).
52 *Guardian,* 20 February 1993.
53 Ibid.
54 Quoted in Durgnat, 'The ploughman's (just) desserts'.

CHAPTER 2: THE VIDEO REVOLUTION

1 Stephen Woolley, interviewed by author, June 2017.
2 Hansard, HC vol. 48, cols. 521–80 (11 November 1983), http://hansard.millbanksystems.com/commons/1983/nov/11/video-recordings-bill.

3   Woolley, interview.
4   *Billboard*, 22 May 1982.
5   Terry Ilott, interviewed by author, London, March 2017.
6   Iain Muspratt, interviewed by author, Pimlico, March 2017.
7   Julian Petley, '"Are we insane?" The "video nasty" moral panic', *Recherches sociologiques et anthropologiques* 43.1 (2012), http://journals. openedition.org/rsa/839.
8   *Sunday Times*, 23 May 1982.
9   'The secret video show', *Daily Mail*, 12 May 1982, cited in Petley, 'Are we insane?'
10 Woolley, interview.
11 Ilott, interview.
12 Muspratt, interview.
13 VCL marketing director Steve Webber, quoted in Julian Upton, 'Electric blues', *Journal of British Cinema and Television* 13.1 (2016), p. 22, http://www.euppublishing.com/doi/pdfplus/10.3366/jbctv.2016. 0294.
14 Ibid.
15 Woolley, interview.
16 Nik Powell, interviewed by author, April 2017.
17 *Billboard*, 17 October 1981.
18 Angus Finney, *The Egos Have Landed: The Rise and Fall of Palace Pictures* (London: Heinemann, 1996), p. 57.
19 Woolley, interview.
20 Powell, interview.
21 Graham Humphreys, interviewed by author, September 2017.
22 Woolley, interview.
23 Powell, interview.
24 Woolley, interview.
25 Robert Jones, interviewed by author, July 2017.
26 Ilott, interview.
27 Muspratt, interview.
28 Powell, interview.
29 David Waterman, *Hollywood's Road to Riches* (Cambridge, MA: Harvard University Press, 2005), p. 73.
30 Ilott, interview.
31 Menahem Golan, quoted in D. Semple, 'Menahem Golan and the Thorn Emi Films Buyout', *Foreign Affairs*, 17 October 2016, http:// www.iridescentvillage.com/politiclass_blog/?p=368.
32 Muspratt, interview.
33 Upton, 'Electric blues', p. 20.

34 *Billboard*, 30 April 1977.
35 Alan Pritchard, interviewed by author, March 2017.
36 *Billboard*, December 1981.
37 Pritchard, interview.
38 Lucas Hilderbrand, *Inherent Vice: Bootleg Histories of Videotape and Copyright* (Durham, NC: Duke University Press, 2009), p. 56.
39 Pritchard, interview.
40 Simon Perry, interviewed by author, London, March 2017.
41 Powell, interview.
42 Ilott, interview.
43 Stan Fishman, interviewed by author, telephone, March 2017.
44 Muspratt, interview.
45 David Puttnam, interviewed by author, Pimlico, March 2017.
46 Pritchard, interview.
47 Brian Robertson, interviewed by author, March 2017.
48 *New York Times*, 22 February 1983.
49 Lavinia Carey, interviewed by author, March 2017.
50 *Billboard*, 30 October 1999.
51 *Billboard*, 2 May 1998.
52 Woolley, interview.
53 Muspratt, interview.
54 Woolley interview.

CHAPTER 3: POLYGRAM FOREVER

1 Michael Kuhn, interviewed by author, April 2017.
2 Kuhn, quoted in *Variety*, 13 January 1991.
3 Eric Fellner and Tim Bevan, Working Title, interviewed by *Moving Pictures*, May 1998.
4 David Puttnam, interviewed by author, Pimlico, March 2017.
5 Julia Short, interviewed by author, March 2017.
6 Stewart Till, interviewed by author, June 2017.
7 Short, interview.
8 Kuhn speaking in 2007 documentary *100 Films and a Funeral*, directed by Michael McNamara and based on Kuhn's 2002 book of the same title.
9 Till, interview.
10 Kuhn, in *100 Weddings and a Funeral*.
11 *Variety*, 29 January 1995.
12 Short, interview.

13 Review of *Four Weddings and a Funeral, Sight & Sound,* June 1994, p. 47.
14 Derek Malcolm, review of *Four Weddings and a Funeral, Guardian,* 12 May 1994, https://www.theguardian.com/film/News_Story/Critic_Review/Guardian_review/0„530826,00.html.
15 Short, interview.
16 '1994 An average year, but a cool and wet spring', London Weather, http://www.london-weather.eu/article.133.html.
17 Till, interview.
18 Short, interview.
19 Mike Newell, interviewed by author, *Sight & Sound,* May 1997.
20 Till, interview.
21 Unpublished telephone interview by author with Eric Fellner, 2009.
22 Till, interview
23 Kuhn, interview.
24 Cor Boonstra, quoted in Christopher A. Bartlett, 'Philips versus Matsushita: the competitive battle continues', Harvard Business School 9-910-410, 11 December 2009, p. 6, http://schallmag.net/wp-content/uploads/2013/01/7306_120705_Case_Philips-vs-Matsushita.pdf.
25 Till, interview.
26 Kuhn, interview.

CHAPTER 4: THE WORKING TITLE MAGIC

1 'The insider interviews: Sarah Radclyffe', Industrial Scripts, 29 December 2016, https://screenplayscripts.com/sarah-radclyffe.
2 Alexander Walker, *Icons in the Fire: The Decline and Fall of Almost Everybody in the British Film Industry* (London: Orion, 2005), p. 21.
3 Stephen Frears, interviewed by author, in *Screen Epiphanies: Filmmakers on the Films that Inspired Them* (London: BFI/Macmillan, 2009).
4 Ate de Jong, interviewed by author, June 2017.
5 Laurence Gornall, interviewed by author, June 2017.
6 Charlotte Higgins, 'The producers', *Guardian,* 16 April 2005, https://www.theguardian.com/film/2005/apr/16/business.hayfilmfestival2005.
7 Gornall, interview.
8 Alex Cox, *X Films: True Confessions of a Radical Filmmaker* (London: I.B.Tauris, 2008), p. 79.
9 Eric Fellner, unpublished interview with author, 2009.

CHAPTER 5: THE GREAT BRITISH LOTTO BONANZA

1   John Major, 'Preface', in Ruth Lea with Dan Lewis, *The Larceny of the Lottery Fund* (London: Centre for Policy Studies, 2006), p. i, https://www.cps.org.uk/files/reports/original/130307152141-TheLarcenyoftheLotteryFund.pdf.

2   John Major, speech at launch of the Lord Attenborough NFTS Charitable Fund, 11 June 2013.

3   Jeremy Newton, interviewed by author, March 2017.

4   Virginia Bottomley, interviewed by author, March 2017.

5   Alexander Walker, *Icons in the Fire: The Decline and Fall of Almost Everybody in the British Film Industry* (London: Orion, 2005), p. 205.

6   Ibid., p. 206.

7   Terry Ilott, interviewed by author, London, March 2017.

8   Quoted in James Caterer, *The People's Pictures: National Lottery Funding and British Cinema* (Newcastle upon Tyne: Cambridge Scholars Publishing, 2011), p. 59.

9   Simon Perry, interviewed by author, London, March 2017.

10 Anonymous executive, interviewed by author.

11 Perry, interview.

12 Marc Samuelson, interviewed by author, March 2017.

13 Ibid.

14 Xan Brooks, 'South side story', *Guardian*, 8 December 2000.

15 Former panellist, interviewed by author.

16 *Variety*, 23 October 1995.

17 David Lister, 'UK films plagued by poor scripts', *Independent*, 19 February 1998.

18 Newton, interview.

19 Perry, interview.

20 Newton, interview.

21 Former panellist, interview.

22 Alexander Walker, *Evening Standard*, 4 May 2000.

23 Samuelson, interview.

24 Newton, interview.

25 Former panellist, interview.

26 Hansard, HC vol. 261, cols 19–28 (6 June 1995), https://publications.parliament.uk/pa/cm199495/cmhansrd/1995-06-06/Debate-1.html.

27 Nick Redfern, 'UK film tax relief, 1992 to 2008', Research into Film (blog), 21 May 2009, https://nickredfern.wordpress.com/2009/05/21/uk-film-tax-relief-1992-to-2008.

28 Hansard, HC vol. 275, col. 10 (1 April 1996), https://publications.parliament.uk/pa/cm199596/cmhansrd/vo960401/debtext/60401-03.htm.

29 Bottomley, interview.

30 Hansard, HC vol. 287, col. 590 (16 December 1996), https://publications.parliament.uk/pa/cm199697/cmhansrd/vo961216/debtext/61216-01.htm#61216-01_spnew5.

31 *Variety*, 18 December 1996.

32 See 'Lottery funding for British films', Harris Tulchin & Associates, http://www.medialawyer.com/article4.php.

33 Jeremy Thomas, interviewed by author, Hanway Street, London, February 2017.

34 A well-placed insider, interviewed by author.

35 Mick Southworth, interviewed by author, February 2017.

36 Anonymous former Arts Council executive, interviewed by author.

37 Andrew Macdonald quoted in Geoffrey Macnab, 'Choose cash', *Guardian*, 13 November 2003, https://www.theguardian.com/film/2003/nov/13/1.

38 Alexis Lloyd, interviewed by *Moving Pictures*, October 1997.

39 Andrea Calderwood, quoted in Geoffrey Macnab, 'Five years of flack', *Guardian*, 25 October 2002, https://www.theguardian.com/culture/2002/oct/25/artsfeatures1.

40 Geoffrey Macnab, 'Five years of flack', *Guardian*, 25 October 2002, https://www.theguardian.com/culture/2002/oct/25/artsfeatures1.

CHAPTER 6: THE LIFE AND DEATH OF THE FILM COUNCIL

1 Hansard, HC vol. 297, col. 299 (2 July 1997), https://publications.parliament.uk/pa/cm199798/cmhansrd/vo970702/debtext/70702-21.htm.

2 Chris Smith, interviewed by author, June 2017.

3 Ibid.

4 David Puttnam, interviewed by author, Pimlico, March 2017.

5 Puttnam, interviewed by Roger Clarke, 'The ego and the agony', *Independent*, 11 May 2000, http://www.independent.co.uk/arts-entertainment/films/features/the-ego-and-the-agony-278628.html.

6 Smith, interview.

7 Department for Culture, Media and Sport, *A Bigger Picture: The Report of the Film Policy Review Group* (London: DCMS, 1998), http://bigpictureresearch.typepad.com/files/a-bigger-picture.pdf.

8   Smith, interview.
9   Stewart Till, interviewed by author, June 2017.
10 *Spectator*, 4 November 1966.
11 Chris Auty, interviewed by author, August 2017.
12 DCMS, 'Summary', *A Bigger Picture*, p. 3.
13 See Dorota Ostrowska and Graham Roberts, *European Cinemas in the Television Age* (Edinburgh: Edinburgh University Press, 2007), p. 14.
14 Smith, interview.
15 Smith, quoted in Geoffrey Macnab, 'The life and death of the UK Film Council', *Sight & Sound*, October 2010, http://old.bfi.org.uk/sightandsound/feature/49647.
16 Smith, interview.
17 John Walsh, 'Interview: Alan Parker: Parker's new suit', *Independent*, 1 November 1997, http://www.independent.co.uk/life-style/interview-alan-parker-parkers-new-suit-1291438.html.
18 Geoffrey Macnab, 'Film: the death-trap London studio that time forgot', *Independent*, 24 June 1999, http://www.independent.co.uk/arts-entertainment/film-the-death-trap-london-studio-that-time-forgot-1102265.html.
19 Alan Parker, email interview with author, July 2017.
20 Till, interview.
21 Smith, interview.
22 Till, interview.
23 Parker, interview.
24 Puttnam, interview.
25 'BFI falls into line', *Arts Professional* , 19 April 2004, https://www.artsprofessional.co.uk/magazine/article/bfi-falls-line.
26 *British Film Institute 2003–2004* (annual report) (London: BFI, 2004), p. 2, http://www.bfi.org.uk/sites/bfi.org.uk/files/downloads/bfi-annual-report-2003-2004.pdf.
27 Film Council, *A Development Strategy for Film and the Moving Image in the English Regions*, November 2000.
28 Ibid.
29 John Woodward, interview by author for *Moving Pictures*, 1999.
30 Ibid.
31 Ibid.
32 Till, interview.
33 British Screen, 'A new strategy for film', internal memo, 2000.
34 Email from Simon Perry to author, London, January 2018.
35 Puttnam, interview.
36 Woodward, interview, *Moving Pictures*.

37 Woodward, quoted in Agnes Poirier, 'Film-making is a business like any other', *Guardian*, 25 August 2000, https://www.theguardian.com/film/2000/aug/25/culture.features2.

38 Interview with author, anonymous.

39 Parker, interview.

40 Perry, interview.

41 Jeremy Thomas, interviewed by author, Hanway Street, London, February 2017.

42 Ibid.

43 Auty, interview.

44 Simon Hattenstone, 'Bigmouth strikes again' (interview with Terence Davies), *Guardian*, 20 October 2006, https://www.theguardian.com/film/2006/oct/20/3.

45 Robert Jones, interviewed by author, July 2017.

46 Woodward, interview, *Moving Pictures*.

47 Till, interview.

48 Perry, interview

49 Julian Fellowes, 'Screenwriters' lecture', BAFTA Guru, 26 September 2012, http://guru.bafta.org/julian-fellowes-screenwriters-lecture.

50 Julian Fellowes, 'Cut the Film Council and end this 1970s navel-gazing', *Daily Telegraph*, 12 August 2010, http://www.telegraph.co.uk/culture/film/7941224/Cut-the-Film-Council-and-end-this-1970s-navel-gazing.html.

51 Jones, interview.

52 Geoffrey Macnab, 'What's an American director doing making an English movie about manners?', *Guardian*, 8 May 2001, https://www.theguardian.com/film/2001/may/08/artsfeatures.

53 *Variety*, 21 April 2002.

54 Jones, interview.

55 Till, interview.

56 Alexander Walker, '*Pandaemonium*' (review), *Evening Standard*, 13 September 2001, https://www.standard.co.uk/go/london/film/pan-daemonium-7433475.html.

57 Alex Cox, *X Films: True Confessions of a Radical Filmmaker* (London: I.B.Tauris, 2008), p. 253.

58 Parker, interview.

59 Alan Parker, 'Building a sustainable film industry: a presentation to the UK film industry', 5 November 2002, http://alanparker.com/essay/building-a-sustainable-uk-film-industry/.

60 Letter from Mick Southworth, Alchymie Ltd, to John Woodward, Film Council, 11 February 2000.

61 Till, interview.
62 Film Council executive, interviewed by author for *Moving Pictures*, 1999.
63 Andi Engel, quoted in Geoffrey Macnab, 'Whatever happened to the rest of the planet?', *Guardian*, 4 June 2003, https://www.theguardian.com/film/2003/jun/04/artsfeatures.
64 Parker, interview.
65 Quoted in Macnab, 'Life and death'.
66 Don Boyd, interviewed by author, April 2009.
67 Pete Buckingham, interviewed by author for Screen Daily, October 2017.
68 Letter from CEA to Department of Trade and Industry, 9 February 2001.
69 Letter from Richard Segal, chief executive of Odeon, to SEDFS consultation, British Film Institute, 11 February 2002.
70 Mimi Turner, 'U.K. Film Council, BFI plan merger', *Hollywood Reporter*, 20 August 2009, https://www.hollywoodreporter.com/news/uk-film-council-bfi-plan-87909.
71 Woodward, quoted in Geoffrey Macnab, 'Merger is not a "done deal", says BFI's Dyke', Screen Daily, 21 August 2009, https://www.screendaily.com/merger-is-not-a-done-deal-says-bfis-dyke/5004761.article.
72 Greg Dyke, ibid.
73 Former Film Council executive, interviewed by author.
74 Jeremy Hunt, 'I've cut the UK Film Council so that money goes to the industry', *Observer*, 8 August 2010, https://www.theguardian.com/business/2010/aug/08/film-council-quangos-cuts-jeremy-hunt.
75 Smith, interview.
76 Parker, interview.
77 Alan Parker, 'Quotes on British cinema', http://alanparker.com/quotes/on-british-cinema.
78 Alan Parker, 'UK film politics: the muddy waters of eternity', http://alanparker.com/cartoon/uk-film-politics.
79 Puttnam, interview.
80 Till, interview.
81 https://www.theguardian.com/business/2010/aug/08/film-council-quangos-cuts-jeremy-hunt
82 Puttnam, interview.
83 Anonymous senior producer, interviewed by author.
84 Iain Smith, interviewed by author, July 2017.

CHAPTER 7: POTTER GOLD

1   Tanya Seghatchian, quoted in Geoffrey Macnab, 'The spell is broken: what will replace Harry Potter?', *Independent*, 30 June 2011, http://www.independent.co.uk/arts-entertainment/films/features/the-spell-is-broken-what-will-replace-harry-potter-2304865.html.

2   *Herald* [Glasgow], 24 June 1997.

3   Seghatchian in Macnab, 'The spell is broken'.

4   *I Was There*, BBC Radio Five Live, June 2017.

5   Christopher Little, interviewed by author, July 2017.

6   *I Was There.*

7   Little, interview.

8   Gary Oldman, interview with author, press junket, *Harry Potter and the Prisoner of Azkaban*, London, 2004.

9   Nisha Parti, quoted in Ryan Gilbey, 'Ten years of making Harry Potter films, by cast and crew', *Guardian*, 7 July 2011, https://www.theguardian.com/film/2011/jul/07/harry-potter-making-the-films-cast-and-crew.

10   Little, interview.

11   Ibid.

12   An executive speaking anonymously, interviewed by author, January 2017.

13   Little, interview.

14   Alan Parker, quoted in Simon Brew, 'Director Alan Parker on how he turned down Harry Potter', Den of Geek, 28 October 2013, http://www.denofgeek.com/movies/harry-potter/27914/director-alan-parker-on-how-he-turned-down-harry-potter.

15   Chris Columbus, interview with author, *Prisoner of Azkaban* press junket, London, 2004.

16   Columbus, speaking in video in 'The Making of Harry Potter', Warner Bros. studio tour, Leavesden.

17   Anonymous executive, interview.

18   Stuart Craig, quoted in *Sight & Sound*, BFI,   August 2005, p. 9.

19   Little, interview.

20   Rick Senat, interviewed by author, January 2017.

21   Mark Batey, quoted in Macnab, 'The spell is broken'.

22   Tim Mullaney, 'A bet on Florida pays off', *New York Times*, 26 May 2014, https://www.nytimes.com/2014/05/27/business/a-bet-on-florida-pays-off.html.

CHAPTER 8: THE NAME IS STILL BOND

1   Albert R. 'Cubby' Broccoli, quoted in *Screen International*, June 1985.
2   Alexander Cockburn, 'The secret agent', in *Corruptions of Empire: Life Studies and the Reagan Era* (London: Verso, 1988), p. 60.
3   Geoffrey Macnab, 'Cubby Broccoli – the man with the golden franchise', *Independent*, 27 March 2009, http://www.independent.co.uk/arts-entertainment/films/features/cubby-broccoli-the-man-with-the-golden-franchise-1655010.html.
4   Ibid.
5   Ibid.
6   Matthew Parker, *Goldeneye: Where Bond Was Born: Ian Fleming's Jamaica* (London: Hutchinson, 2014), p. 273.
7   Albert R. Broccoli with Donald Zec, *When the Snow Melts: The Autobiography of Cubby Broccoli* (London: Boxtree, 1998), p.105.
8   Michael G. Wilson, interview with author, *Quantum of Solace* junket, 2008.
9   John Boorman, quoted in 'Sean Connery before Bond', *Sight & Sound*, October 1992.
10 Broccoli, *When the Snow Melts* (quoting a memo from Ian Fleming); see http://www.007.com/the-inside-story-of-bond/.
11 'Octopussy™ Barbie® Doll', http://barbie.mattel.com/shop/en-us/ba/barbie-loves-bond-collection/octopussy-barbie-doll-t4550.
12 Richard Maibaum on adapting *Goldfinger*, April 1963, special collections, University of Iowa libraries.
13 Sam Mendes, quoted in Geoffrey Macnab, '*Spectre*: Daniel Craig's fourth outing as James Bond is likely to delve into 007's past – this is a worrying prospect', *Independent*, 11 October 2015, http://www.independent.co.uk/arts-entertainment/films/features/spectre-daniel-craigs-fourth-outing-as-james-bond-is-likely-to-delve-into-007s-past-this-is-a-a6689751.html.
14 Michael G. Wilson, speech at BSAC Film Conference, 14 March 2013.
15 Mark Batey, interviewed by author, July 2017.
16 Sandra Echeverri, 'Industry report: marketing: case study: branding James Bond', Cineuropa, 13 October 2016, http://cineuropa.org/dd.aspx?t=dossier&l=en&tid=1366&did=318278.
17 Todd McCarthy, '*Die Another Day*' (review), *Variety*, 15 November 2002, http://variety.com/2002/film/awards/die-another-day-1200544820/.

18 'Casino Royale' (review), *Variety*, 31 December 1966, http://variety.
com/1966/film/reviews/casino-royale-1200421405/.

CHAPTER 9: AN UNEASY PARTNERSHIP – BRITISH FILM AND TV

1 Geoffrey Macnab, 'MIPCOM: UK indies embracing high-end
TV', Screen Daily, 12 October 2016, https://www.screendaily.
com/features/mipcom-uk-indies-embracing-high-end-tv/5110013.
article.
2 Stephen Evans, interviewed by author, August 2017.
3 Stewart Mackinnon, quoted in Macnab, 'MIPCOM'.
4 David Puttnam, interviewed by author, Pimlico, March 2017.
5 Simon Perry, interviewed by author, London, March 2017.
6 Jeremy Isaacs, quoted in Geoffrey Macnab, 'Jeremy Isaacs talks
Channel 4 privatisation, "The World at War" and director Jack Gold',
Screen Daily, 25 July 2016, https://www.screendaily.com/features/
jeremy-isaacs-talks-channel-4-privatisation-the-world-at-war-and-
director-jack-gold/5106994.article.
7 Justin Dukes, quoted in Dominique Joyeux, 'Une bouffée d'oxygène
pour le cinéma britannique', *Cahiers du cinéma* 342, December 1982
(in French), English translation at http://100pages.me/film-writing/
british-film-production.aspx.
8 Paul Bonner with Lesley Aston, *Independent Television in Britain,
Volume 6: New Developments in Independent Television 1981–92* (Basingstoke:
Palgrave Macmillan, 2003), p. 197.
9 Perry, interview.
10 'TV since 1981', Broadcasters' Audience Research Board (BARB),
http://www.barb.co.uk/resources/tv-facts/tv-since-1981/1981/
top10/.
11 Antony Root, interviewed by author, September 2017.
12 Mark Shivas, quoted in Kevin Jackson, 'The transformer', *Independent*,
4 January 1996, http://www.independent.co.uk/arts-entertainment/
the-transformer-1322297.html.
13 David M. Thompson, interviewed by author, September 2017.
14 Ibid.
15 Paul Webster, quoted in David Gritten, 'Four goes to Hollywood',
Daily Telegraph, 13 January 2001, http://www.telegraph.co.uk/cul-
ture/4721023/Four-goes-to-Hollywood.html.
16 Ibid.

17 Thompson, interview.

18 Iain Smith, interviewed by author, July 2017.

19 Thompson, interview.

20 Root, interview.

21 Thompson, interview.

22 Tessa Ross, quoted in Mike Goodridge, 'A dog's path to glory: The ups and downs of financing and producing *Slumdog Millionaire*', Screen Daily, 13 February 2009, https://www.screendaily.com/a-dogs-path-to-glory-the-ups-and-downs-of-financing-and-producing-slumdog-millionaire/4043301.article.

CHAPTER 10: A TAXING BUSINESS

1 Josie Bevan, 'How it feels… to be a prison wife', *The Times*, 8 January 2017, https://www.thetimes.co.uk/article/how-it-feels-to-be-a-prison-wife-zlt255wsv.

2 Josie Bevan, 'Halloween Heart', *Prison Bag* (blog), 23 November 2017, http://prisonbag.com/?m=201711.

3 Adam Dawtrey, 'Tax law ruling rocks U.K. production biz', *Variety*, 15 February 2004, http://variety.com/2004/film/columns/tax-law-ruling-rocks-u-k-production-biz-1117900114/.

4 Letter to HM Treasury from the producers of *The Truth About Love*, 11 February 2004.

5 Email from Sarah Curtis to Dawn Primarolo MP, 11 February 2004.

6 John Hill, 'Government policy and the British film industry, 1979–90', *European Journal of Communication* 8 (1993), pp. 203–24, https://pure.royalholloway.ac.uk/portal/files/23887812/filmpolicy_001.pdf.

7 For more information on tax reliefs and write-offs see Antony Seely, 'Tax reliefs for production of British films', House of Commons Library Standard Note SN/BT/3927, 16 March 2007, researchbriefings.files.parliament.uk/documents/SN03927/SN03927.pdf.

8 Advisory Committee on Film Finance, chair: Sir Peter Middleton, 1996 Report to the Secretary of State for National Heritage.

9 Helen Pidd, 'Guy Hands sues experts who advised investment in giant shrimp film', *Guardian*, 5 July 2008, https://www.theguardian.com/business/2008/jul/05/emi.taxavoidance.

10 Cannes dailies, *Moving Pictures*, May 2001.

11 Alexander Walker, *Icons in the Fire: The Decline and Fall of Almost Everybody in the British Film Industry* (London: Orion, 2005), p. 261.

12 Simon Perry, quoted in *Moving Pictures*, May 2001.

13 Adam Minns, 'Cannes flooded by low-budget Brits', Screen Daily, 15 May 2001, https://www.screendaily.com/cannes-flooded-by-low-budget-brits/405738.article.

14 Anonymous executive, interviewed by author.

15 Cannes Dailies, *Moving Pictures*, May 2003.

16 Quoted ibid.

17 Adam Dawtrey, 'Evolution evolving prod'n', *Variety*, 16 January 2001, http://variety.com/2001/film/news/evolution-evolving-prod-n-1117792160/.

18 Guy Hands, quoted in *Financial Times*, 10 July 2008.

19 https://www.accountancyage.com/aa/news/1758408/claim-shipwright-baker-tilly-settled

20 Letter from Richard Segal to SEDS Consultation, c/o Simon Duffy, Exhibition Development Unit, BFI, dated 11 February 2002.

21 Tim Levy, *Screen International*, February 2002.

22 Anonymous executive, interviewed by author.

23 Simon Perry, interviewed by author, London, March 2017.

24 Mike Kelly, quoted in *Moving Pictures*, May 2002.

25 Dawn Primarolo, interviewed by author, July 2017.

26 Anonymous Treasury official, interviewed by author.

27 Primarolo, interview.

28 Ibid.

29 David Puttnam, interviewed by author, Pimlico, March 2017.

30 Primarolo, interview.

31 Stewart Till, interviewed by author, June 2017.

32 Primarolo, interview.

33 Alexi Mostrous, 'Top taxman targeted film "scams for scumbags"', *The Times*, 26 October 2013, https://www.thetimes.co.uk/article/top-taxman-targeted-film-scams-for-scumbags-nsdjzmkrsv3.

34 'Investors in film partnerships schemes face financial ruin as HMRC issues multi million pound shock tax demands of up to 10 times their original investment', Pannone press release, 25 June 2012, http://www.pannone.com/media-centre/press-releases/professional-negligence-news/investors-film-partnerships-schemes-face.

35 Stephen Bristow, interviewed by author, April 2017.

36 *The Economic Impact of the UK Film Industry* (Oxford: Oxford Economics, September 2012), http://www.bfi.org.uk/sites/bfi.org.uk/files/downloads/bfi-economic-impact-of-the-uk-film-industry-2012-09-17.pdf.

37 Primarolo, interview.

316 | STAIRWAYS TO HEAVEN

CHAPTER 11: FLYING THE FLAG – MARKETING BRITAIN ON SCREEN

1   Richard Attenborough, quoted in Aljean Harmetz, 'New life for Britain's movie houses', *New York Times*, 18 June 1985, http://www.nytimes.com/1985/06/18/movies/new-life-for-britain-s-movie-houses.html.

2   *Screen International*, 22 June 1985.

3   *Screen International*, 9 February 1985.

4   *Screen International*, May 1984.

5   Fiona Halton, interviewed by author, London, July 2017.

6   David Puttnam, quoted in *Screen International*, 9 February 1985.

7   Harmetz, 'New life for Britain's movie houses'.

8   Halton, interview.

9   *An Independent Review of British Film Year Activities March–November 1985*, prepared by Deloitte, Haskins & Sells Management Consultancy Division, November 1985.

10 John Mahony, interviewed by author, July 2017.

11 Address given by John Mahony to the Danish Film Association, November 1998.

12 Mahony, interview.

13 Anonymous film executive, interviewed by author.

14 Ibid.

15 Audit Bureau of Circulations figures cited in Wikipedia, 'List of newspapers in the United Kingdom by circulation', https://en.wikipedia.org/wiki/List_of_newspapers_in_the_United_Kingdom_by_circulation#1950%E2%80%931999.

16 Kezia Williams, interviewed by author, August 2017.

17 Ian George, interviewed by author, July 2017.

18 Angus Finney, *The Egos Have Landed: The Rise and Fall of Palace Pictures* (London: Heinemann, 1996), p. 179.

19 Daniel Battsek, interviewed by author, July 2017.

20 Nigel Sharrocks, interviewed by author, July 2017.

21 Ibid.

22 George, interview.

23 Williams, interview.

24 Stephen Follows, 'How important is international box office to Hollywood?' (blog), 15 May 2017, https://stephenfollows.com/important-international-box-office-hollywood/.

25 Sharrocks, interview.

26 George, interview.

27 Paul Lewis, interviewed by author, August 2017.

28 Ken Loach, quoted in Geoffrey Macnab, 'Ken Loach: keeper of the flame', Screen Daily, 13 June 2016, https://www.screendaily.com/features/ken-loach-keeper-of-the-flame/5104790.article.

29 Williams, interview.

30 Hansard, HC vol. 616, col. 417 (27 October 2016).

31 Hansard, HC vol. 616, col. 882 (2 November 2016).

32 Melanie McDonagh, 'Why Paddington is anti-Ukip propaganda', *Spectator* (blog), 19 December 2014, https://blogs.spectator.co.uk/2014/11/why-paddington-is-anti-ukip-propaganda/.

33 Ron Halpern, quoted in Ali Jaafar, '"Paddington": potential game-changer for StudioCanal; Euro major bares ambition', *Deadline*, 28 November 2014, http://deadline.com/2014/11/paddington-potential-game-changer-for-studio-canal-1201300308/.

CHAPTER 12: STEPPING UP

1 'Statistical bulletin: gross domestic product, preliminary estimate: Apr to June 2017', Office for National Statistics, https://www.ons.gov.uk/economy/grossdomesticproductgdp/bulletins/grossdomesticproductpreliminaryestimate/aprtojune2017.

2 Barbara Broccoli and Amanda Nevill, 'Foreword', *Future Film Skills: An Action Plan* (London: BFI, 2017), p. 5, http://www.bfi.org.uk/sites/bfi.org.uk/files/downloads/future-film-skills-an-action-plan-2017.pdf.

3 Amanda Nevill speaking at the launch of the BFI's Future Film Skills Action Plan, June 2017.

4 David Puttnam, interviewed by author, Pimlico, March 2017.

5 Andy Paterson quoted in Geoffrey Macnab, 'PACT proposes 40% UK tax credit for British independent films', Screen Daily, 28 April 2017, https://www.screendaily.com/news/pact-proposes-40-uk-tax-credit-for-british-independent-films/5117213.article.

6 *The State of the UK Independent Film Sector: A Study for PACT by Olsberg SPI* (London: Olsberg SPI), 28 April 2017, http://www.o-spi.co.uk/wp-content/uploads/2017/04/The-State-of-the-UK-Independent-Film-Sector.pdf.

7 Michael Brooke, 'The BFI Production Board: The Features', *BFI Screenonline*, n.d., http://www.screenonline.org.uk/film/id/1348538/index.html.

8 Colin MacCabe, interviewed by author, July 2017.

9   *FDA Yearbooks*, 2015 and 2016 (London: Film Distributors' Association).

10 Philip Knatchbull, interviewed by author, May 2017.

11 Ibid.

12 John Bullen, quoted in *Screen International*, July 2016.

13 Ben Luxford, quoted in *Sight & Sound*, August 2016.

14 Paul Brett, quoted in Geoffrey Macnab, 'UK industry fears "devastating" loss of EIS funding (exclusive)', Screen Daily, 26 September 2017, https://www.screendaily.com/news/uk-industry-fears-devastating-loss-of-eis-funding-exclusive-/5122616.article.

15 David Garrett, quoted in Diana Lodderhose, 'Europe's digital single market: what you need to know & how it could kill the indie biz', *Deadline*, 21 November 2016, http://deadline.com/2016/11/europe-digital-single-market-what-you-need-to-know-how-it-could-kill-the-indie-business-1201857973/.

16 Sir Peter Bazalgette, *Independent Review of the Creative Industries* (London: DCMS, September 2017), p. 13, https://www.gov.uk/government/uploads/system/uploads/attachment_data/file/649980/Independent_Review_of_the_Creative_Industries.pdf.

17 Bazalgette, quoted in Marcus Fairs, 'Creative careers seen as "worse than drug dealing or prostitution" says Peter Bazalgette', Dezeen, 22 September 2017, https://www.dezeen.com/2017/09/22/creative-careers-seen-as-worse-than-drug-dealing-prostitution-peter-bazalgette/.

18 Alan Parker, email interview with author, July 2017.

19 Department for Culture, Media and Sport, *A Bigger Picture: The Report of the Film Policy Review Group* (London: DCMS, 1998), http://bigpictureresearch.typepad.com/files/a-bigger-picture.pdf.

20 Sean Perkins, interviewed by author, October 2017.

21 *BFI Film and Television Handbook 1993* (London: BFI, 1993).

22 Perkins, interview.

23 Amanda Berry, interviewed by author for *Sight & Sound*, January 2013.

24 Stephen Follows, 'The shocking state of corporate finance among UK film companies' (blog), 11 December 2017, https://stephenfollows.com/corporate-finance-among-uk-film-companies/.

25 Anushka Asthana, 'So long, Slumdog? Film studio chief says Brexit threatens British cinema', *Guardian*, 15 October 2017, https://www.theguardian.com/film/2017/oct/15/brexit-threatens-british-cinema-lionsgate-zygi-kamasa.

SELECT BIBLIOGRAPHY

Baker, Kenneth, *The Turbulent Years: My Life in Politics* (London: Faber, 1993).

Bruck, Connie, *When Hollywood Had a King: The Reign of Lew Wasserman, Who Leveraged Talent into Power and Influence* (New York: Random House, 2003).

Campbell, John, *The Iron Lady: Margaret Thatcher: From Grocer's Daughter to Iron Lady* (London: Vintage, 2012).

Cox, Alex, *X Films: True Confessions of a Radical Filmmaker* (London: I.B.Tauris, 2008).

Drazin, Charles, *A Bond for Bond: Film Finances and Dr No* (London: Film Finances, 2011).

Finney, Angus, *The Egos Have Landed: The Rise and Fall of Palace Pictures* (London: Heinemann, 1996).

Kuhn, Michael, *One Hundred Films and a Funeral: The Life and Death of Polygram Films* (London: Thorogood, 2002).

Macnab, Geoffrey, *J. Arthur Rank and the British Film Industry* (London: Routledge, 1993).

――― *Searching for Stars: Stardom and Screen Acting in British Cinema* (London: Continuum, 2000).

――― *Screen Epiphanies: Filmmakers on the Films That Inspired Them* (London: BFI/Macmillan, 2009).

――― *Delivering Dreams: A Century of British Film Distribution* (London: I.B.Tauris, 2015).

Moore, Charles, *Margaret Thatcher, the Authorised Biography, Volume One: Not for Turning* (London: Allen Lane 2013).

Murphy, Robert (ed.), *British Cinema of the 90s* (London: BFI, 1999).

Thatcher, Margaret, *The Downing Street Years* (London: HarperCollins, 1993).

――― *The Path to Power* (London: HarperCollins, 1995).

Walker, Alexander, *National Heroes: British Cinema in the Seventies and Eighties* (London: Harrap, 1985).

——— *Icons in the Fire: The Decline and Fall of Almost Everybody in the British Film Industry 1984–2000* (London: Orion, 2005).

Waterman, David, *Hollywood's Road to Riches* (Cambridge, MA: Harvard University Press, 2005).

INDEX